The Manuscripts of Statius

III

HARALD ANDERSON

THE MANUSCRIPTS OF
STATIUS

REVISED EDITION

VOLUME III

RECEPTION:
THE VITAE AND ACCESSUS

Arlington, Virginia
MMIX

TABLE OF CONTENTS
VOLUME III

PREFACE

Publius Papinius Statius was one of the most popular classical Latin poets through the mid-eighteenth century. His epics—the *Thebaid* and *Achilleid*—were among the most influential works in the Middle Ages, with the former being the inspiration for countless versions of the story of Thebes, including the *Roman de Thèbes*, and the latter forming part of the most common Latin "textbook," the *liber Catonianus*. In medieval literature, he is best known for being Dante's co-chaperone through Purgatory and his sole chaperone into Paradise. Through the *Silvae*, Statius wielded an even stronger influence in the early modern period, introducing a previously unknown ancient genre at a time when literature was starting to break away from medieval traditions and giving birth to the concept of "writing while the fire is hot," which set a classical precedent for what would become the Romantic movement.

This volume discusses Statius' reception, interpretation, and popularity through the beginning of the sixteenth century. The discussion and analysis is based on the richest primary source of this type of information, biographical details found in the manuscripts and printed volumes, which are listed and described in the first two volumes. The purpose of this discussion is to (1) illustrate the most important issue in medieval criticism of Statius, one that crops up in most manuscripts in one form or another: the question of his biography; and (2) to shed light on the very peculiar circumstances of Statius' biographical tradition, which, given the lack of information available to medieval scholars, shows much more clearly the use of sources and the development of academic methodologies and scholarly interests than the traditions of other poets. This information will also help illustrate the state of academic inquiry in the late fifteenth century, a period about which much has been assumed but for which little concrete information is available.

While this volume is an integral part of the catalog and indices in Volumes I and II, it is intended to be partially free-standing, since it will have the most appeal to a non-Statian audience. It thus includes its own bibliography and indices. Some references to other volumes are included, however, in the form of references to the Incipitarium in Volume II and brief references to manuscripts in Volume I. The most important piece of information lacking from this volume is an extended discussion of Statius' biography as we now know it. The reasons for not including more than a brief summary here were that it was already discussed at length in Volume I and that it was medieval scholars' ignorance of Statius' life that played the formative role in the medieval biographical tradition. This notwithstanding, details of his life are discussed in the analysis this volume when appropriate. A detailed life of Statius can be found in most commentaries since 1898, but I should reiterate that most biographies that go beyond the brief outline I provide below rely on autobiographic and programmatic interpretations of passages in the *Silvae*.

This volume is a full revision of my PhD dissertation, *Medieval Accessus to Statius* (The Ohio State University, 1997), and includes some new texts and witnesses, as well as references to manuscript materials that discovered since then. It was originally printed in its current form in the first edition of this work, although the bibliography was subsequently updated and references to a few newly discovered texts have been added. This volume reached its final form in 2004, and some studies have appeared since that date that I was not able to incorporate in my analysis or the bibliography.

In addition to the individuals to whom I express my gratitude in Volume I, I am very grateful to Frank Coulson, who served as my adviser, and to my readers at Ohio State—Charles Babcock and Kirk Freudenberg—who provided very insightful comments and guidance. Portions of this were presented in papers delivered at the American Philological Association convention in San Diego in December 1996; the Statius conference held at Trinity College, Dublin, in March 1998; and seminars at the Pontifical Institute of Mediaeval Studies, Toronto, in 1998 and 1999. I am grateful to the session chairs, attendees, and participants at these events, as well as to individuals who commented on my dissertation or on the first edition of this work, for their invaluable criticism and corrections. In the end, the responsibility for errors and omissions remains my own.

December 17, 2009

SHORT TITLE BIBLIOGRAPHY

Allen, J.B. 1982. *The Ethical Poetic of the Later Middle Ages: A Decorum of Convenient Distinction*. Toronto.

Alston, R.C. 1994. *Books with Manuscript: A Short Title Catalogue of Books with Manuscript Notes in the British Library*. London.

Anderson, D. 1994. "Boccaccio's Glosses on Statius." *Studi sul Boccaccio* 22, 3–134.

Anderson, H. 1998. "Note sur les manuscrits du commentaire de Fulgence sur la Thébaïde." *RHT* 28, 235–38.

_____. 2000. "Newly Discovered Metrical Arguments to the *Thebaid*." *MS* 62, 219–53.

Bischoff, B. 1954. "Wendepunkte in der Geschichte der lateinischen Exegese im Frühmittelalter." *Sacris erudiri* 6, 189–279 (*Mittelalterliche Studien* 1 [Stuttgart, 1966], 205–73).

Bozzolo, C. and C. Jeudy. 1979. "Stace et Laurent de Premierfait." *IMU* 22, 413–47.

Brugnoli, G. 1965. "Due note dantesche." *RCCM* 7 (Studi in onore di A. Schiaffini), 246–51.

_____. 1969. "Stazio in Dante." *Cultura Neolatina* 29, 117–25.

_____. 1988. *Identikit di Lattanzio Placido: Studi sulla scolastica staziana*. Testi e studi di cultura classica 3.

Cesarini Martinelli, L. 1975. "Le Selve di Stazio nella critica testuale del Poliziano." *SIFC* 47, 130–74.

_____. 1978. *Angelo Poliziano: Commento inedito alle Selve di Stazio*. INSR Studi e Testi 5. Firenze.

_____. 1982. "Un ritrovamento polizianesco: il fascicolo perduto del commento alle Selve di Stazio." *Rinascimento* 22, 183–212.

Clogan, P.M. 1964. "A Preliminary List of Manuscripts of Statius' *Achilleid*." *Manuscripta* 8, 175–78.

_____. 1964. "Chaucer and the *Thebaid* Scholia." *SPh* 61, 599–615.

_____. 1965a. "A Preliminary List of Anonymous Glosses on Statius' *Achilleid*." *Manuscripta* 9, 104–109.

_____. 1965b. "Medieval and Renaissance Latin Commentaries on Statius." Proposal in *APS Yearbook*, 498–500.

_____. 1967. "Medieval Glossed Manuscripts of the *Thebaid*." *Manuscripta* 11, 102–12.

_____. 1968. *The Medieval Achilleid of Statius*. Leiden.

_____. 1970. "The Planctus of Oedipus." *M&H* 1, 233–39.

Comparetti, D. 1941. *Virgilio nel Medio evo*. Vol. 2. Firenze. (Reprinted Firenze, 1981.)

Constans, L. 1881. *Légendes d'Œdipe*. Paris. (Reprinted Genève, 1974.)

Coulson, F.T. 1997. "Hitherto Unedited Medieval and Renaissance Lives of Ovid (II)." *Mediaeval Studies* 59, 111–53.

_____. and B. Roy. 2000. *Incipitarium Ovidianum*. Publications of the Journal of Medieval Latin 3. Turnhout.[*]

de Angelis, V. 1984. "Magna questio preposita coram Dante et Domino Francisco Petrarca et Virgilio." *Studi Petrarcheschi* n.s. 1, 103–209.

_____. 1985. "Petrarca, Stazio, Liegi." *Studi Petrarcheschi* n.s. 2, 53–84.

_____. 1997. "I commenti medievali alla *Tebaide* di Stazio: Anselmo di Laon, Goffredo Babione, Ilario d'Orléans." Pp. 75–136 in N. Mann and B. Munk Olsen, edd., *Medieval and Renaissance Scholarship*. Mittellateinische Studien und Texte 21. Leiden.

du Cange, A. 1883–87. *Glossarium mediae et infimae latinitatis*. Paris.

Curtius, E. 1954². *Europäische Literatur und lateinisches Mittelalter*. Bern.

Freytag, W. 1912. "Otfrieds Briefvorrede 'Ad Liutbertum' und die 'Accessus ad auctores.'" *ZfdA* 111, 168–93.

Ghisalberti, F. 1946. "Mediaeval Biographies of Ovid." *Journal of the Warburg and Courtauld Institutes* 9–10 (1946–47), 10–59.

Grafton, A. 1983. *Joseph Scaliger: A Study in the History of Classical Scholarship, Vol. I: Textual Criticism and Exegesis*. Oxford.

_____. 1993. *Joseph Scaliger: A Study in the History of Classical Scholarship, Vol. II: Historical Chronology*. Oxford.

Hagen, H. 1870. *Anecdota Helvetica*. GLK supp. 1. Leipzig.

Hardie, A. 1983. *Statius and the Silvae: Poets, Patrons, and Epideixis in the Greco-Roman World*. ARCA 9. Liverpool.

Hardie, W.R. 1916. "Virgil, Statius, and Dante." *JRS*, 1–12.

Heil, A. 2002. *Alma Aeneis: Studien zur Vergil- und Statiusreception Dante Alighieris*. Studien zur klassischen Philologie 135. Frankfurt am Main.

Hunt, R.W. 1948. "Introductions to the «Artes» in the Twelfth Century." Pp. 85–112 in *Studia mediaevalia in honorem... Raymundi Josephi Martin*. Bruges.

Huygens, R.B.C. 1970. *Accessus ad auctores — Bernard d'Utrecht — Conrad d'Hirsau, Dialogus super auctores*. Leiden.

Jeudy, C., and Y.-F. Riou. 1974. "L'Achilléide de Stace au moyen-âge: Abrégés et arguments." *RHT* 4, 143–80.

Klopsch, P. 1980. "Die mittelalterlichen Lehren a: *Accessus ad auctores*." Pp. 48–64 in *Einführung in die Dichtungslehren des lateinischen Mittelalters*. Darmstadt.

Kulcsár, P. 1987. *Mythographi vaticani I et II*. Corpus Christianorum series latina 91c. Turnholdt.

Landi, C. 1913. "Sulla leggenda del cristianesimo di Stazio." *Atti e Memorie del R. Accademia di scienze, lettere ed arti in Padova* 29, 231–66. (Reprinted in *Atti e Memorie Padova* [Padova: Gian. Batt. Randi, 1913].)

_____. 1914. "Di un commento medievale inedito della «Tebaida» di Stazio." *Atti e Memorie del R. Accademia di scienze, lettere ed arti in Padova* 30, 315–44.

---

[*] References to Coulson-Roy refer to entry numbers, not to pages.

_____. 1921. "Intorno a Stazio nel medio evo e nel purgatorio Dantesco." *Atti e Memorie del R. Accademia di scienze, lettere ed arti in Padova* 37.

Löfstedt, B. 1995. *Vier Juvenal-Kommentare aus dem 12. Jh.* Amsterdam.

Mariotti, S. 1975. "Il cristianesimo di Stazio in Dante secondo il Poliziano." Pp. 149–61 in *Letteratura e critica, Studi in onore di N. Sapegno*. Vol. 2. Roma. (Reprinted in *Scritti medievali e umanisti*. Storia e letteratura 137 [Roma, 1976], 71–85.)

Minnis, A.J. 1984. *Medieval Theory of Authorship: Scholastic Literary Attitudes in the Later Middle Ages*. London.

_____ and A.B. Scott. 1991. *Medieval Literary Theory and Criticism c. 1100-c. 1375*. Oxford.

Robathan, D.M. 1968. *The Pseudo-Ovidian De Vetula*. Amsterdam.

Ross, B. 1970. "Giovanni Colonna, Historian at Avignon." *Speculum* 45, 533–63.

Sabbadini, R. 1910. "Giovanni Colonna biografo e bibliografo del sec. XIV." *Atti della reale Accademia di Torino* 46 (1910–11), 846.

_____. 1914. *Le scoperte dei codici latini e greci ne' secoli XIV e XV*. Vol. 2. Biblioteca storica del Rinascimento, n.s. 4. Firenze. (Reprinted Firenze, 1967.)

Sanford, E.M. 1934. "The Manuscripts of Lucan: *Accessus* and *Marginalia*." *Speculum* 9, 178–95.

Scaliger, J.C. 1561. "Hypercriticus." *Poetices*. Book 7. Lyon. (Reprinted Stuttgart, 1964.)

Suerbaum, W. 1981. "Von der «Vita Vergiliana» über die «Accessus Vergiliani» zum Zauberer Vergilius." *ANRW* 2.31.2, 1156–262.

Sweeney, R.D. 1969. *Prolegomena to an Edition of the Scholia to Statius*. Mnemosyne Suppl. 8. Leiden.

Venini, P. 1969. "Stazio poeta doctus?" *RIL* 103, 461–76.

Wasserstein, A. 1956. "Politian's Commentary on the *Silvae* of Statius." *Scriptorium* 10, 83–89.

Weber, C.F. 1856. *Vitae M. Annaei Lucani collectae*. Indices lectionum... in Academia Marburgensi. In three parts. Marburg, 1856, 1857, 1858.

Wessner, P. 1931. *Scholia in Juvenalem vetustiora*. Leipzig.

Zabughin, Z. 1909. *Giulio Pomponio Leto*. 2 voll. Roma.

INTRODUCTION

Accessus, *Vitae*, and Medieval Scholarship: A Brief Introduction

From the fourth until the seventeenth century, the interpretation of a work of literature was intertwined with and inextricable from the biography of its author. Not only was the meaning of a work a function of the author's life, but conscious fabrications and false etymologies were employed to make the author's identity a function of his work. The key vehicles for this are the *accessus* (an academic introduction)[1] and *vita* (a biography).[2] These texts served not only as introductions to a text but also, when collected, as a type of literary survey.

The medieval tradition of *accessus* began, for all intents and purposes, with Servius,[3] and remained an important part of scholarship until the mid-sixteenth century.[4] An *accessus* is, formally, a discussion of the background of a specific text mostly based on the author's life, with the information usually divided into different rubrics or *circumstantiae*, with the rubrics listed at the beginning of the text. Servius' commentary on the *Aeneid*, for example, begins (*ad Aen.1.praef.* 1–3):

> *In exponendis auctoribus haec consideranda sunt: poetae vita, titulus operis, qualitas carminis, scribentis intentio, numerus librorum, ordo librorum, explanatio*

and provides us with the seven types of information that we need in order to study an author. The rest of the *accessus* is spent expositorily answering these questions.

In their ancient usage, these *accessus* served as prefaces to commentaries, but there are only a few examples that date from antiquity.[5] *Accessus* first become widespread as a genre in the ninth century, possibly as an intentional scholarly archaism that developed independent of the new and largely insular scholarship of the day.[6] In their earliest medieval usage, *accessus* were attached to a commentary or some other exegetical text and provided the reader with the basic terminology and framework within which the commentary would operate.[7] After the tenth century, however, their usage changed, and *accessus* began to exist as independent entities,

---

[1] Literally, an approach. The term is commonly found in medieval texts (see Curtius 1954.228 n. 2). Another term, *didascalia*, seems to have been used only by Boethius and his direct scholarly descendants.

[2] The key difference between the two texts is that *vitae* discuss the author's life in and of itself, whereas *accessus* discuss the biography in the context of the work in question, but interpretation in the two developed in parallel.

[3] On Servius' terminological and methodological dominance in the Middle Ages, see O.B. Hardison, Jr., "Toward a History of Medieval Literary Criticism," *M&H* 7 (1976), 1–12 [5].

[4] The latest formal *accessus* that I have come across is the early–seventeenth century one in London, BL, 11355.aa.26, A1v (*P. Ovidii Nasonis poetae Sulmonensis poemata amatoria* [Antwerpen: Joannis Loeus, 1566]; the volume is not listed in Alston's catalog), *inc.* "Est familiaris amicorum absentium et quasi mutuus sermo, ut faceremus amicos absentes certiores si quid esset quod eos scire aut nostra aut ipsorum interesset. In exponendis autoribus...." According to T.W. Baldwin (*William Shakspere's Small Latine and Lesse Greeke* [Urbana, IL, 1944], 2.423), this text was copied by Jacob Butler, but another hand (possibly the one that later signs the name Christopher Phillipsome) wrote, "Jacob Butler est uerus professor huius." Thus, Butler may actually have been the lecturer on whom the notes are based.

[5] We have only (1) *accessus* to Virgil by Donatus, Probus, and Servius; (2) the *vita* of Horace by Porphyry; and (3) the *accessus* to Porphyry by Boethius. Many of the *accessus* and *vitae* that are found in editions of other early commentaries are later accretions. Cf. O. Keller, ed. *Pseudacron Scholia in Horatium Vetustiora* (Leipzig, 1902), 1–3.

[6] This is the conclusion reached by B. Bischoff 1954.201–203.

[7] Cf. the *accessus* to the B commentary to Juvenal (Löfstedt 1995.3.1–4): "Ante adiacentis littere istius operis expositionem quedam inquisicione digna videntur, quibus expositis, post intellegentiam memorie infixis, tocius libri series ad intelligendum erit facilior et sentencia ad retinendum elucidior."

forming a genre that was growing independent of the genre of their commentaries.[8] *Accessus* in the Middle Ages were essentially used as introductory lectures in university courses, which thus allowed them to maintain tradition while showing some academic originality. The *accessus* were more than just a discussion of the author and text at hand; rather, they became the lens through which students would read and learn to read an author. As such, these texts provide us with an awkward mixture of specific and peripheral interpretation. In discussing a text, the typical late *accessus* mixes the *circumstantiae* with notes on literary genres, lists of authors or emperors, as well as other information that was useful to the medieval professor and student, but seems superfluous to us. *Accessus* thus enjoyed three forms of transmission: as attached to a commentary, as a self-standing text, or as part of a collection of *accessus ad auctores*.[9] In spite of these developments, *accessus* always remained formally and stylistically close to their origin, such that in many manuscripts it is very difficult to ascertain where the *accessus* ends and the commentary begins.[10]

Servius is the ultimate generic source for *accessus*, but he is not the only one. In spite of his proclamation, "in exponendis auctoribus," it was clear from the very beginning that different authors required different approaches, and different scholars preferred different scientific methods. So, scholars felt free to syncopate, expand, and combine different traditions, depending on how they viewed the text at hand. At any rate, by the beginning of the "high" Middle Ages, there were four sources at hand for scholars to use: Servius, Boethius, Ps.-Augustine, and the Aristotelian *causae*. These four sources provide different taxonomies and methodologies to the *accessus*. These differences are more than stylistic. While most *accessus* in practice will obfuscate the boundaries between the different schemata, the texts will preserve the language of the elements that they take from each schema, and the use of the verbiage may entail the adoption of the rationale and logic behind it, resulting in overlapping critical and logical structures.

Servius

As mentioned above, Servius lists seven *circumstantiae*: *poetae vita, titulus operis, qualitas carminis, scribentis intentio, numerus librorum, ordo librorum,* and *explanatio*. The *vita* begins with brief notes on the author's parents, his nationality, his education (4–7) and a list of his character attributes (7–10). The bulk of the *vita* (and of the *accessus* as well) is a discussion of the author's activities and the condition of the text (10–74).

The *titulus* is simply a grammatical or etymological explanation of the title of the present work. While Servius just provides us with the name of the work, *Aeneis*, in later *accessus*, later *accessus* expand the title to include the full *incipit* of the work, e.g., *Virgilii Maronis Aeneidis liber primus incipit*. The title, especially the fuller title, was an important aspect of *accessus*, and is transmitted "with considerable uniformity."[11]

---

[8] For a fuller discussion of the development of self-standing *accessus*, see Suerbaum 1981. As the index of commentaries and Incipitarium in Volume II illustrate, a given commentary could be transmitted with any one of a number of *accessus*. In some cases, *accessus* appear to be transmitted independently of the accompanying glossary tradition.

[9] These *accessus ad auctores* are puzzling entities. For some reason that has yet to be explained, *accessus* to dozens of authors were collected together, separate from their related texts. There are only a few traditional instances (one of which was most recently edited in Huygens 1970), but there are scores of manuscripts that contain collections of *accessus*, often by several hands.

[10] Many *accessus* end, for example, with a discussion of the *propositio, invocatio,* and *narratio,* although many commentaries begin with a similar discussion. This narrative division of the work derives either from Quintilian (3.3.9, 7.*praef.* 4, and 7.1.1–2) or from a reading in the two P manuscripts of Servius (1.*praef.*89–96: "tribus modis omnis auctoritas poetica constat: praefatione, inuocatione, <narratione>, ueluti hic abentur [*sic*] praefatio 'Arma uirum,' inuocatio 'Musa mihi,' narratio 'Urbs antiqua'"). See Curtius 1954.491.

[11] Sanford 1934.286

The *qualitas carminis*, or genre, is always defined along metrical lines. Virgil writes in a heroic meter (*metricum heroicum*, 77). Servius (and many other *accessus* authors) further defines the *heroicum metrum* as consisting of factual (*manifestum*, 79) and fictional (*compositum*, 81) details.[12] Lastly, he subdivides this *circumstantia* into the *actus* and *stilus* of the poem. The *actus* is the narratological relationship between the *actor* and the narrator of the poem. In the *Aeneid*, the *actus* is *mixtus*: Virgil himself narrates as well as introduces other (or "imbedded") narrators.[13] The *stilus*, or tone, is divided into three groups, *humile* (which later scholars would use to describe the *Eclogues*), *mediocre* (later used to describe the *Georgics*) and *grandiloquum*.

Servius' last four *circumstantiae* can be discussed more briefly. The *intentio* represents the intention of the author, and usually has some connection with the *vita*. The *numerus librorum*, *ordo*, and *explanatio* are details necessary for proving the integrity of the text at hand. In most *accessus*, these are discarded or are relegated to the *titulus* or to a plot summary.

Boethius

Our second source, Boethius, began his commentary *In Porph. Dial.* 1[14] with six *circumstantiae*: *intentio, utilitas, ordo, germanitas, inscriptio,* and *ad quam partem philosophiae cuiuscumque libri ducatur intentio*. While the first three and the fifth *circumstantiae* are familiar from Servius' commentary, the other two show the difference between Boethius' approach and that of his predecessor. The first difference between the two approaches resides in the texts in question. The authenticity of the *Aeneid* was never in question; with Porphyry, that was not the case. *Germanitas* reflects the question as to whether a text is genuine; or, as Boethius wrote:[15]

> *si eius cuius esse opus dicitur, germanus propriusque liber est, quod* γνήσιον *interpretari solet.*

In later *accessus*, this *circumstantia* would only be used, often under the rubric of *auctenticitas*, for works whose authority was in question.

Secondly, the question of the *pars philosophiae* represents a different approach to genres from what we saw in Servius above, and reflects the developments in education since Servius' time. Here, instead of classifying a text on meter alone, Boethius classifies it on the basis of the *septem artes liberales* into three *partes*: *logica, physica,* and *ethica*. Logic, which corresponded to the *trivium*, was divided into grammar, rhetoric, and logic; *physica*, corresponding to the *quadrivium*, into music, astronomy, geometry, and arithmetic; *ethica*, which was never divided, was simply explained as *moralis scientia*, and later came to encompass most literature.[16]

---

[12] For a full discussion of the *metra* and *stili*, see F. Quadlbauer, *Die antike Theorie der Genera dicendi in lateinischen Mittelalter*, Österreichischer Akademie der Wissenschaften, Philosophisch-historische Klasse, 241.2 (Wien, 1962).

[13] Cf. Isidore, *Etymologiae* 8.7.11: "Apud poetas autem tres characteres esse dicendi: unum in quo tantum poeta loquitur, ut est in libris Vergilii Georgicorum; alium dramaticum, in quo nusquam poeta loquitur, ut est in comoediis et tragoediis; tertium mixtum, ut est in Aeneide. Nam poeta illic et introductae personae loquuntur."

[14] Migne, *PL* 64 (1847), col. 1A–C

[15] 64.1B–C

[16] See Clogan 1968.9. This seems to have been a matter of some debate. The *accessus* to the P commentary to Juvenal (Löfstedt 1995.217.19–26; cf. Conrad of Hirsau [Huygens 1970.19.228–9]), notes: "Magister vero Bernardus dicebat hoc [*sc.* que pars philosophie] non esse in auctoribus querendum, cum ipsi nec partes philosophie nec de philosophia tractant. Magister Wilelmus de Conchis dicit auctores omnes, quamvis nec partes sint philosophie nec de ipsa agant, philosophie suponi, propter quam tractant, et omnes illi parti philosophie suponi, propter quam tractant. Utraque ergo lectio falsa est: auctores suponuntur philosophie, id est propter ethicam, que pars est philosophie, tractant, ut scilicet moralem comparent instructionem" (cf. the *accessus* of William of Conches [ed. B. Wilson, *Glosae in Iuvenalem* (Paris, 1980)]).

Ps.-Augustine

The third source for *circumstantiae* is in Ps.-Augustine, *Rhetorica* 7, which provides the list *quis, quid, quando, ubi, cur, quem ad modum*, and *quibus adminiculis*. Here, after the first four rubrics, which are self-explanatory, *cur* corresponds to the *intentio* of Servius; *quem ad modum* (later also termed the *modus tractandi*) to his *stilus*; lastly, the rubric *quibus adminiculis* (more often termed *quibus auxiliis*) designated the patronage and literary friends of the author.[17]

The *Aristotelian* causae

The final source for *circumstantiae* were the four Aristotelian *causae* (the *causa efficiens*, the *causa formalis*, the *causa materialis*, and the *causa finalis*).[18] The *causa efficiens* usually identified either the author or the patron and could be subdivided into two groups, the *mediata* and the *immediata*. The former was usually ascribed to God as the prime mover of all things, and the second to the author, who moves the text.

The *causa formalis*, corresponding to the Servian *stilus* and the Ps.-Augustinian *modus*, was subdivided into the *forma tractatus* and the *forma tractandi*.[19] The *Casualis euentus accessus* to Statius' *Achilleid* explains the difference between the two:[20]

> *Forma tractatus est compositio seu diuisio libri in suas partes. Forma trac-*
> *tandi est modus agendi quem seruab<a>t autor, qui est metricus.*

The *causa finalis* is the *intentio*, and can be divided into two groups, the *intrinseca* and the *extrinseca*. The *intrinseca intentio* was the plot. The *extrinseca intentio* was usually tied to some event contemporary to the author's writing. Again, the *Casualis euentus accessus* to Statius (Incipitarium 38) shows us how these categories worked in practice:

> *Causa uero finalis est duplex, scilicet intrinseca et extrinseca. Intrinseca est cognitio*
> *eorum que fecit Thetis ut Achilles filius suus non moreretur. Extrinseca fuit triplex.*
> *Prima fuit ut ostenderet Statius quod nullus potest obstare diuinis. Secunda fuit ut os-*
> *tenderet quod quelibet mater sine patre deberet instruere suos filios. Tertia fuit ut se-*
> *ruiret Domiciano filio Vespesiani et hoc de primo.*

Modern classifications and the critical role of accessus

Though *accessus* can be delineated into these groups in theory, in practice they appear quite different. As *accessus* became more detached from commentaries, scholars freely picked and chose from the systems of *circumstantiae* depending on the work at hand, the goal of the scholar, and the depth of the exegesis that followed, if there was any.[21] What I have just depicted as delineated groups are only seldom found purely intact in individual *accessus*. In practice, actual *accessus* tend to borrow and adapt from all traditions.

One scholar, R.W. Hunt (1948), made a preliminary analysis and classification of the varied patterns of *circumstantiae*, and found four groups, which he labeled A, B, C, and D. Unfor-

---

[17] This methodology is used in only one *accessus* to Statius, the early–sixteenth century one by Janus Parrhasius (Incipitarium 215).

[18] *Physica* 2.194v–95a; cf. *Aristoteles Latinus* (München, 1995 [Berlin, 1831]), 107a.

[19] On these two elements, see Allen 1982.67–178.

[20] This unedited *accessus*, which de Angelis classified as a *recollecta* (1984.117), was likely written in the 1380s.

[21] *Accessus* that preface full commentaries tend to be more detailed than those before glossaries or texts without notes. This is, however, not a robust tendency, and it is not uncommon for a lengthy *accessus* to precede a very simple commentary or a very simple *accessus* to precede a detailed commentary.

tunately, three of these groups are tied to the sources of the *circumstantiae* I listed above (groups B, C, and D are simply the schema of Servius, Ps.-Augustine, and Boethius, respectively), and afford us little practical aid in classifying actual *accessus*. His group A, however, does represent actual *accessus*, not because of its *circumstantiae*, but because of its methodology.

Group A, which is chronologically the last of Hunt's groups,[22] gives three *circumstantiae*: *persona*, *locus*, and *tempus*. While ultimately a simplification of the Servian scheme, this group is derived from the early–fifth century *De nuptiis Mercurii et Philologiae* of Martianus Capella (§ 552), where we see the *circumstantiae* of *persona, causa, modus, locus, tempus*, and *res*.[23] In order to form Hunt's group A, the *circumstantiae* of *causa, modus*, and *res* were collected under the rubric *persona*. It is this simplification of groups, together with conflation, that governs the formation of actual *accessus*. Unfortunately, not enough *accessus* have been edited to allow an adequate scientific study of the *circumstantiae* used by individual scholars or to create a useful classification guide.[24] From our current perspective, then, the one critical tool available to us is to pay heed to the language used in each *accessus* and to see whether the logic implied by the source still applies.

Accessus are our best tool for understanding popular medieval criticism, much better than scholia and commentaries.[25] This is because most of the medieval commentaries that we have are aimed at school students and provide us with more glosses and etymologies than they do criticism.[26] General interpretation, especially biographical interpretation, is stated most succinctly in the *accessus*, and often only there. So, one thread that passes through all of the *circumstantiae* I have discussed is the importance of the *auctor*.[27] In practice, it is the *vita* of the *auctor* that governs the *accessus*, in that most of the *circumstantiae* are answered on the basis of the *vita*. Put briefly, non-allegorical interpretation of an author was then, as it is today, intimately tied to the biography of the author. It is not surprising, then, that our modern interpretations and the medieval interpretations often overlap, even though our methodology does not.

Before beginning, there is one more aspect of *accessus* that I should mention. We must remember that the intended academic audience of these texts was students and we should not see *accessus* as showing more than generally held opinions; they were certainly not intended to be original or to demonstrate any advanced theoretical skills.

---

[22] Scholars first seem to use this group in the early-to-mid-eleventh century (see Klopsch 1980.52). There are a few examples of the *circumstantiae locus, tempus*, and *persona* before this time. B. Bischoff 1954.202 notes that they can be found in a few Evangelical commentaries as early as the eighth century (he did not specify which ones), and also cites two tenth-century Donatus commentaries: Vaticano, Pal. lat. 1754 (H. Keil, *Analecta grammatica*, prog. Königliche Pädagogium zu Halle [Halle, 1848], 21, which begins, "Notandum est quia in capite uniuscuiusque libri tria sunt requirenda, id est locus, tempus, persona") and the so-called *Quae sunt, quae* commentary (Hagen 1870), XLI; discussed below, p. 4).

[23] Hugh of St. Victor discusses and refines these categories in his *De tribus maximis circumstantiis* (I use the edition of W.M. Green, *Speculum* 18 [1943], 488–92).

[24] At the end of the Incipitarium in Volume II, there is a table listing the *curcumstantiae* in the *accessus* to Statius.

[25] This is the one beneficial aspect of medieval introductions that did not survive into the age of the printing press, where introductions contain very little methological nor scientific information and "forbade too much discussion of technical problems as boring and inelegant" (Grafton 1983.6).

[26] The commentary to Statius in Vaticano, Pal. lat. 1695, for example, is simply a collection of extracts from Isidore's *Etymologiae*. The *accessus* that precedes it, however, is extensive and shows evidence of much more research. See below, p. 28.

[27] We also find the variants *autor* and *author*. I found no evidence of the pejorative/laudatory distinctions between *auctor, autor*, and *author* that Minnis saw (see Minnis 1984.10). Indeed, we find that different witnesses of the same *accessus*, use different forms.

Statius' Biography and the *Accessus* Model

On the basis of a few passages in the *Silvae* (mostly 3.5, 5.3, and 5.5), we now know that Statius, the son of an emigree from Magna Graecia, was born and seems to have spent most of his life in Naples, coming to Rome only later in life, where he sought out patrons, performed in competitions, and received some interest from the Flavian emperor Domitian. He was born in about AD 45, and seems to have died before Domitian, who died in 96 (or, if he outlived Domitian, he seems not to have composed any poems for the Nervan-Antonian emperors). Of his family we know little. His father was a *grammaticus*, but we know nothing of his mother. Statius' wife was a widow named Claudia (whose previous husband was a poet or a musician), and adopted her daughter. Their marriage was a happy one but without fruit and the couple adopted a son, who died at a young age. Other than Claudia, we know the name of none of his family members.

Now, as I noted in the introduction to Volume I, Statius' *Silvae* were lost between the mid-fifth century and 1417–18.[28] For this reason, Statius, who was one of the most popular ancient authors during the Middle Ages, posed a severe problem for the *accessus*-based approach to literary criticism: he did not have a traditional *vita*, such as Virgil had, and, without the *Silvae*, very few biographical details could be gleaned from his texts, such as scholars did with Ovid[29] and, much later, Pindar.[30] Rather, Statius was known in the Middle Ages through his epic poems only, the only external source for his life being a passage from Juvenal (6.82–87):[31]

> *Curritur ad uocem iucundam et carmen amicae*
> *Thebaidos, laetam cum fecit Statius urbem,*
> *Promisitque diem, tanta dulcedine captos*
> *Adficit ille animos, tantaque libidine uolgi*
> *Auditur, sed cum fregit subsellia uersu*
> *Esurit, intactam Paridi nisi uendat Agauen.*

Even with the *Silvae*, Statius poses a serious problem for biographical criticism, since he is what we might term a detached narrator. The *Thebaid* and *Achilleid* deal with events that are in no way contemporary to him;[32] and in these epics, outside of generic apostrophes, he is personally present only at the very beginning and the very end. Likewise, in the *Silvae*, his narrative personality is always subordinated to his subject.[33] While a few poems provide some personal details, the details are very thin and only invite the reader to read other passages of the poems programmatically or autobiographically.

Without the *Silvae*, our knowledge of Statius' biography is very limited. From the epics, we can ascertain only that his patron was a Roman emperor (*Theb.* 12.814) who had had several successes against the Germans (1.18–33), that Statius had worked on the *Thebaid* for twelve

---

[28] The title *Silvarum* as a Statius work occurs in Priscian, *Inst.* 13.15 (*GLK* 3.10.21), but this is noted in only one manuscript: Vaticano, Barb. lat. 74.

[29] The best discussion of the formation of Ovidian biographies is Ghisalberti 1946. For other biographies and *accessus* to Ovid, see B. Nogara, "Di alcune vite e commenti medioevali di Ovidio," in *Miscellanea Ceriani; Raccolta di scritti originali per onorare la memoria di Mr. Antonio Maria Ceriani* (Milan, 1910), 413–31; G. Przychocki, *Accessus Ovidiani*, Rozprawy Akademii Umiejętności, Wydział Filologiczny, ser. 3, vol. 4 (Kraków, 1911) ["Symbolae ad veterum auctorum historiam atque Medii Aevi studia philologa", I, 65–126]; F.T. Coulson, "Hitherto Unedited Medieval and Renaissance Lives of Ovid (I)," *Mediaeval Studies* 49 (1987), 152–207; Coulson 1997; and Coulson-Roy.

[30] See M. Lefkowitz, "The Influential Fictions in the Scholia to Pindar's *Pythian 8*," *CP* 70 (1975), 173–85 (reprinted in *First Person Fictions* [Oxford, 1991], pp. 72–88).

[31] Some of Statius' patron sin the *Silvae* were also patrons of Martial, but the two do not mention each other and no information on Statius' biography can be gleaned directly from Martial's poems.

[32] See D. Vessey, *Statius and the* Thebaid (Cambridge, 1973), p. 57.

[33] For this assessment, see A. Hardie 1983.138–51.

years before publishing it (12.811), that he was so successful that students in the schools already were reading his works (12.815), and lastly, that he respected the *Aeneid* (12.816) and therefore post-dated Virgil.

This brief information, combined with the lines from Juvenal, was all that the medieval scholar definitely knew about the poet,[34] and it is from this that scholars constructed a biography for him.

Statius is, then, an extreme instance of medieval scholars "getting the facts wrong," not because of a difference of interpretation or methodology, but simply because of a lack of information. This situation is exacerbated by his popularity, such that we have a great number of manuscripts providing us with a wide array of interpretation. My purpose in editing these texts is to demonstrate how criticism of Statius evolved. This will highlight not only how readers interpreted Statius' poems, but also changing academic tastes and methodological developments throughout the Middle Ages.[35]

Editorial Principles

The texts presented here reflect the most traditional interpretations as well as the most radical. The choice of texts was made in order to give the reader an understanding of how the tradition changed, highlighting the ways that scholars approached and solved problems, for better or for worse. Texts that were simply derivative of other accessus were not included unless they showed a development in thinking.

In editing the texts, I have taken a very conservative approach to emending the texts at hand. In my recension, I chose to favor two types of manuscripts: the oldest and those witnesses that preserve the longest, most complete text (without visible interpolation). I have sometimes favored witnesses that contain the wording that is preserved in *accessus* of other traditions. I have done this (albeit only occasionally) because of the close relationship among all *accessus* to Statius; the phraseology that persists through most of the witnesses of all *accessus* is sometimes logically preferable to that found in one or two anomalous manuscripts, although not always.

In emending these manuscripts, I follow the modern epigraphical rules: emendations of words lost due to physical problems with the manuscript, such as a hole or a tight binding, are surrounded by square brackets ([]); text that has been interpolated into a manuscript of tradition is written in *italics*; my own emending insertions are surrounded by triangular brackets (<>). The deduced presence of lacunae is indicated by asterisks (***), and text which does not make sense and I have been unable to correct is obelized (†). I also strive to preserve the spelling and the distinction between u and v found in the oldest or best manuscripts, even when that flows

---

[34] Oddly, medieval scholars never seem to have paid mind to the poems that Sidonius Apollinaris praises and names. There is no mention of that poet in the notes to Statius, and in the manuscripts of Sidonius Apollinaris' poetical works (which are admittedly few), there are no notes that mark the problem. Sidonius Apollinaris' prose works are cited in the *accessus* to Lucan, that begins *Equalis uero ideoque familiaris...* (edited by Weber 2, pp. 12–15 as the *Laur. cod. vita*): "memoriter hoc Sidonius in epistolis refert."

[35] The *accessus* to Statius have not been fully studied heretofore. The only scholarly discussions are those of de Angelis 1984 and 1985, in which she sought to investigate the completeness or incompleteness of the *Achilleid* in the medieval school; and those of C. Jeudy (with Y.-F. Riou and with C. Bozzolo), which treat the *compendia* of Laurent de Premierfait (Laurentius Campanus) to Statius' epics. For the scholarly reception of the *Silvae* since 1898, a period not covered in this study but no less important for Statius' reception, see H. Cancik, "Statius, Silvae: Ein Bericht ueber die Forschung seit Friedrich Vollmer (1898)," *ANRW* 2.42.5 (1986), 2681–726 and H.-J. van Dam, "Statius, Silvae: Forschungsbericht 1974–1984," *ANRW* 2.32.5 (1986), 2727–53. For the recent popular reception of the *Thebaid*, see W.J. Dominik, "Statius' *Thebaid* in the twentieth century," in R. Faber und B. Seidensticker, edd., *Worte, Bilder, Töne: Studien zur Antike und Antikerezeption Bernhard Kytzler zu ehren* (Würzburg, 1996), 129–41. See too J. Tolkiehn, "Bibliographie critique, 1911–1914," *JAW* 171 (1915), 53–59; J. Tolkiehn, "Bibliographie critique, 1908–1920," *JAW* 188 (1921), 228–34; and M. Schuster, "Literaturbericht, 1915–1925," *JAW* 212 (1927), 131–44.

contrary to our sense (such as the retention of a medial σ when used terminally). I have resolved the manuscript abbreviations in accordance with the general pattern of the best manuscripts. When, in the narrative portions of this volume, a reading requires clarification (but not correction), I surround the added letters with round brackets, e.g. *ill(a)e*, to distinguish it from *ille*.

In citing manuscripts, I have chosen to follow a kind of short-hand method in the text of my commentary; full citations will be found before the edited text. For the sigla of each edition, I follow the traditional practice of using Roman letters to represent extant manuscripts, Greek letters to represent non-extant archetypes, and fracture letters (e.g. 𝕽 and 𝕾) to represent extant witnesses whose authority can be somewhat undermined (such as revisions and *florilegia*). I have adopted the newer practice of using *ac* and *pc* after a siglum to indicate *ante correctionem* and *post correctionem*.

Three appendices are added to the study. Appendix A (pp. 131 ff.) shows the relationships between the various texts in a graphic form. Appendix B (on pp. 135 ff.) lists the edited texts chronologically. Appendix C contains editions of some epitaphs and poems on Statius found in the manuscripts in the belief that these will add some less techinical evidence for Statius' reception, particularly in the fifteenth century.

ACCESSUS TO STATIUS THROUGH THE TWELFTH CENTURY

The *Thebaid*

The *Quaeritur accessus*

Exegesis is very common in the Statian manuscripts. Of the thirteen earliest manuscripts containing Statius' epic poems or commentaries thereon, six transmit marginal commentary to a poem,[1] while another three transmit self-standing commentaries.[2] Beginning in the tenth century, most glossed manuscripts include an *accessus* of some sort, the earliest of which is the *Quaeritur accessus* to the *Thebaid* (Incipitarium 226).[3] From the beginning, this *accessus* is associated with the commentary of Lactantius Placidus.[4] The earliest manuscript of this *accessus*, which is of north-central Italian origin and dates to the tenth century,[5] is also our oldest complete manuscript of Lactantius Placidus.

Our only clue for the date and origin of this *accessus* is its phraseology. The language of the text is classical, for the most part, except from the phrase "supra taxati... tempore" (15). To take *taxati* first, "to mention" or "to cite" is an uncommon usage for the verb *taxo*. It is used by Tertullian (*pr.* 6 *advers. Marc.* 4.20 and 27), Cyprianus (*Epist.* 63.7), and Commodianus (*Apol.* 386); Latham cites further uses in 786, 939, and c. 1146;[6] but these instances are sporadic. The greatest concentration comes in the mid-ninth century, in the *Benedicti regula* 18 (ca. 840),[7] Charlemagne 1.6 (ca. 858—Migne 98.1019 D), and Eulogius' *Memorialia Sanctorum* 3.6 (ca. 860—Migne 115.803 D). This evidence would point to a date in the ninth century for the composition of the *accessus*. Next, the usage of *supra* meaning "in the time of" or "back then when" seems to be a uniquely Gallic usage.[8] This helps us pinpoint the origin of the text; the only documented usage of *supra* in this time period is by St. Remigius of Reims, *Polyptychum* 3.1 (mid-ninth century).[9] From this scanty evidence, it is possible to argue that the *accessus* was

---

[1] Five transmit Lactantius Placidus : the Worcester fragments (add.7 and Q.8 [X s.]), Gotha, Memb. I 129 (X s.); Düsseldorf, K2: F.49 (X–XI s.); Halle, Qu. Cod. 86 (XI s.); Leipzig, Rep. I. 12a (XI s.); Montpellier, Ms. H. 62 (X s.); and a tenth/eleventh-century fragment, now in a private collection in Pavia (see G. Bezola, "Un fragmento di codice della *Tebaide* di Stazio," *Athenaeum* 18 [1940], 51–53). One transmits a commentary from a different tradition: Paris, BnF, n.a.l. 1627 (X s.).

[2] Two of these transmit Lactantius Placidus: Valenciennes, 394 (IX–X s.) and Vaticano, Pal. lat. 1694 (X s.). One transmits a commentary from another tradition: Berlin, Staatsbibliothek—Preußischer Kulturbesitz, Ms. lat. qu. 228 (XI s.).

[3] Manuscripts often call this the *vita Statii* (e.g., Bruxelles, BR, 5337–38, [XI s., but the title was added by a later hand]), and Clogan and Sweeney classified it as such, but it is clearly an *accessus*, as it deals exclusively with the *Thebaid*. The only modern discussions of this *accessus* (which has yet to be critically edited) are those of Brugnoli 1965 and 1969. For his text, Brugnoli simply copied the *accessus* from the Lindenbrog edition (Paris, 1600), without understanding the printing and abbreviation conventions of the time.

[4] For colometrical reasons, it is unlikely that that the *accessus* was a part of the original Lactantian commentary; however, in the Middle Ages, it was assumed that it was. In the "Glosula magistri Martini a S. Benedicto super Statium Thebaidos" in Paris, BnF, lat. 5137 (XIII s.), for example, we find the note, "Lactencius [sic] uero nomina sic exponit: 'Papinius est cognomen, quoniam de genere Papinorum fuit. Surculus agnomen ab euentu, ut dictum est, quasi sursum canens. Statius proprium nomen,'" which is a recasting of the *Quaeritur*. The error perpetuated even into the twentieth century: in 1902, H.F. Tozer (*Notes on the Purgatorio* [Oxford], 321) wrote, "Statius was a native of Naples. Dante's error as to his having been born at Toulouse was derived from Lactantius, who in his commentary on the *Thebaid* confounds him with a rhetorician at Toulouse of the same name."

[5] Vaticano, Pal. lat. 1694. The scribe writes *ae* uniquely as *ę* in the *accessus*, but in the commentary to Lactantius Placidus that follows, *æ* is heavily favored; it is possible, then, that the scribe copied the *accessus* and the commentary from different parents.

[6] R.E. Latham, *Revised Medieval Latin Word-List* (London, 1965)

[7] Ed. J. Semmler, *Corp. consuet. monast.*, vol. 1 (Siegburg, 1963), 513–36

[8] du Cange, s.v. *taxo*.

[9] See B. Guérard, *Polyptique de l'abbaye de Saint-Remi de Reims* (Paris, 1853), 4, col. 1.

written some time in the mid-ninth century in France, perhaps northern France, but since most modern medieval lexica have not yet reached the letters S or T, this conclusion cannot be fully substantiated.

The sources of the biographical section of this *accessus* have been studied and criticized since the rediscovery of the *Silvae*, most copiously by Gevartius in 1616, whose treatise was frequently reprinted and cited throughout the seventeenth century.[10] In the *accessus*, the date for Statius' poetic activity was derived from the presence of Domitian in the poems[11] and from Juvenal's contemporary reference to him.[12] His presumed birth-place and name stem from confusion with L. Statius Ursulus, a rhetor from Toulouse who is mentioned in Suetonius' *De Rhetoribus* (12) and Jerome's translation of Eusebius' *Chronica*.[13]

The sources for Statius' character are more conjectural: the assumption of his noble stock ("nobili ortus prosapia," 7) may stem from a misunderstanding of *prisca parentum nomina* (*Ach.* 1.12–13)[14] or from his patronage; he was "clarus ingenio, doctus eloquio" (7) either because in the poem in which Juvenal praised him, *ingenium* and *eloquium* are mentioned as important virtues of a poet,[15] or because of some unstated assessment of the poems. Lastly, the cognomen "Surculus"[16] is explained as meaning he sang *sursum* (18), which is usually explained as "iocundam et altam habebat uocem" (London, BL, Burney 258) or "super omnes poetas" (London, BL, Royal 15.C.X).[17]

Although short and simple, the *accessus* poses serious taxonomic problems. Formally, the *accessus* follows Hunt's schema A, giving the *tempus*, the *locus*, and *persona* of the author, each appropriately framed by the word *autem*. At the end is a concluding note on the *opus*. However, Hunt's schema A is representative of later medieval *accessus*, usually after the eleventh century.[18] Before then, we would expect to see a more Servian structure, in which the text

---

[10] First edition: 1616, Leiden: J. Marcus; the second followed in 1618. It is reproduced in Cruceus' 1618 edition (Paris: Thomas Blaise), Thomas Stephens' 1651 edition (Cambridge: Thomas Buck), and Johann Veenhusen's 1671 edition (Leiden: Hackniana). The last reproduction I have found is that in A.J. Valpy's Delphine edition (London, 1824), vol. 3. In his notebook (now London, BL, Sloane 1173 [XVII s.]), S. Byfield rewrote Gevartius' introduction for a school lecture.

[11] Domitian is nowhere named; *Thebaid* 1.17–33 summarize the achievements of some emperor against the Germans; he is mentioned still more generally in *Achilleid* 1.14–19 and *Thebaid* 12.814. In a XV s. commentary on the *Achilleid* in London, BL, Harley 4869, Vespasian is noted as the dedicatee of the poems, and a gloss in the XII s. manuscript 's-Gravenhage, Koninklijke Bibliotheek, 128.A.38, Statius is noted as having lived under the reign of Diocletian, but I suspect that both of these are scribal errors and do not reflect traditions.

[12] Many of *accessus* transmit variant readings in the entire Juvenal passage, especially line 83. I have been unable to find any of these in the standard critical editions or in the manuscrits of Juvenal I have consulted.

[13] *Olymp.* 209 (R. Helm, *Die Chronik des Hieronymus,* Eusebius Werke, vol. 7, Die Griechischen christlichen Schriftsteller der ersten Jahrhunderte, 47 [Berlin, 1956], 182.11; in Migne [*PG* 19.542], the entry is in the 210th Olympiad.)

[14] Cf. the note to 1.12 in Venezia, BNM, Lat. XII.10 (=3973) (XIII s.): "prisca, notandum quod iste Stacius nobilis estiterat genere a primo auis."

[15] *Sat.* 7.19: *eloquium*; 7.63: *ingenio*

[16] The difference between *Sursulus* and *Surculus* is one of methodology. Both were seen as etymologically descended from *sursum canens,* but *Sursulus* was derived from *sursus canens* and *Surculus* from *sursum canens.*

[17] The scholia to Juvenal reflect the first of these, saying, "poema ipsud [*sc.* Thebais] delectabile et ipse dicitur bonam vocem habuisse" (Schol. *ad* Juv. 7.83 [Wessner 1931.126]). Huguccio of Pisa (c. 1140–1210) explains this assessment in his *Liber de derivationibus,* s.v. *sursum*: "Surculus ille dictus est quasi surcum canens, quia post Virgilium inter ceteros poetas principatum obtinuit" (München, Clm. 14056).

[18] Hunt 1948. Another scheme of three *circumstantiae* is found in the late–eleventh/early–twelfth century *accessus* to Ovid's *Metamorphoses* of Manegold of Lautenbach: "... moderni quadam gaudentes brevitate tria principaliter inquirenda statuere, id est materiam, intentionem et cui parti philosophiae supponatur." See Ghisalberti 1946.17 n. 3; Coulson-Roy 72; and C. Meiser, "Ueber einen Commentar zu den Metamorphosen des Ovids," *Sitzungsberichte der philosophisch-philologischen und historischen Classe der k.b. Akademie der Wissenschaften zu München* (München, 1885), 47–89 [49].

began with some sort of preface and discussed the work under some rubricated plan, including details from the author's life. Surprisingly, none of these elements is present here. But that is not the only anomaly.

Before the twelfth century, the incipit "quaeritur" is found only in our text and in introductions and commentaries to Priscian.[19] In later manuscripts, the incipit "quaeritur" is found in medical, scientific, and religious treatises, on such topics as why water evaporates, why we need to confess, etc. There are a few early literary instances, one being Rabanus' thirteenth-century preface to the *Judith* in the Bibliothèque Mazarine in Paris.[20] Rabanus' preface dates the events of the text by interrelating Assyrian, Hebrew, and Persian king-lists and then counting the number of years each king ruled.[21] Now, what Rabanus' investigation and the scientific treatises[22] have in common is that the information they give us is not available to the average reader. To connect three calendar systems or to answer a scientific problem, such as the nature of confession,[23] requires knowledge, perhaps access to a library, and, most importantly, authority.

In the other *accessus* of the tenth century, authority posed no problem. For readers of Ovid and Horace (that is, poetry in which the narrative persona plays a central role), the material for the author's biography was easily verifiable—it was in the text in front of them. For readers of Virgil, in addition to the autobiographically programmatic passages in the *Eclogues*, there was also Servius' preface to the *Aeneid*, which had the added authority that comes with age. Scholars could also arrogate the authority of Servius by borrowing his schema and then inserting their own material, which was based upon verifiable facts. Without a biography or enough information to fill in the Servian scheme, however, scholars of Statius could claim authority from none of these sources. The question arises, then, how can research, especially "new" research, have authority?

In the mid-thirteenth century, Dante, following Boethius' lead, would solve this problem by arguing in favor of a new authority (and nobility) that does not come from age, but from reason,[24] even if this reason is that of the fallible individual. But Dante lived a good three centuries after the composition of the *Quaeritur accessus*, and we must ask ourselves if the *Quaeritur accessus* embraces this "new" authority long before Dante's time, or if it only uses reason because age is lacking. To answer this, we must look at the methodology of the *Quaeritur accessus*.

The *accessus* to the *Thebaid* is succinct. Its rubrics are clearly delineated, and it is connected by a running narrative, in the tone of a lecturer. There is no information that could not have come from research (that is, there is no inferential material), and the *accessus* makes a

---

[19] The genre of the *quaestio* has a long history in classical literature, with the most famous authors being Cicero, Plutarch, and Papinian. The incipit *quaeritur*, however, is a much later development, reportedly appearing first in the eleventh century ("Quaeritur cur omne studiorum genus sapientiae dixit" [Barcelona, Archivio de la Corona de Aragon, Cod. Ripoll 59 (XI s.) 1r]; see G.L. Bursill-Hall, *A Census of Medieval Latin Grammatical Manuscripts*, Gammatica Speculativa 4 [Stuttgart, 1981], 18.1.1). Its common presence in literary *accessus* is a later development, beginning in the thirteenth century, as in an *accessus* to the Ps.-Ovidian *De Vetula* (Coulson-Roy 400), incipit "Queritur unde mihi quod opus processit istud... ." The word *quaeritur* is found within in a few *accessus* before then (cf. that to Boethius edited by Huygens 1970.47–48.26: "queritur tempore cuius imperatoris fuit iste Boetius"), but never at the beginning.

[20] Ms. 199, 2va, "Prefatio quedam Rabini de tempore Iudith," *inc.* "Queritur quo tempore quibusue regibus hystoria Iudith fuerit"

[21] On the methodologies of chronologists before Scaliger, see Grafton 1993.25–75 and 145–357.

[22] We should remember that these treatises, like *accessus*, were at heart scholarly lectures.

[23] Dublin, Trinity College Library, 312, 24r: "Queritur utrum qui habet mortalia plura et confitetur alique et alique non... "

[24] *Conv.* 4.8.12–14. This is germane to Augustine's precept that his readers accept only those things in his works that, upon examination, they found to be true. Both of these passages are discussed more fully in Minnis and Scott 68.

point of making a division between what is common knowledge (*constat ueraciter*, 1) and what is not (*inuenitur*, 4). Further, the life does not give any methodology or allegory for interpreting the epic or understanding its composition. A good parallel to this is the tenth-century so-called *Quae sunt, quae* commentary.[25] The commentary begins:

> *Quae sunt, quae omnem ueritatem scripturae commendant? Tria: locus, tempus, persona. Donati requiretur locus, tempus et persona. Locus scribendi Roma et dicitur "urbis Romae," persona "Donati grammatici," tempus Liberii episcopi, qui fuit XXXVI post sanctum Petrum. I littera quomodo dicitur in Hebreo, in Graeco, in Latino?...*

This is a very simple commentary that is formed around a series of questions, without expansion. Like our *accessus*, it is sparse and keeps very close to the material at hand. It is succinct like our text, but it lacks the narrative tone.

It is the sparseness that we find in the *Quaeritur accessus*, combined with its keen scholarly responsibility, that leads me to believe that the author deliberately composed the *accessus* as a scientific *quaestio*, both because of the dearth of available information on Statius and to lend the life a scientific or even scholarly authority. The incipit *quaeritur* emphasizes this, and if this is not the earliest use of this incipit, then the author deliberately chose it to identify the genre of the *accessus*; if not then we can see that the author saw his[26] work as more appropriate for the genre of a *quaestio* than for the genre of an *accessus*.

My answer is a problematic one. Accurate scholarship and honest reasoning are usually seen as late developments, beginning in the early thirteenth century.[27] To argue, as I have done, that a scholarly treatise that dates at least to the ninth century, embraces reason and logic to the exclusion of all else, suggests either that the piece is an anomaly or that it gives us a glimpse into a poorly represented period of intellectual history that seems to have been much richer in scholarly ideas than we had thought.

The *Quaeritur accessus* was a bold undertaking, especially given its early date. It may be this, combined with its scholarly attitude, that made the *accessus* such a formidable and tenacious force in medieval scholarship on Statius. It eclipsed all other contemporary and earlier biographies of the poet—if there were any—and gained so much authority that out of the 253 extant witnesses of the *Thebaid*, 50 transmit the text. It is by far the most common *accessus* to Statius, and with the exception of one *accessus* to the *Achilleid*, which I discuss below, all medieval *accessus* to the poet were based on it.[28] It was reproduced in several printed editions (although never edited from more than one manuscript) and proved so contentious that in the first two centuries of the printed book, most editors and commentators occupied themselves with the biographical problems posed by this text.[29]

---

[25] Hagen 1870.XLI

[26] I say "his" because, from what we know of medieval schooling, it is more likely that these *accessus* were composed by males. Women were certainly involved in writing and illuminating manuscripts, although their presence is usually noted indirectly, either by means of tax-roles or by feminine endings in colopha (see C. de Hamel, *A History of Illuminated Manuscripts* [Oxford, 1986], 130 and 172 for some examples). There is no direct evidence of female scribes in manuscripts of Statius.

[27] Minnis and Scott, *passim* and 373–94

[28] *Pace* de Angelis, who believes that a thirteenth-century *accessus* that names Statius' mother and notes his schooling in Narbonne and Bordeaux represented a second tradition. I discuss this problem below.

[29] Cf. the somewhat exaggerated claim by Thomas Stephens (*An Essay upon Statius* [London 1648], A3v): "For those criticall pens which have published their ingenuous disputes, between Ursulus and Surculus, (although, I conceive, neither were of kin to our Statius) would have deserv'd better of the Commonwealth of Learning, if they held a torch to the darke and mysterious places of the poem: which, I dare say, would not be so much neglected, but that it is so little understood."

The stemma of the text divides the witnesses into two families and betrays what appears to be several recensions, most noteworthily to form the readings of P and Q.

Figure 1. Stemma of Manuscripts of the *Quaeritur accessus*

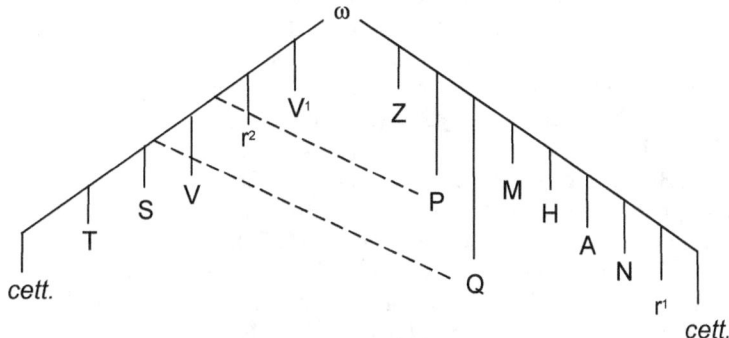

Text 1. The *Quaeritur accessus*

A = London, British Library, Harley 2665 (XII s.), 1r
B = Bruxelles, Bibliothèque Royale Albert 1ᵉʳ, 5337–38 (XI s.), 1r
H = London, British Library, Harley 2636 (XIII s.), 108v
M = München, Bayerische Staatsbibliothek, Clm. 312 (XII s.), 1v
N = Reims, Bibliothèque municipale, ms. 1265 (XII s.)
P = Paris, Bibliothèque nationale de France, lat. 14140 (XIII s. in.), 1r
Q = London, British Library, Burney 258 (XII/XIII s.), 3r
R¹ = London, British Library, Royal 15.C.X (XII s.), 1rc
R² = London, British Library, Royal 15.C.X (X/XI s.), 2r
S = Paris, Bibliothèque national de France, lat. 13046 (X/XI s.), 1ra
T = Paris, Bibliothèque national de France, n.a.l. 1627 (X/XI s.), 1ra
V = Vaticano, Città del, Biblioteca Apostolica Vaticana, Pal. lat. 1694 (X s.), 1r
V¹ = Vaticano, Città del, Biblioteca Apostolica Vaticana, Barb. lat. 84 (XV s.)
Z = Zürich, Zentralbibliothek, Rh. 53 (420) (XII s.), p. 69a

     Queritur quo tempore fuerit iste Statius, sed constat ueraciter
     fuisse eum temporibus Uespasiani imperatoris et peruenisse usque
     ad imperium Domitiani fratris Titi, qui etiam et Titus iunior dictus
     est. Si quis autem unde fuerit querat, inuenitur fuisse Tholosensis,
5   que ciuitas est Gallię. Ideoque in Gallia celeberrime docuit
     rethoricam, sed postea ueniens Romam ad poetriam se transtulit.
     Fuit autem nobili ortus prosapia, clarus ingenio et doctus eloquio.
     Cuius Iuuenalis sic meminit dicens <*Sat.* 7.82–86>:

          Curritur ad uocem iocundam et carmen amicę
10   Thebaidos, lętam cum facit Statius urbem,
          Promisitque diem tanta dulcedine captos
          Afficit ille animos, tantaque libidine uulgi
          Auditur, sed cum fregit subsellia uersu
          Esurit, intactam Paridi nisi uendat Agauen.

15   Scripsit autem Thebaiden supra taxati imperatoris tempore. Est
     autem Thebais femininum patronomicum sicut Ęneis et Theseis.
     Dictus est autem proprio nomine Statius, Papinius autem
     cognomine, Surculus autem agnomine quasi sursum canens.

---

5 quę... Gallię] cf. Servium *ad. Aen.* 1.*praef.*5: quae civitas est Venetiae.
5–6 in... rethoricam] cf. Hieronymum-Eusebium, *Chronicon* (*Olymp.* 209): Statius Surculus
     Tolosanus celeberrime in Gallia rhetoricam docet.
7 ingenio... eloquio] cf. Juvenalis *Sat.* 7.19 (eloquium) et 63 (ingenio).
16 Ęneis... Theseis] cf. Servium *ad Aen.* 1.*praef.*75.

---

1 sed *om.* HN   statius iste fuerit R¹   statius iste V¹   eum ueraciter fuisse R¹   **2** eum *om.* q
eum fuisse BHNqR¹S   imperatoris *om.* N   et] atque HV   uenisse H   usque... domitiani
(3)] ad imperium usque ad domiciani H   **3** imperium] tempus V¹ : *om.* N   et] ac R²S : *om.*
AHNPR¹   ad domitianum fratrem N   iunior*om.* BHMNR¹Z   **4** aliquis querat R¹   autem
om. PV   querat unde fuerit R¹   inde V   fuit A   fuerit... inuenitur *om.* N   tolonensis
HR¹1 : tolossensis R² : colosensis MqZ : tholonensem N   **5** uocata tholosa *post* gallie *add.* R¹
ideoque... gallia] ibique R¹   celeberrimæ R¹   decuit S*ac*   rethoricam docuit R¹   **6** romam
ueniens H   poetam H   contulit HNR¹   **7** autem] enim AqSTVV¹ : *om.* PNZ   ortu R¹ :

natus B   prosapia ortus AP   et *om.* HN   et doctus] edoctus R[1]   **8** cuius] de quo R[1]   sic]
in libro suo N   dicens *om.* APR[1]   **9** iucundam V   ad *post* et *add.* R[1]   **10** statius *post* cum
dist. A   cum *ante* statius *dist.* PZ   fecit BMPR[1]R[2]STV *rectius*   facit cum Z   urbem facit
H   **11** promisitque... agauen (14) *om.* BHMNR[1]   que *om.* T   misitque S   **12** que *om.* A
13 aditur A   **14** exurit V[1]   **15** scripsit... theseis (16) *om.* N   scripsit] sumpsit r1   sub Br1
taxati] tanti R[1]   tempore imperatoris A   **16** sic R[2]S   **17** est *om.* NS   autem[1]] a H : *om.*
MNR[1]   statius proprio nomine cognomine papinius N   pampinus R[1]   autem[2] *om.* ABHNR[1]
18 cognomen... agnomen V[1]   sursulus A*ac*BTV   autem] uero ABHMN *fort. rectius* : *om.*
PR[1]

The Zürich *accessus*

Outside of the *Quaeritur accessus* and two rewritings of it,[30] there are no other *accessus* to the *Thebaid* before the end of the eleventh century. After the eleventh century, interest in *accessus* seems to increase greatly,[31] and in the twelfth century, we find some eleven individual *accessus* to Statius, which, although they are mostly brief, do show us the new critical problem faced in that age. As I noted above, the *Quaeritur accessus* gives us very little information. In the twelfth century, scholars, likely influenced by the development of *accessus* as a genre, sought to expand the *Quaeritur accessus* along the lines of the *accessus* to other authors. A good demonstration of such an attempt is a short *accessus* in Zürich, Zentralbibliothek, Rh. 53 (XII s.; Incipitarium 98). On page 96 of the manuscript, we see traces of several *accessus*, both to Statius and in general: aside from two *accessus* to the *Thebaid*, there are also some notes on rhetorical devices, and an *accessus* to Ovid's *Metamorphoses*.[32] Further, across the top of the page is a fragment of an *accessus*:

> *incipiendis auctoribus* VII *inquiruntur, uita poetii, titulus operis, qualitas carminis, intentio scribentis, numerus librorum, naco,*[33] *ordo lib<rorum>.*[34]

The first *accessus* to Statius is the *Quaeritur accessus*; the second, which is separated only by an initial,[35] reads:

> *Tria primitus inquiruntur in hoc libro, sicut in aliis, materia, intentio, utilitas. Materia eius est fraternum bellum pro Thebis quod fuit inter Ethioclem et Polinicem. Intentio eius dissuadere fraternum odium ne tale incurramus periculum. Vtilitas eius est ut perlectis istis libris pulchras et ornatas sententiarum positiones imitemur.*

Here, the *Thebaid* is given an educational role. First, we should avoid fraternal enmity, and second, as students, we ought to imitate the rhetorical passages and *sententiae* in the work. As such, this *accessus* suggests that the *Thebaid* (and perhaps, too, the *accessus ad auctores* this *accessus* may have been extracted from) was read by younger students, and represents as well the growing interest in the rhetorical nature of Statius' works.[36]

The Bern-Burney *accessus*

Fraternal enmity is commonly seen as the essential *materia* of the *Thebaid* not only in this century, but throughout the Middle Ages, and most *accessus* make some connection between the theme of the *Thebaid* and the rivalry between the imperial brothers Titus and Domitian that

---

[30] The exceptions are the brief *accessus* in London, BL, Royal 15.C.X (X–XI s.) and the lengthy one in Paris, BnF, lat. 13046, which confuses Domitian with Nero. Both of these *accessus* are simply adaptations of the *Quaeritur accessus* with lengthy expansions explaining why Statius chose his material. It is worth noting that before the discovery of Tacitus' *Historiae*, Domitian was depicted either as a benevolent, philanthropic emperor or as a conceited one (the later on the testimony of Suetonius), and the manuscripts differ on whether Statius' praise is honest or false (cf. London, BL, Add. 22314).

[31] Five of the Ovidian *accessus* cataloged by Coulson-Roy can be dated before the twelfth century; some 32 can be dated to the twelfth century.

[32] Coulson-Roy 407

[33] This is likely a mistranscription of *explanatio*, rather than of *natio*.

[34] Cf. the *accessus* of Servius. Here, only the order of the last two *circumstantiae* is changed (*ordo librorum* and *eiusdem explanatio*).

[35] It is common to find a second, often shorter *accessus* to Statius appended to the *Quaeritur accessus*.

[36] This last detail, *pulchras... positiones* is also found in the second *accessus* to Ovid's *Amores* edited in Huygens (1970.37.3). A rhetorical emphasis on classical poetry seems to have been present since the beginning of the Middle Ages, as most of the manuscripts have various marginal rhetorical guides, of which *comparatio* is the most common (cf. Sanford 1934).

Suetonius records. The more advanced *accessus* normally see Statius as operating more in a socio-political framework: he is seen as a teacher of morals and values to both the crown and the Roman people. This latter group is best evidenced by the *accessus* preserved in Bern, cod. 528, and London, BL, Burney 258 (Incipitarium 310).

The most noteworthy aspect of this *accessus* is not its interpretation, however, but is its tradition. Both witnesses preserve the first 22 lines of text, which provide us with the *locus*, *intentio*, and a brief discussion of the *materia*, but diverge thereafter. In the Bern manuscript, we find 20 lines in which the author expands on the *materia* and discusses the *pars philosophiae*. The Burney manuscript, on the other hand, provides us with the *utilitas*, *titulus*, and a plot summary. Since the later lines in the two witnesses do not overlap, but seem more to complement one another, it seems likely that both manuscripts preserve only part of the original *accessus*. The scribe of the Burney manuscript skipped over lines 23–41 possibly because of their lengthy, tangential nature, whereas the scribe of the Bern witness apparently stopped writing in the middle, or was working from a damaged parent.[37] Alternatively, it is possible that the material in the Bern witness is simply a rambling interpolation.[38]

According to this *accessus*, Rome herself was plagued by civil wars and strife during the time of Domitian (who is given the epithet *nequissimus imperator*),[39] and Statius wrote this poem as an exemplum to bring concord back to the people.[40] The emperor, however, in his desire to intensify his own crimes, decreed that no one be allowed to insult the Roman nobility. The penalty for this is a gory death (13–14):

> *facta fossa circumque illuminato igne, fixo palo in*
> *guture uiuus conbureretur,*

which is derived from Juvenal's hypothetical description of the fate of a poet writing about Nero's favorite Tigellinus (1.155–57):

> *taeda lucebis in illa*
> *qua stantes ardent, qui fixo gutture fumant,*
> *et latum media sulcum dedulcis harena.*

Statius, the *accessus* continues, who is of noble stock,[41] decides to save his city. He chose the history of the Theban war, not only because of its historical relevance, but also to rescue the myth from oblivion (19–20). But first and foremost, Statius' aim is the "correctio malorum et per hec exempla ab eis [*sc.* malis] continere" (39–40).

The *accessus* in our witness then continues with a plot summary, which begins: *Laius rex Thebanorum*. Nine manuscripts of Statius (representing five *accessus*) contain plot summaries

---

[37] The Bern version shows many textual problems. There is a lacuna at line 40, and the scribe mistakenly copied "in<de> ethica moralis sciencia" out of sequence (line 32). A second *accessus* to the *Thebaid* (1v) is also incomplete.

[38] I do not favor this explanation because the witnesses do not provide contradictory or redundant statements (except for the repetition of *materia* in 21 and 23), and it is not uncommon for *accessus* to discuss the *partes philosophiae* at length (such discussions are found in the *accessus* in Oxford, Lincoln College 27 and Sankt Florian, XI.58).

[39] References to Domitian as a bad emperor are rare this early in the *accessus* tradition. I suspect that the statement is a lingering trace of the confusion in the *accessus* in Paris, BnF, lat. 13046, to which this *accessus* is indebted, which claims that Statius wrote under Nero.

[40] The *accessus* then adds the confusing note "etsi naturalem Thebanorum et Grecorum exitum minetur" (10–11). This seems to be an extension of the oft expressed idea that Statius' poem has an applicability to the Romans, even though it has nothing thematically to do with Rome. Here, Statius seeks to correct the Romans, "even though he discusses the natural demise of the Greeks and Thebans" (for *minor* as a synonym of *mino* [*agere, trahere*], see J.W. Fuchs, *et al.*, *Lexicon latinitatis nederlandicae medii aevi* [Leiden, 1991], vol. 5, col. M 312).

[41] The relation of *decui genere iste descenderat* (16) to its surrounding text is puzzling. It might be the result of a lacuna or of a marginal note that was incorporated into the text.

of the *Thebaid* that have this or a similar incipit,[42] all of which are derived from the second Vatican mythographer.[43]

The summary spends some 20 lines on the myth of Oedipus, 5 lines in summary of Books 1–6,[44] 1 line on Books 7–11 and 3 lines on Book 12. What is interesting about this summary is the version of the myth of Oedipus. The only lengthy versions of the myth of Oedipus that circulated in the Middle Ages were those of Ovid, Seneca, Statius, and the French *Roman de Thèbes*, each of which varies in many details.[45] In the Bern-Burney *accessus*, the version of the myth is a rewriting of the Vatican mythographer's story, with some minor variations. Oedipus hears from Delphi that he is the son of a king of Greece (59). He asks Polibus, who tells him he must be the son of Laius (60–61). War then breaks out between the people of Corinth and the people of Thebes, and Oedipus unwittingly kills his own father and marries his mother.[46] The revelation in this version is the same as in the source: one day when Oedipus is putting his shoes on, Jocasta "pedes illius considerans" (66), notices the scars and tells him who he is.

The most interesting aspect of this *accessus*, however, is the identification of Statius. There was, as I shall discuss in my next chapter, a great deal of confusion regarding Statius' origin. Here, the Bern exemplar tells us that he came from *Tullum* and the Burney, that he was from *Tul* (which is either a shortening for *Tulosa* or a variant for *Toul*, the vulgar name for *Tullum*). Next, under the rubric of the *titulus*, the names *Surculus* and *Papinianus* are to be attributed to Statius' voice, *Surculus* being derived from *sursum canens* (as we saw in the *Quaeritur accessus*) and *Papinianus* from *pape*, meaning *mirabilis*.[47]

The two manuscripts seem to transmit the beginning of the original *accessus* and half of the following material. I suspect further that they are descended from a second archetype that added the puzzling *decui... descenderat* (16; see above, p. 9), resulting in the following stemma.

Figure 2. Stemma of the Bern-Burney *accessus*

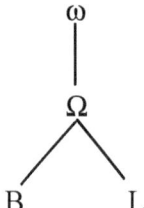

[42] Outside of this *accessus*, Assisi, 302 (XV s.); Augsburg, 4° cod. 21 (XV s.); Edinburgh, 18.5.12 (XII s.); Genève, Bibliothèque publique et universitaire, Lat. 96 (XII–XIII s.); Leiden, BPL 136K (XIII s.); London, BL, Burney 258 (XII/XIII s.); London, BL, Harley 2693 (XV s.); and Napoli, Biblioteca Oratoriana dei Girolamini, CF 2.14 (dated 1478).

[43] *Laius res Thebarum habuit uxorem nomine Iocastam, cui precepit ut omnes filios ex se genitos necaret...* (Kulcsár 1987.331–32 nr. 320).

[44] The only noteworthy part of the summary is the misidentification of Aphareus, Tydeus' brother, as Meleager. This is a common confusion that we also find in Padova, Vescovile 41, Ms. .

[45] The various versions of the myth in the Middle Ages are discussed in Constans 1881.

[46] In the Vat. Myth. version (2.230), Oedipus goes to Delphi because of impugned stock ("improperatum fuisset se genus suum ignorare," 7–8), and kills his father accidentally on the way.

[47] Cf. Remigius, *Expositio de celebratione misse* (Migne, *PL* 101, col. 1257[d]): "papa autem secundum quosdam dicitur admirabilis vel coronatus." Du Cange cites the definition "papa: admirabilis, major, pater, et custos" as being in Walafridus Strabo, *De rebus ecclesiasticis* 7, but I could not find the reading either in Migne (*PL* 113) or in the edition of A. Boretius and V. Krause (*De exordiis et incrementis quorundam in observationibus ecclesiasticis rerum*, Capitula regum Francorum, vol. 2 [*MGH* 2.2] [Hannover, 1897], 474–516).

Text 2. The Bern-Burney *accessus*

B = Bern, Burgerbibliothek, Cod. 528 (XII s.), 1r
L = London, British Library, Burney 258 (XII/XIII s.), 2r

Tullum est ciuitas Gallie, vnde auctor iste oriundus Tulosensis dictus est.
Inde Romam ueniens rethoricam didicit, quam etiam in Gallia celeberrime
docuit. Sed quoniam ex ciuilibus guerris et dissensionibus contentiones et
discidia magna per omnia mouebantur, maxime suo tempore, cum regnaret
5   nequissimus imperator Domitianus, uoluit Romanos a discordiis ciuilibus
reuocare. Sed quum imperator Domitianus ut suę iniquitates liberius
augerentur, edictum fecerat ne aliquis poeta aliquem nobilem
Romanum publice reprehenderet, historiam Romanam assumere
non audens, Thebanam incepit, vt saltim per alienum exemplum et bellorum
10   effectum Romanos corrigat, etsi naturalem Thebanorum et Grecorum exitum
minetur, neque enim si Romanorum historiam scriberet omnino
reprehensionem eorum uitare posset. Pęna autem reprehensionis
talis erat, vt scilicet facta fossa circumque illuminato igne, fixo palo in
guture uiuus conbureretur. Quod uiderat per effectum Lucani qui concisis
15   uenis utriusque brachii iussu eiusdem imperatoris occisus est quod uitium
Cesarem aliquando notasset. †Decui genere iste descenderat;† et cum itaque
nichil Romanum audeat, intendit in hoc opere describere ciuilia facta inter
duos fratres, scilicet Ethioclem et Polynicem et infortunia tum ex una parte
ut periculum uitaret supradictum, tum, quia populus Romanus, cum illam
20   historiam non satis frequentasset, multum habere in cognitionem optabat.
Hec est causa intentionis.

   Materia constat e tribus partibus que sunt he: fratres, eorum fautores,
regnum Thebanum. Materia alia principalis, alia secundaria. Principalis est
illa de qua auctor principaliter tractare intendit. Secundaria est illa que
25   incidit, sicut digressio, que, nisi principali materie conueniat,
superflua iudicetur. Materia alia de qua fit, alia per quam fit, alia in
qua fit. De qua fit, sicuti de ferro fit cultus; per quam fit sicuti
per macellum fit culltelus; in qua fit, sicuti in incude fit cultus. Ethice
supponitur quia loquitur de moribus. Ethos Grece, Latine dicitur mos.
30   Inde ethica, moralis sciencia. Philosophia est amor sapiencie (philo
Grece, Latine dicitur amor, sophia sapiencia). Philosophia diuiditur
in tres partes, in logicam, in phisicam, in eticam. Logos Grece, sermo
dicitur Latine. Logica diuiditur in tres partes, [in gram]maticam, in
rectoricam, in dialecticam. Gramma Grece, lumen dicitur Latine, inde
35   grammatica, litteralis sciencia. Grammatica docet nos iungere casum
[cum] casu, genus cum genere. Dialogica dicitur dualis sermo.
Dialogica docet nos uere et probabiliter loqui. Rethorica docet apte
et habiliter loqui. Phisis Grece, Latine natura, inde naturalis sciencia.
Phisica diuiditur in quatuor partes, in musicam, in astronomicam, in
40   geometricam, in arithmeticam. Musica loquitur de tonis, astronomia
de astris, arithmetica de numero, geometria de mensura. *** in<de>
ethica moralis sciencia.

   Vtilitas siue finis est correctio malorum et per hec exempla ab eis
continere. Titulus est Statii Papiniani Surculi liber Thebaidos incipit. Statius
45   prenomen suum, Papinianus uero dictus est propter quod et Surculus, quasi
sursum canens, quia iocundam et altam habebat uocem et in hoc ipso
Papinianus id est mirabilis in recitatione, cum etiam in dictamine satis ualuit.

Pape enim uox est mirabilis.

Hec est historia de commento tracta. Laius rex Thebanorum filius
50   Labdacii cum a fatis accepisset manu filii se moriturum, uxori sue Iocaste
praecepit ut omnes partus exponeret. Quare illa pariens filium plantis
perforatis, dedit pedisequis, quem ille in nemus portantes opertum foliis
inter truncos dimiserunt. Casu autem contigit dum quidam diues Polibus
nomine in illa silua uel uenaretur uel aliud ageret, puerum inuenit et
55   inuentum pro suo nutriuit. Sed cum adoleuisset uirtute pollens, per inuidiam
ei imperatum est quod inuenticis esset. Quare ira commotus a rege
sciscitans sic esse reperit. Regem itaque relinquens et scrutatus deum
Appollinem de patre consultum iret, monstri scilicet Spingis in cauerna,
uerba soluit, ipsamque interfecit et ad Apollinem perueniens cum se
60   filium regis Grecie accepisset, ad Polibum rediens ei retulit. Ad quem ille,
"Scio quod si filius regis es, cuius regis sis, scilicet Laii cum in eius regno
te inuenirem." Ductis ergo secum conpluribus hoc ipsum a Laio perscrutari
uoluit. Cum interim orta seditione inter suas ciuitates et Laium, cum alii
alios, ipse patrem interfecit inscius et capta ciuitate uxor matrem
65   duxit, de qua duos filios, scilicet Ethioclem et Polinicem et duas filias,
scilicet Antigonem et Himenem procreauit. Quodam autem mane dum ille
in lecto se calciaret, uxor pedes illius considerans, calces perforatas aduertit
et filium esse agnouit. Eique rem patefecit. Miserum ille se clamans oculos
sibi eruit et in fossa propter pudorem ab illa die latuit. Filii autem cum se in
70   regno pati non possunt, iacta sorte ut alternis regnarunt annis, Ethiocles
primus regnauit, Polinices exulans ad Adrastum eius filiam duxit Argiam.
Alteram autem, id est Deiphilem, habuit Tideus, qui ideo de patria eiectus
erat quia fratrem Mel<eagrum> interfecerat. Preterito itaque anno, cum
missus esset Tideus ut regnum a fratre requireret et ille negaret, motus
75   Adrastus cum VII ducibus et finito bello cum Thebis uix solus refugere
potuit. Fratres autem postquam se mutuis uulneribus occiderent, rex Creon
est factus. Ipse etiam quia cremari Grecos prohibuerat, a Theseo est
interfectus et hic est finis.

More scribentium, prologum facit in quo materie sue partes aperit et
80   geminam excusationem facit, vnam erga Romanos, quia de historiis eorum
non scribat, alteram ad imperatorem quod facta eius non decantat.

2–3 in... docuit] *Quaeritur* accessus, l. 5

3 dissensio] cf. Sallustius, *BJ* 41 fin.

13 facta... conbureretur (16)] cf. Juvenalem 1.155–57; cf. accessum in Paris, BnF, lat. 13046, ll.
        14–16

45 quasi... canens (46)] *Quaeritur* accessus 18

46 iocundam] Juvenalis 7.82

46 mirabilis... pape (48)] cf. Paris, BnF lat. 13046, ll. 24–25

48 pape] cf. Remigius, *Expositio de celebratione misse* (*PL* 101) col. 1257d

49–78 cf. *Mythogr. vat.* [Kulcsár] 2.230

49 Laius... Thebanorum] *ibid.* 1

51 illa... perforatis (52)] *ibid.* 4

68 oculos... eruit (69)] *ibid.* 20: sibimet oculos eruit

76 mutuis... occiderent] *ibid.* 26–27

1 tul L   in gallia B   thulosensis L   **2** addidicit L   **3** guerris] vverris L   contriciones B
4 discordia B   cum *post* maxime *dist.* B   **5** nequissimus imperator] titus L   ciuilibus discordiis L   **6** extemporaniter *post* suę *add.* L   iniquitates *post* augerentur (7) *dist.* L   augerentur liberius L   **8** cum ob hec *ante* historiam *add.* L   romanorum B   **9** auderet L   saltim
om. L   alienum] aliud B   et *om.* B   **10** effectum *om.* B   etsi... posset (12) *om.* B   **12**
reprehensionis] propter reprehensionem L   **13** talis] hec L   scilicet... igne *om.* B   **14** uiuus
om. B   quod... intentionis (21) *om.* B   **21** constat... he] eius est triplex B   **22** eorum
fautores] fautores et adiutores eorum B   regnum thebanum *om.* B   **23** materia... mensura
(41) *om.* L   **25** dicgressio B   **33** moralis].....emalis *subpunct.* B   **38** habiliter] probabiliter B
40 arithmeticam] ar̊monicam B   **41** arithmetica] armonica B   in... sciencia (42) *post* latine
(32) *dist.* B   **43** vtilitas... decantat (81) *om.* B   **45** pronomen L   **47** ualore L   **48** mirabilis]
narantis L   **58** cauerne L   **61** es] est L   **62** perscrutari *ex* perscrutare L   **66** ille | ille L

The *Achilleid*

The earliest *accessus* to the *Achilleid* are much more consistent in approach than was the case with the earliest *accessus* to the *Thebaid* and they present us with an entirely different set of issues as well as a very different academic approach. Authorship here was not an issue, and the earliest *accessus* seem unfamiliar with the problems behind or even the solutions reached by the *Quaeritur accessus*. What was at issue was the structure of the *Achilleid* and, in particular, why the poem ends where it does. In order to answer this question, scholars paid close attention to two aspects of the poem: the *intentio auctoris* and the end of the poem (likely in the belief that the end of the poem and the completion of the *intentio* would coincide). Scholars noted three elements at the end of the poem that suggested various *intentiones*. The first is that the poem ends, thematically, with the triumph of Fate over Thetis' scheming; second, the end of the poem is occupied by Achilles' lengthy discussion of his education;[48] lastly, the poem ends with reference to Thetis with the emphatic *mater*. In the earliest *accessus* to the *Achilleid*, scholars focused their attention on the first of these, the triumph of Fate.

The *accessus* in Firenze, BML, plut. 24 sin. 12

The earliest extant *accessus* to the *Achilleid* is found in Firenze, BML, plut. 24 sin. 12 (XI s.) and Bruxelles, BR, IV 719 (dated 1418; Incipitarium 267). In it, we learn that Statius was born in Thebes, where he wrote the *Thebaid*, whereafter he was crowned and then drank from the fountain from which poets normally drank after the publication of a poem.[49] The identification of Thebes as Statius' home occurs only in this *accessus*,[50] and stems either from some unexpressed etiological explanation of why Statius wrote the *Thebaid* or from a scribe's mistransmission of *Tholosa*.[51] As the point is never elaborated, we cannot be sure; however, as the *accessus* is nowhere else related to the *Quaeritur accessus*, I think it unlikely that its author knew of the tradition that Statius came from Toulouse.

The rest (and the bulk) of the *accessus* is an etiological explanation of why Statius chose his material. Statius, after coming to Rome, received great honors and was invited into the emperor's court to aid in the discussion of whether one can escape destiny.[52] Statius, in answering the question, composed this poem.

In this *accessus*, we see the beginning of an important theme that will persist throughout later *accessus* to Statius, the idea of the *poeta doctus*, that is, the poet whose wisdom is recognized through his poetry. As is the case here, this is usually indicated by the emperor's asking

---

[48] Z. Pavlovskis ("The Education of Achilles, as Treated in the Literature of Late Antiquity," *PP* 20 [1965], 281–97) notes that authors after Statius tended to focus on the childhood and formative experiences of heroes. See too H.W. Fortgens, "Publius Papinius Statius, de latijnse dichter van het kinderleven," *Hermeneus* 31 (1959), 52–59.

[49] The crowning and drinking from the fountain are literal interpretations of the invocation of Apollo (*Ach.* 1.8–10):

> tu modo, si veterem digno deplevimus haustu,
> da fontes mihi. novos ac fronde secunda
> necte comas.

The laureate poet is a common motif in *accessus* (cf. the so-called *Vacca accessus* to Lucan, ed. C. Hosius, *Lucani Pharsalia* [Leipzig, 1913], 334–36).

[50] In Leiden, Gronov. 143, there is a note claiming that he studied at Rome and Athens.

[51] The confusion *Tholosensis > Theb[s]ensis* is possible in the Gothic hand in which the Florence witness of this *accessus* is written. In the manuscript Oxford, MS. Auct. F.5.6 (XIII s.), Domitian is called "imperator Troie," which may also represent an untransmitted explanation for Statius' choice of material, but is more likely an error.

[52] The parallels to events in the life of Johannes Eriugena, who was summoned by Hinkmar of Reims in ca. 850 to aid in a debate on predestination, are probably only a coincidence.

for Statius' help in some matter. The source of this judgment is unclear; it may stem from the same source as the claims of his intelligence (such as *clarus ingenio, doctus eloquio,* and *tenacis memorie*) or from the invocation of the emperor at 1.17–19, in which Statius suggests that he has been requested to write an imperial *res gestae*. In any case, it is important that Statius is personally associated with the emperor. In *accessus* to the *Thebaid*, he is in a position to chastise or instruct the emperor; here, the emperor turns to him for philosophical advice.

This *accessus* does have one aspect in common with the *Quaeritur accessus*, its conservatism. Even though the *accessus* provides us with a fanciful, etiological myth, it does not extend into the realm of tropological allegory. The interpretation here, as we saw in the earliest *accessus* to the *Thebaid*, stems entirely from evidence that can be found in the text. The author of the *accessus* adapted this information to what he knew about Rome during Statius' lifetime.

Text 3. The Firenze, plut. 24 sin. 12 *accessus*

B = Bruxelles, Bibliothèque royale Albert 1er, IV 719, 21v (dated 1418), 21r
F = Firenze, Biblioteca Medicea Laurenziana, plut. 24, sin. 12 (XI s.), 49r

Stacius iste Thebanus fuit poeta qui librum Thebaidos conposuit, quare
coronatus fuit et de fonte ex quo alii poete in fine libri bibebant potauit. Postea
uero Romam ueniens a Domitiano imperatore oneste susceptus est. Interea
in eius curia questio talis facta est, utrum ea que predestinata sunt euitari
5   queant necne. Ad quam soluendam Stacius a Domiciano inuitatus est. Qui
imperatori suisque fidelibus questionem soluere cupiens hunc libellum
composuit, ostendendo qualiter Thetis fatis resistere uoluit et nequiuit.
Presagium enim fuerat quod si aliquis deorum Thetidem uxorem acciperet, ex
ea filium nasciturum qui eum de regno expelleret. Vnde dii perterriti noluerunt
10   eam accipere. Ipsa uero uidens nullum deorum eam accipere uelle, terreno
homini se coniunxit. Cuius nuptiis omnes dii et dee interfuerunt. Discordia
uero, que non affuit, pomum aureum inter Iunonem et Paladem et Uenerem
proiecisse dicitur, in quo scriptum erat "pulcriori debetur." Unde quia litigium
erat inter illas, Carpatius uates pro pomo magnum malum fore nasciturum
15   Thetidi predestinauit. Quod malum filius qui ex ea nasceretur uindicaret et
postremo inde uitam amitteret. Quod Thetis minime tradidit obliuioni. Nuptiis
peractis adiuere Paridem qui Uenerem pulcriorem asseruit, quia Elenam
uxorem Menelai sibi promiserat. Puero nato Thetis fatis resistere cupiens illum
Chironi detulit, deprecans ut eum nutriat atque studiose conseruet. Exinde
20   Paris iuit pro Helena et rapuit eam. Thetis uero uidens illum eam deferentem
adiuit Neptunum ut sibi licenciam daret obruendi nauim illam, quia mortis filii
sui causa erat. Quod quia Neptunus non sibi concessit, filium suum Chironi
abstulit eumque femineo more uestiens ad Licomedem regem Sciros detulit
ut inter filias suas illum nutriret atque custodiret. Interea Menelaus suum
25   suique regni dedecus uindicare cupiens Troiam armata manu porrexit.
Vaticinatum autem fuerat quod numquam sine Achille ciuitas caperetur.
Quocirca omnes unanimiter preces ad Apolinem fuderunt ut eis quo in loco
Achilles absconditus esset patefaceret. Qui ore Calcantis inter Licomedis filias
illum muliebria indumenta deferentem esse patefecit.

---

1 ipse *post* quare *add.* B   **2** ex *om.* F   alii *om.* B   in fine libri | in fine F   **3** domicio B
oneste] honorifice B   **4** eius incuria F   quesipo F   **5** domicio B   **6** questionibus F   **7**
fuerit F   **8** fuerit F   in vxorem B   **9** noluerunt *post* accipere (10) *dist.* B   **10** ipsa... accipere *om.* F   **11** omnes *post* deę *dist.* B   et] atque B   **12** que... affuit] quia non ad nuptias
inuitata fuit B   et¹ *om.* B   **13** detur B   **14** Carphanius F   illo *post* pomo *add.* B   **15** filius
om. F   ex ea] exuę(?) F   et *om.* F   **16** tradididit F   obluioni tradidit B   nuptum F   **17**
helenam B   **18** uero *post* puero *add.* B   **19** deprecans... conseruet *om.* F   **21** illam] suam B
22 quod quia] et qua F   **23** eamque F   Sciros *om.* F   **24** filiam suam F   atque custodiret
om. F   **25** armatam F   autem *om.* F   **26** sine] absque B   **27** apollinem B   eis | eis F
esset F   **28** patefaceret B   filiam F   **29** deferentem indumenta F

The KP *accessus*

The solution to the structure of the *Achilleid* posited in the Plut. 24 sin. 12 *accessus* found a more formal version in the twelfth century, in what is our next oldest tradition[53] of *accessus* to the *Achilleid*, which I term the KP *accessus* (Incipitarium 116). This *accessus*, which is extant in five manuscripts, is the earliest *accessus* to Statius that follows the more traditional form of medieval *accessus*, in that it is prefaced by a catalog of *circumstantiae*.

The text of the *accessus* is problematic, even in its earliest witness. In most of the witnesses, we see the conflation of two distinct *accessus*, Ω and ω. The author of the former *accessus*, Ω, sought to answer only the questions of the *intentio scribentis*, the *materia*, the *vtilitas*, and the *titulus* (1–2), and in the discussion of the *titulus*, notes the debate of the number of books into which the poem is divided (18–20). Between the *materia* (5) and *utilitas* (16), however, is a lengthy interpolation from a second *accessus*, ω. This second *accessus* is transmitted outside of this context only in the fifteenth-century manuscript, Napoli, Bn, V.F.21 (Incipitarium 156).[54] Here, we find a different (albeit germane *intentio* (5–12), a brief discussion of the *pars philosophiae* (12), and a summary of the poem, broken into books (13–16). Two later manuscripts, A and Z, lack the interpolated lines 5–16.[55] We could thus imagine that the witnesses are descended from the "pure" Ω. However, since A also has close relations to R, and Z is related to P and K (and since P and K are closer to ω than the other witnesses are), it is more logical that the scribes of these manuscripts realized that the lines were interpolated and deleted the supposedly superfluous material. All of our extant witnesses of the "full" *accessus*, then, are descended from one archetype, γ, and our stemma appears as on the next page.[56]

The original *accessus* (Ω) was based closely on Statius' words in the beginning of the poem, and quotes him almost verbatim: the *intentio scribentis*, for example, simply states that Statius wanted to expand the story of Achilles as told by Homer (3–5):[57]

> *forcia et bellicosa Achillis facta describere nec in Hectore tracto more Homerico desistere, sed supplendo ea que minus ab eo dicta sunt plene de omnibus tractare,*

which is itself simply a restatement of *Achilleid* 1.3–7:

---

[53] The *accessus* in Oxford, Lincoln College, MS. 42, which seems to exist only in one manuscript, is older, but its findings and results are not further transmitted. I discuss this manuscript below.

[54] In this manuscript, the *accessus* is preceded by a few lines on the *titulus* which may come from another tradition: "Liber iste intitulatur Statius Achilleydos. Statius nomen autoris est. Liber Achylleydos, id est opus factum de Achille. Achilleis est patronomicum nomen et formatur a patronomico masculino, quod est Achilleydes, per adiectionem -d-, et Achilleides formatur a Greco nominis quod est Achillei per additionem -des."

[55] This is also the case with a few rewritten versions of the KP *accessus*, such as that in Paris, BnF, lat. 8207 (XIV s.).

[56] The separation of K and P is suggested by the borrowings from this *accessus* in Firenze, BML, Plut. 38.10 (dated 1394) (see below, p. 90).

[57] The words used in common are italicized.

Figure 3. Stemma of the KP *accessus*

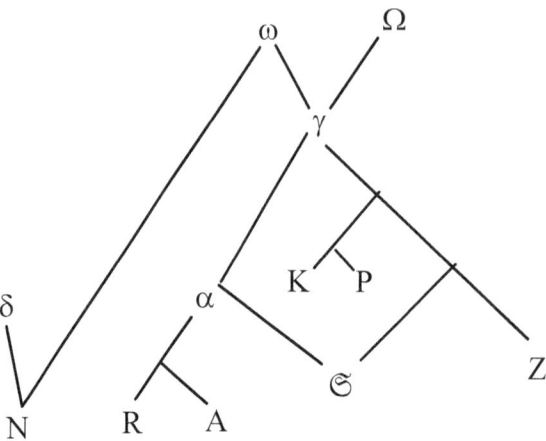

> *quamquam acta viri multum inclita cantu*
> *Maeonio (sed plura vacant), nos ire per omnem—*
> *sic amor est—heroa velis Scyroque latentem*
> *Dulichia proferre tuba nec in Hectore tracto*
> *sistere, sed tota iuvenem deducere Troia.*

The major importance of this *accessus resides* in the *utilitas*, which follows the interpolated passage in lines 16–17: "Vtilitas est ne fatis obuiare temptemus, cum Thetidem eis obuiantem nichil profecisse nouerimus." Now in the Plut. 24 sin. 12 *accessus*, Statius' *intentio* was to demonstrate that Thetis sought to resist fate, but was unable (*qualiter Thetis fatis resistere uoluit et nequiuit*, 6). In this *accessus*, the same idea is given under the *utilitas* in a slightly modified form: Statius tells us the story so that we can avoid the frustration Thetis faced.[58]

The ω interpolation provides us with two *intentiones*, the first of which (5–6) is germane to the *utilitas* of Ω; that is, Statius wanted to write Achilles' *gesta*. The second (6–12) states that Statius specifically wrote what he did with the intent to keep us from avoiding fate (*ut retrahat nos ab hoc vitio, ne velimus resistere fatis*, 8–9) and to help us avoid frustration (*et quod nil illi dee profuit, multo minus nobis mortalibus prodesset*, 11–12).

The interpolation then continues and gives information that was not in the Ω *accessus*, including an answer to the question *cui parti philosophie supponatur* (11), and a plot summary, which is similar to the periochae in the commentary that follows in K, P, and R.[59]

The solution reached by these two *accessus*—Ω and ω—as to why the *Achilleid* ended where it did is influenced by the end of the poem, and betrays a very neat structural division of the poem: the *Achilleid* begins with Thetis' worries and the beginning of her scheming, then continues with Achilles' education, and concludes with a scene in which Thetis' scheming is undone, whereafter Achilles relates the details of his education; the last word of the epic reminds us of Thetis' governing role.

---

[58] Negative exempla are a common topos in *accessus*. Cf. the *accessus* to Arator edited by Huygens (1970.27–28.15–16): "utilitas... ne perverse eos imitando dampnationem Ananiae et Saphirae incurramus."

[59] The summary is similar to several others in thirteenth-century manuscripts, including Paris, BnF, lat. 8207 and 8559, Escorial, El, Real Biblioteca, ms. f.III.11, and Oxford, Bodleian Library, Lat. class. e.47.

The central interpretation of the resulting *accessus*—the inexorability of Fate—reflects a wider topos in antiquity and the Middle Ages. The most common classical examples of this are passages from Horace and Seneca:

> *Tu ne quaesieris, scire nefas, quem mihi, quem tibi*
> *Finem di dederint, Leuconoe, nec Babylonios*
> *Temptaris numeros* (Horace, *Odes* 1.11.1–3).

> *Sed siue quidquid evenit faciunt, quid inmutabilis rei notitia proficiet? Sive significant, quid refert providere quod effugere non possis? Scias ista, nescias, fient* (Seneca, *Ep.* 88.15.3–6).

> *Ducunt uolentem fata, nolentem trahunt* (Seneca, *Ep.* 107.11.5).[60]

This motif was also popular in the Middle Ages. There is, for example, buried in the Ps.-Catonian *Liber distichorum*, the maxim (Duff, *MLP* 2.12):

> *Quid deus intendat, noli perquirere sorte.*
> *Quid statuit de te, sine te deliberat Ille.*

Now, it was not until a century later that the *Achilleid* was included in the *Liber catonianus*, but the similarities between the moral of this *accessus* and this distich show that there was already some moralizing interpretation of the *Achilleid* already in the twelfth-century. That the *Achilleid* was so well integrated into this popular wisdom may have been one reason for its inclusion in the *Liber catonianus*.

---

[60] This line had further exposure by virtue of being quoted by Augustine, *Civ. Dei* 5.8.

Text 4. The KP *accessus*

A = Antwerpen, Museum Plantin-Moretus, M 357 (XIII s.), 1r
K = København, Kongelige Bibliotek, Fab. 29 2° (XII s.), 19rb
N = Napoli, Biblioteca nazionale "Vittorio Emanuele III," V.F.21 (XV s.), 50v
P = Pommersfelden, Graf von Schönborn, Schloss Bibliothek, Schloss Weissenstein, 84 (2804)
    (XIII–XIV s.), 125ra
R = Vaticano, Città del, Biblioteca Apostolica Vaticana, Reg. lat. 1556 (XIII s. med.), 75rb
Z = Venezia, Biblioteca nazionale Marciana, Zan. Lat. 541 (1560) (XIV s.), 2rüft
ᚷ = Sankt Florian, Augustiner-Chorherren Stiftsbibliothek, XI.587 (XIII s.) 133r (continens *titulus* [17] usque ad finem)

In principio huius auctoris quatuor sunt inquirenda: intentio scribentis,
materia, vtilitas, titulus. De hiis propositis ordinem videamus. Intentio sua
est forcia et bellicosa Achillis facta describere nec in Hectore tracto more
Homerico desistere, sed supplendo ea que minus ab eo dicta sunt plene de
5 omnibus tractare. *Materia eius est Achilles et eius forcia facta. Intentio*
sua est non tantum de illis agere que egit Achilles circa Troiam sed quomodo
Chiron eum nutriuit et mater sua Thetis in aula Licomedis eum abscondidit,
quod facit hac intentione, ut retrahat nos ab hoc vitio, ne velimus resistere
fatis, quia Thetis cognito quod fata filium suum apud Troiam moriturum
10 *predestinassent, volens hoc differre filium suum abscondidit. Qui postea a*
Grecis inuentus est et ad Troiam deductus interiit; et quod nil illi dee
profuit, multo minus nobis mortalibus prodesset. Liber iste ethicus est.
Notandum est Stacium de hoc opere quinque libros composuisse. In primo
sollicitudinem matris et causam sollicitudinis describit. In secundo filii
15 *absconsionem. In tercio inquisitionem Grecorum. In quarto inuentionem.*
In quinto adductionem ad Troiam. Vtilitas est ne fatis obuiare temptemus,
cum Thetidem eis obuiantem nichil profecisse nouerimus. Titulus talis est:
Stacii Achilleidos liber primus incipit. Bene dicitur primus quia sequitur
secundus. Sunt enim quatuor, secundum alios quinque, qui unum in duos
20 diuidunt. Achilleis patronomicum femininum ab Achille, sicut Eneis ab
Enea. More aliorum poetarum, opus suum in tria diuidit: proponit, inuocat,
narrat. Proponit cum de quo tractat ostendit, vt ibi "Magnanimum" et
cetera. Inuocat vt ibi, "Tu modo" et cetera; narrat vbi materiam suam
explanat, vt ibi, "Soluerat ebalio" et cetera.

---

2 ordinem] cf. accessum In principio in *Thebaidem* (inf., p. 33), 8–10: *Horum unumquodque eo*
    ordine quo proposuimus exequamur.
3 in... desistere (4)] cf. *Ach.* 1.6–7
22 *Ach.* 1.1
23 *ibid.* 1.8
23 vbi... vt (24)] cf. inter al., Vat. lat. 1663, ll. 18–19
24 *Ach.* 1.20

---

1 in... tractare (5) *om.* N   inquirenda sunt PZ   scilicet *post* inquirenda *add.* AZ   scribentis]
actoris P   **2** de hiis] quibus A   de hoc proposicionis Z   ordinem *om.* K : ordine Z : in ordine A   sua] itaque ipsius A : ipsius itaque Z   **3** facta] acta AR : *om.* P   facta achillis KZ
describere facta R   tracto *om.* A   homerico more KP   **4** homeri A   implendo Z   que
minus] quamuis KPZ   ab eo (ab illo Z) *post* sunt *dist.* AZ   sint KPZ   **5** materia... facta *om.*
K   eius] huius autoris N   et... facta *om.* N   intentio... troiam (16) *om.* AZ   uel intentio K

6 sua] eiusdem Z   agere *post* est *dist.* KN   non] nec P   tantum *om.* KP   bellis *post* illis *add.* P   achilles egit AR : gessit (*om.* achilles) N   *post* sed *add.* de illis que uacant ab homero scilicet de illis que fecit antequam ueniret ad Troiam et N   **7** chiron... nutriuit] nutritus a chirone K   nutriuit eum PN   mater... abscondidit] absconsus a matre in chiro insula licomedis K   mater *post* licomedis *dist.* P   sua Thetis *om.* PN   lycomedis regis N   eum *post* et *dist.* P   abscondit *post* mater *dist.* N   **8** quod] hoc autem N   quod... fatis] utilitas... nouerimus (*ex inf. ll. 16–17*) K   **9** fatis] predestinationi deorum PN   quia thetis] thetis enim dea N   quia... troiam] que thetis erat quedam dea que conmota quia filium achillem P : que sciens filium suum troie K   fata *post* moriturum *dist.* P   achillem *post* suum *add.* N   moriturum apud troiam N   **10** predestinassent... suum *om.* K   volens... abscondidit] predestinationem ipsam volens desistere filium frustra recondidit N   hoc differre] predestinationem desistere P *fort. rectius* : *om.* K   frustra *post* suum *add.* P   recondit R   postea... troiam (11)] tunc illuc K   *post* N   **11** est *om.* ANR   adductus ad troiam interiit N   ductus KP   et quod] quod ergo P   et²... est (12)] illa que erat dea nil profuit multo minus proficeremus et nos sic liber est ethicus quia bonis moribus instruit nos prologum facit in quo proponit de quo agat et inuocat musam et apollinem, et excusat se domiciano [*ex* de-] imperatore cuius tempore claruit N   nil *post* dee *dist.* P   et... prodesset (12) *om.* K   **12** prodesset *om.* P   iste liber P   **13** notandum... composuisse *om.* K : notandum hunc librum quinque libris constari N   et *post* composuisse *dist.* P   in primo... troiam (16) *post* diuidunt (l. 20) *dist.* K   in quorum primo N   **14** matris sollicitudinem ARZ   describit *post* primo (11) *dist.* N   filii *om.* K   absconsionem filii N   **15** grecorum inquisicionem ARZ   eius *post* inuentionem *add.* N   **16** maxima *post* vtilitas *add.* Z   vtilitas... nouerimus (17) *in l.* 8 *dist.* K   **17** Thetidi K : Thetide R : Thetiee Z   eis *post* cum *dist.* A   obuiantem] obuiasse et R : obuiare uolentem P : obuiare K   profecisse *post* conononimus [sic] *dist.* A   profuisse P   cognouerimus Z conononimus A   titulus... diuidunt (20) *post* est (12) *dist.* K   **18** Papinii Surculi *post* Stacii *add.* ℭ   liber... achilleis (20) *om.* A   primus liber ARℭ   dicit Pℭ   **19** etiam P   quatuor] quinque ℭ   quinque... quattuor P   secundum... diuidunt (20) *om.* ℭ   duo Z   **20** diuiudunt] computant P   Achilleidos P   est *post* achileis *add.* Z   parronomius R   femininum patronomicum AZℭ   ab Achille *om.* ℭ   sicut] ut A : quemadmodum P : quomodo ℭ   eneis] eneas Z   eneis eneidos *post* enea (l. 21) *dist.* P   **21** poetarum *om.* Zℭ   diuidit in tria Z   et *post* inuocat *add.* PZℭ   **22** cum] enim ℭ   tractum P   ostendit *om.* ℭ   et cetera] eacidem RZ   **23** vt ibi] ubi dicit P : ubi ait ℭ : ibi ubi dicit Z   et cetera] si ueteres ARZ : *om.* ℭ   vbi... vt (24) *om.* K   **24** ibi vbi dicit K   Ebalio *om.* Kℭ   et cetera] classem Z *om.* ARℭ

The Lincoln College *accessus*

The second explanation of the structure of the *Achilleid* is based on the last 73 lines of the poem, in which Achilles gives the details of his education. Statius Ursulus, as Jerome and Suetonius tell us, was a celebrated teacher of rhetoric in Gaul. As a teacher, Statius the poet had the authority to write on the education of children, and the *Achilleid*, according to this interpretation, was seen partially as a treatise on the raising of children.[61]

The earliest such approach is found in a twelfth-century manuscript now housed in Oxford, Bodleian Library, Ms. Lincoln College lat. 27 (dated 1119; Incipitarium 238). The *accessus* in this unique witness portrays Statius as a moral man and a teacher of rhetoric. The two allegories of his name illustrate this. First, *Statius* is derived from the verb *stare* (16–20):

> *Vocabatur nomine proprio Statius, quod tunc eius probitati quasi quodam presagio congruebat, quia enim Statius a stando dicitur. Recte fuit hoc nomen eius proprium, qui per omnia scripta sua non solum tamquam in uertice litterarum, sed in morum dignitate stetit et eminentia uirtutum.*

Second, the name *Pampinius*[62] attests the rhetorical aspect of his poetry (20–25):

> *Cognominabatur etiam Pampinius, a Pampino, folio uitis, quia sicut pampinus sui densitate uitem circumtegit et uestit, sic iste poeta totum opus suum uariis arborum ornamentis et maxime comparationum uenustate compaginat. Appellabatur preterea Surculus ad modum tenere uirgule pullulantis ab arbore, quia in omnibus que scripsit prenimia stili elegantia recens semper et nouus apparuit.*

Based on Statius' role as a teacher and a moral person, the author of this *accessus* argues that Statius is a teacher of morals, i.e., the *poeta doctor*. From this come two conclusions: first, that Statius wrote the *Achilleid* to counteract the effeminacy that had come to be typical of the Romans and to urge the Romans to arms (8–11):

> *Arbitrabatur enim utilius fore rei publice alicuius magni et bellicosi uiri facta describere, cuius exemplo ciues Romani prouocarentur ad amorem milicie et usum armorum, sine quibus non potest res publica salua consistere.*

These are not the *arma* of war, however. Under the rubric of *utilitas*, the *accessus* allegorically defines these *arma* based on *Proverbs* 16.32 (41–46):

> *Cum enim dicat Salomon, "Melior est patiens uiro forti et qui dominatur animo suo expugnatore urbium," patet profecto quia sicut est milicia armorum, ita est et milicia morum. In milicia armorum decertatur uiribus corporis; in milicia morum contenditur uiribus mentis. Igitur preter emulationem corporalis militie, que plurima est in hoc libro, etiam spiritualis milicie doctrinalia sunt gesta Achillis.*

The *Achilleid*, then, seeks to teach us to train ourselves for moral combat, as opposed to Achilles' mortal combat.

---

[61] Outside of these *accessus*, we have much indirect evidence for the *Achilleid* being read in such a manner, including Baltimore, Walters Art Gallery, MS W.358 (a fifteenth-century composite manuscript containing St. Basel's *De poetis legendis*, Guarinus' translation of Plutarch's *De liberis educandis*, and the *Achilleid*) and Oxford, Bodleian Library, MS. D'Orville 182 (a late–fifteenth century manuscript containing the *Achilleid*; Guarinus Veronensis' *Regule grammaticales*; Guarinus' translation of Plutarch's *De liberis educandis*; Jerome's *Life of Paul the Heremite*; and a biography of Malchus), both of which bind the *Achilleid* together with works which promise *exampla* for raising young boys.

[62] This variant for *Papinius* occurs in about 60 manuscripts.

The second interpretation, found in the *intentio*, is that Statius put forth an *exemplum* of magnanimity for the Romans to imitate: "magnanimitatem discerent imitari" (30–31). In this regard, the *Achilleid* is seen as a collection of character exempla, and Statius is seen again as a *poeta doctor* (73–81):

> *Ergo et hic liber Statii merito subponitur ethice, id est morali parti. Agit enim de moribus multipliciter: agit de affectu materne pietatis in Thetide, de magisterio sedule eruditionis in Chirone, de culpando adulterio in raptu Helene, de zelo iuste ultionis in Menelao et Agamemnone, de malo prescriptionis et preceptacionis in Prothesilao milite, de consilio et prudentia in Ulixe, de animositate et fiducia in Diomede, de honore regie mansuetudinis in Licomede, de titulo uerecundie puellaris in Deidamia uirgine, de uirilis animi constantia in iam reperto et mutato Achille.*

There is, however, one other important facet of this *accessus*, the realization that the *Achilleid* is incomplete (26–28):

> *Materia huius libri gesta sunt Achillis, que omnia quidem Statius a primeua etate usque ad eius obitum scribere proposuit, sed morte preuentus opus incepit, non expleuit.*

While this is the first mention of the incomplete state of the poem, it is noteworthy that this—like all *accessus* that claim that the poem is incomplete—notes it is only the content of the poem that is affected by its incompleteness. In no *accessus* to the *Achilleid* do we find that the style, structure, or language of the poem was affected by its incompleteness.[63] Indeed, the texts infers that the poem was planned beforehand, even down to the length of the individual books, which Statius intentionally shortened to keep his audience[64] from being overwhelmed (83–85):[65]

> *et sunt... libelli longe breuiores quam in Thebaide, ne populus audiens recitantem prolixitate grauaretur.*

---

[63] We note in *accessus* to other authors that the death of the author affects the style of the poem. Cf. the *accessus* to Theodolus, edited by Huygens (1970.26–27): "morte praeventus non emendauit."

[64] Note that the scholars, likely because of Juvenal, see Statius as singing his poetry, not necessarily as writing it to be read.

[65] The avoidance of *prolixitas* is a common topos in *accessus* to Ovid. See F.T. Coulson, "New Manuscripts of the Medieval Interpretations of Ovid's Metamorphoses," *Scriptorium* 44 (1990), 272–75 [273–75]; F.T. Coulson and L. Jones, "A Newly Acquired Manuscript of Alan of Lille's *De planctu naturae* in the Ohio State Library," *Scriptorium* 45 (1991), 84–88; and Coulson-Roy 274, 412, 413, and 421.

Text 5. The Lincoln College *accessus*

L = Oxford, Bodleian Library, Ms. Lincoln College Lat. 27 (dated 1119), 62ra–vb

Inscr.   Materialis prelibatio in Achilleida Statii

Quis sit auctor huius libri, que materia, que scribentis intentio, quis modus uel
ordo scribendi, que legentium utilitas, que causa suscepti operis, cui parti
philosophie supponatur, quis sit titulus eiusdem libri uideamus. Auctor huius
libri Statius poeta est. Qui cum Rome positus Thebaida, id est historiam de
5   bello Thebano, XII annis elucubratam per dies XII recitasset, singulis
uidelicet diebus libellos, rogatus est a Domiciano [imper]ato[re] ut gesta sua
imperialia describeret. At ille secum deliberans seque excusans quod petebatur
facere supersedit. Arbitrabatur enim utilius fore rei publice alicuius magni et
bellicosi uiri facta describere, cuius exemplo ciues Romani prouocarentur ad
10   amorem milicie et usum armorum, sine quibus non potest res publica salua
consistere. Et quoniam eo tempore nondum subiecto Romanis orbe terrarum,
sed bellis undique consurgentibus, uiribus opus erat, non ocio, et armis potius
decertandum quam legibus, Achillis militum fortissimi et uirorum strenuissimi
gesta scribere aggressus est quatinus et ipsi Domiciano magnificentiam animi
15   et populo Romano circa usum bellandi conciliaret affectum.

Erat autem idem poeta trinomi<n>us. Vocabatur nomine proprio
Statius, quod tunc eius probitati quasi quodam presagio congruebat, quia enim
Statius a stando dicitur. Recte fuit hoc nomen eius proprium, qui per omnia
scripta sua non solum tamquam in uertice litterarum, sed in morum dignitate
20   stetit et eminentia uirtutum. Cognominabatur etiam Pampinius, a Pampino,
folio uitis, quia sicut pampinus sui densitate uitem circumtegit et uestit,
sic iste poeta totum opus suum uariis arborum ornamentis et maxime
comparationum uenustate compaginat. Appellabatur preterea Surculus
ad modum tenere uirgule pullulantis ab arbore, quia in omnibus que scripsit
25   prenimia stili elegantia recens semper et nouus apparuit.

Hec de auctore et ipsius uocabulis. Materia huius libri gesta sunt
Achillis, que omnia quidem Statius a primeua etate usque ad eius obitum
scribere proposuit, sed morte preuentus opus incepit, non expleuit. Intentio
Stacii in hoc opere fuit ipsum Achillem uelut exemplar ciuibus Romanis uelle
30   proponere, | quatinus dum eiusdem facta legerent, etiam magnaminitatem   62rb
discerent imitari. Modus uel ordo scribendi quadripartitus est. Est enim
propositorius, est inuocatorius, est excusatorius, est narratorius. Primo loco
proponit unde uelit agere, videlicet ab hoc uersu, "Magnanimum Eacidem"
usque ad hunc uersum, "Tu modo si ueteres." Deinceps inuocat
35   Phebum deum Musarum et poetarum, uidelicet ab hoc uersu, "Tu modo si
ueteres" usque ad hunc uersum, "At tu quem primum." Dein
excusat se apud Domicianum imperatorem ab eodem uersu usque ad illum,
"Soluerat Ebalio." Exinde uero usque ad finem totius operis seriem
narrationis exequitur. Utilitas legentium in hoc opere est ad exemplum et
40   imitationem tanti iuuenis uicium corporis abicere et effeminati cordis habitu
conscisso in castris uirtutum fortiter militare. Cum enim dicat Salomon,
"melior est patiens uiro forti et qui dominatur animo suo expugnatore urbium,"
patet profecto quia sicut est milicia armorum, ita est et milicia morum. In
milicia armorum decertatur uiribus corporis; in milicia morum contenditur
45   uiribus mentis. Igitur preter emulationem corporalis militie, que plurima est in
hoc libro, etiam spiritualis milicie doctrinalia sunt gesta Achillis. De similibus

etiam idem iudicium et ut Simmachus ait, "Familiare sibi est omne quod simile est." Siquidem nichil est unde potius ad fastigia uirtutum animus assurgat quam eorum qui uiriliter egerunt frequentata memoria. Dum alterum recolit
50 quis iam egisse quod ipse intendit, nec diffidit uires sibi defuturas, per quas alterum iam meminit fuisse uictorem. Causa suscepti operis hec est: Homerus quondam librum Achilleidos ediderat sed breuem et particularem. Quia plura ipsius facta digna relatu omiserat, ad supplendum ergo quod ille minus dixerat iste huic operi potius quam alteri instabat, propositum habens omnia facta
55 ipsius militaria plenius enarrare. Quod enim morte preuentus implere non potuit. Cvi parti philosophie supponatur uideamus. Ethice procul dubio subponitur. Tres enim sunt partes philosophie: phisica id est naturale, a phisis Greco, quod est natura; logica, id est rationalis a logos quod est ratio uel sermo; ethica id est moralis ab ethis quod est mos uel mores. Prime parti
60 philosophie, | id est phisice, subponuntur omnes libri de quadriwio,   62va
uidelicet astrologici, geometrici, arismetici, musici, et omnes libri Galieni uel Ypocratis uel aliorum quorumlibet de arte medicine et omnes libri quorumcumque auctorum de naturis rerum, bestiarum, auium, lapidum, herbarum, et arborum, ipsius etiam terre, vt Georgica Virgilii. Secunde parti
65 philosophie id est logice supponuntur omnes libri de triuio, uidelicet grammatica, rethorica, dialectica, et omnes libri legum et canonum et omnes libri in quibus agitur de ratione rerum aut uerborum. Tertie parti philosophie, id est ethice, supponuntur in primis omnes libri diuine pagine et omnes libri historici de rebus gestis siue ecclesiastici siue seculares, etiam hii qui fabulose
70 scripti sunt, ut carmina poetarum. Et ut breuiter dicam, omnes omnino libri in quibus aliquo modo de moribus agitur, siue per fugam uiciorum, siue per electionem uirtutum. Legimus enim bona ut imitemur, legimus mala ut caueamus, quia non potest uitari malum nisi cognitum. Ergo et hic liber Statii merito subponitur ethice, id est morali parti. Agit enim de moribus
75 multipliciter: agit de affectu materne pietatis in Thetide, de magisterio sedule eruditionis in Chirone, de culpando adulterio in raptu Helene, de zelo iuste ultionis in Menelao et Agamemnone, de malo presumptionis et precipitacionis in Prothesilao milite, de consilio et prudentia in Ulixe, de animositate et fiducia in Diomede, de honore regie mansuetudinis in
80 Licomede, de titulo uerecundie puellaris in Deidamia uirgine, de uirilis animi constantia in iam reperto et mutato Achille. Titulus talis est: Pampinii Surculi Statii liber Achilleidos incipit. Sunt autem eiusdem libri quinque distinctiones, quas thomos uocant, a Greco thomos, quod est diuisio, et sunt idem | 62vb
thomi seu libelli longe breuiores quam in Thebaide, ne populus audiens
85 recitantem prolixitate grauaretur. Quid autem unusquisque thomos in se contineat, subscripti uersus breuiter intimabunt:

Panditur istorum breuitas succincta libr[orum]

de primo:

Primus deducit Thetidem [Chironis ad antra]

90 de secundo:

Induit Eacidem muliebri ueste [secundus]

de tercio:

Tercius arma parat Danais et querit [Achillem]

de qua[rto]:

95   Quartus femineo Pelidem nudat amictu

        de q[uinto]:

            Quintus narrantem sua facta abdu[xit Achillem].

---

12 armis... legibus (13)] cf. Cicero, *Pro Plancio* 36.87: *Sed erat non iure, non legibus, non dis-*
    ceptando decertandum... armis fuit, armis inquam fuit dimicandum.
33 *Ach.* 1.1
34 *ibid.* 1.8
35–36 *ibid.* 1.8
36 *ibid.* 1.14
38 *ibid.* 1.20
42 *Prov.* 16.32
47–48 Simmachus, *Ep.* 1.43.2
89–97 *ed.* Jeudy-Riou 170

---

25 prenimia] pro nimia L

The *Universitatis bruxellensis accessus*

The idea of *Statius doctor* providing lessons to imitate is similarly expressed in an *accessus* that had a much wider circulation, particularly in the thirteenth century, but is fully extant in only two manuscripts: Bruxelles, Bibliothèque de l'Université libre, LPB 1418 and Leiden, Bibliotheek der Rijksuniversiteit, Gronov. lat. 143 (Incipitarium 167).[66] The *accessus* is also transmitted in a slightly modified form in Paris, BnF, lat. 7996 (XIV s.). What is important in this *accessus* is the adaptation of ideas similar to ones in the Lincoln *accessus* to the more traditional ideas we saw in the KP *accessus*.

After a brief note on the *materia*,[67] we find an *intentio* that is, in essence, a paraphrase of the *intentio* in the KP *accessus*. Here, the *intentio* reads (2–4):

> *Intentio sua est dehortari quemlibet ne contraire velit diuine dispositioni, quod conabat* [sic] *facere Thetis.*

Statius is again seen as *praeceptor*, but a second *intentio* (which follows this statement) portrays him as a teacher, especially for youths. Just as Homer and Virgil gave us models of virtue, Statius gives us, in the *Thebaid*, an anti-exemplum in the form of Etheocles and Polynices (4–9):

> *Aliter intentio sua est cum in Homero exemplum datum sit sapientie per Vlixem, in Virgilio exemplum pietatis in homines et religionis in deos per Eneam, cum etiam iste autor in maiori opere suo exemplum det iuuenibus per Pollinicem et Ethioclem (omnia exempla enim sunt ad imitandum uel dehortandum)[68]...*

This last detail establishes Statius' interest in educating children. Therefore, the *accessus* continues, Statius wrote the *Achilleid* to teach people how to raise children:

> *... inde hoc libro puerilis uite instructionem instruit per Achillem a Chirone nutritum.*

The third *intentio* states that Statius wrote the *Achilleid* to refine his poetic abilities for the greater poetic task that lay ahead (9–11):

> *Altera intentio sua est animum suum exercere ut facta Domitiani imperatoris, sicut rogauerat, posset digne describere.*

This detail reflects the close association between the poet and the emperor that we saw in the *accessus* in Firenze, BML, Plut. 24, sin. 12, and is likely based on *Ach.* 1.17–19.

The *finalis causa* of the work, which this and many *accessus* link to the *utilitas* and *intentio*, is simply a restatement of the *intentiones* given above, that we not impede fate and that we learn to educate children through the example of Achilles (15–17):

> *Consequimur autem hanc utilitatem ut non obstemus diuine dispositioni, uel consequimur puerilis uite erudicionem exemplo Achillis.*

Lastly, the work belongs to ethical philosophy (as is normal for epic works), or logical philosophy, "quia rethorice loquitur totaliter" (19–20). This stresses the other half of Statius' background: in addition to a teacher, he was also a rhetorician, and this emphasis often influenced criticism of his works.

---

[66] The Leiden witness appends the *accessus* to the end of a simple *accessus* based on the seven *circumstantiae* in a Ps.-Augustine schema.

[67] The Leiden witness begins with the *intentio*.

[68] These last few words resemble 72–73 of the Lincoln College 27 *accessus*: "Legimus enim bona ut imitemur, legimus mala ut caueamus, quia non potest uitari malum nisi cognitum."

The two fullest versions of the *accessus*, B and L, have some minor differences in wording at points. Although I favor the B readings in my edition, those in L were clearly not anomalous. The fifteenth-century commentary in Vaticano, Pal. lat. 1695 and the now-lost Strasbourg, BU, C.VIII.35, for example, borrows heavily from this *accessus*, but the two witnesses of the commentary preserve the readings of B and L, respectively.[69]

---

[69] In Appendix I, these are represented by the sigla Ps and Pv.

Text 6. The *Universitatis bruxellensis accessus*

B = Bruxelles, Bibliothèque de l'Université libre, LPB 1418 (XIII s.), 17r
L = Leiden, Bibliotheek der Rijksuniversiteit, Gronov. lat. 143 (XIII s.), 1ra

Materia Statii in hoc opere principaliter sunt Thetis et Achilles.
Secundaria eius materia Vlixes et Diomedes. Intentio sua est dehortari
quemlibet ne contraire uelit diuine disposicioni, quod conabat facere
Thetis. Aliter intentio sua est cum in Homero exemplum datum sit
5 sapientie per Vlixem, cum et in Virgilio datum sit exemplum pietatis in
homines et religionis in deos per Eneam, cum etiam iste autor in maiori
opere suo exemplum det iuuenibus per Polinicem et Ethioclem (omnia enim
exempla aut ad imitandum aut ad dehortandum data sunt), in hoc libro
puerilis vite erudicionem instruit per Achillem a Chirone nutritum. Aliter
10 intentio sua est animum suum exercere vt facta Domitiani imperatoris, sicut
rogatus erat ab eo, posset digne describere. Domitianus uero et Titus filii erant
Vespasiani. Mortuo autem Domitiano, uel secundum quosdam
Statio, facta eius non sunt scripta, nec Achilleis perfecta est. Finalis
causa sequitur intentionem, quia vtilitas circa intentionem <uersatur>.

15 Consequimur autem hanc vtilitatem ut non obstemus diuine
dispositioni vel consequimur puerilis uite eruditionem exemplo
Achillis, vel consequimur ingenii exercitium exemplo autoris. Ethice
supponitur quia ad morum honestatem spectat, vel etiam supponitur
phisice, quia de naturalibus etiam loquitur. Vel etiam suponitur
20 loyce quia rethorice loquitur totaliter.

More quoque aliorum poetarum opus suum in tria diuidit, in
propositionem, inuocationem, et narrationem. Miscet autem
propositionem et inuocationem.

---

1 materia... Diomedes (2)] materia eius est principaliter Thetis et Achilles secundaria vero
  Ulixes et Diomedes *post* est (13) *dist.* L
2 intentio... est] intentio autem Stacii est in hoc opere L
5 ut cum aliqui sint in adversitate sapientia eam euadant *post* Ulixem *add.* L
8 aut ad... sunt] sunt ad imitandum uel deortandum B
12 mortuo... est (13)] mortvus est autem Domicianus (*ex* uespasianus) et remanserunt inscripta
  eius gesta L
14 sequitur... uersatur] est utilitas et respicit ad singulas intentiones L
21 in propositionem... narrationem (22)] prefationem siue propositionem; inuocat; narrat. Hic
  autem miscet propositionem inuocationi et Musam inuocat L

---

3 conabat facere] nitebatur L   4 aliter... sua] uel eius intencio L   cum *om.* B   fatvm exemplum L   5 et *om.* B   6 etiam] et L   in maiori... suo (7)] in stacio maiore L   7 det] sit L
enim *post* exempla (8) *dist.* L   9 erudicionem] institionem B   9 aliter... sua (10)] uel eius
intencio L   10 suum *om.* L   exercere] exercitatvm reddere L   imperatoris *om.* L   11 rogauerat B   digne posset L   uero *om.* B   et *om.* L   erant filii L   15 dispositioni diuine L
17 vel] aut L   consequimur *om.* L   exemplo achillis *om.* L   17 vel] aut L   consequimur...
autoris] animum exercitatum L   18 quia] nam L   ad mores honestatem (*uel* honestare) (*ex*
honestatvm) pertinet L   uel... totaliter (20)] *om.* L   21 quoque *om.* L   poetarum aliorum L
poetarum *om.* B   opus] carmen L

Conclusion

By the end of the twelfth century, *accessus* began to become established as a genre, and two cornerstones to criticism on the *Achilleid* in the Middle Ages had been laid. First, Statius was seen foremost as *doctus* and a *doctor* or *praeceptor*, whether morally or rhetorically, and this idea will predominate in all later interpretations of the poet and his works. Second, the *Achilleid* took on the physical shape it would have in the following centuries: as de Angelis has shown,[70] by this time, it had been divided into five books, and scholars began to widely recognize that the poem was incomplete.

---

[70] de Angelis 1984.142–43; cf. A. Klotz, "Probleme der Textgeschichte des Statius," *Hermes* 40 (1905), 341–72.

THE THIRTEENTH CENTURY

The *Thebaid*

The most noteworthy development in the *accessus* to the *Thebaid* in the thirteenth century is the sudden appearance of new details concerning Statius' life. The first of these is that he studied at Burdigala (Bordeaux) and Narbo (Narbonne); and second, that his mother was named Agilina. To de Angelis, these were sure evidence of a second, competing biographical tradition that has not been transmitted to us.[1] I find her solution questionable for the following reasons. The so-called *In principio accessus*, which is the only independent source for these details, is, with five witnesses, one of our best transmitted *accessus* to Statius. Moreover, the manuscript witnesses of the *In principio accessus* show us that two recensions of the text were present already in the beginning of the thirteenth century. So there was, from the beginning, already a good deal of scholarly activity on the *accessus*. Now, as we saw above, the biographical information available to Statian scholars was thin, especially in comparison to the information about other authors, and the most used aspect of his biography was his role as a teacher. We would expect, then, that if a second tradition existed in which more details about Statius' own education and upbringing were available, this information would be interpolated into some of these *accessus*.[2] This is, however, not the case. The details taken from de Angelis' supposed "other" tradition are markedly thin, providing us only with the names of the cities where Statius studied and his mother's name, without any elaboration or explanation whatsoever. Likewise, before the end of the fifteenth century, these details are only found in the *In principio accessus* and in other *accessus* that are themselves descended from the *In principio accessus*.

A close look at these two "new" details shows that neither is particularly astounding, and they only betray a growing interest in Statius' background in the thirteenth century, corresponding to the oft unstated *circumstantiae, ubi et quando/quid studuit*[3] and *a quibus originem duxit*. That this interest arises rather suddenly in the thirteenth century is by no means surprising. Statius' sudden appearance in schools and the wild proliferation of his texts attest to his popularity, and along with this popularity comes, naturally, some accretions to his biography. But the origin of these details remains a question.

The association of Tolosa with Burdigala and Narbo is easily answered. In Ausonius' *Commemoratio professorum Burdigalensium*, we see a frequently occurring link between the three cities, such that all of Ausonius' professors from Tolosa taught in Narbo and Burdigala. In 4.17,[4] for example, a certain Exuperius, who was born and raised at Tolosa, became a *rhetor* in Narbo and then in Burdigala. Likewise in 4.19, Sedatus, also a *rhetor* from Tolosa, studied at

---

[1] de Angelis 1984.161 n. 106

[2] The only evidence for a tradition that de Angelis could find is that of Petrarch (*Laurea occidens* 341–46), who preserves Narbo and Bordeaux as the places of Statius' education. See de Angelis 1997.109. I see no evidence for excluding the *In principio accessus* as a source for Petrarch's comment. The *vita Statii* in Sicco Polenton's *Vitae poetarum* adds some details: "Operam doctrinis optimis sed principaliter eloquentię dedit. Apud Gallos rhethoricam docuit atque in foro causas complures easdemque multa cum laude egit. Multum quidem in dicendo et metro et prosa hic potuit" (transcribed from Firenze, BML, Plut 53.15 [XV s. ex.]). However, this claim stems from some misunderstanding of the prefaces to the *Silvae*, which the author apparently knew only second-hand (we read later in the text, "epistulę habentur quędam familiariter ad amicos soluta oratione scriptę").

[3] We find notes on Statius' education in the following *accessus* (thirteenth century) the Freiburg *accessus* edited below; Leiden, Gronov. 143 and Lips. 36; Wolfenbuttel, 228 Gud. lat. 4°; and the *In principio accessus* edited below; (fourteenth century) Padova, Biblioteca del Seminario Vescovile, 56 and Wolfenbuttel, cod. Guelf. 146 Gud. lat. 2°; (fifteenth century) Vaticano, Reg. lat. 1375 and Archivio di S. Pietro 15.

[4] I am using the edition of Prete (Teubner, 1978).

Narbo and Rome (*Narbonem ac Romam nobilitat studiis*, 12), and eventually came to Burdigala.[5]

It seems likely to me that the author of this *accessus*, taking Servius as his model and noting from his reading of Ausonius the close academic association among the three cities, assumed that the same was the case with Statius. The only reason that Statius is reported to have studied at Burdigala and did not teach there is because Jerome-Eusebius' *Chronica* and the pre-existing scholarly tradition state that Statius taught at Tolosa.[6] This is more likely than de Angelis' attempts to see a lost tradition.

More problematic is the emphasis on Statius' family that we see in this century. As important a role as the family played in the *vitae* of most other authors, it seems to have had little importance for Statian scholars.

We find but two details about the poet's family here: his father was named Papinius,[7] and his mother was named Agilina,[8] a name that does not occur in antiquity and seems to occur in the Middle Ages in the biography of Statius. In any case, Agilina, like her husband, is present in the *accessus* in name only, without details of how the two raised their poet-son; thus, her name does not seem to have its origin in some allegorical explanation. So, the name must arise from some other source.

I find five possibilities for the origin of her name. First, that it was simply invented; second, that it was taken from a source that listed some Statius with his mother's name (and perhaps his place of study) only, without mention of who he was or what he did; third, that there was a reference to a *Statius Agyllinus*[9] or *Statius de Agillina*[10] that has not been transmitted to us; or fourth, that her name arose from some confusion with *Aquitania*.[11] None of these answers the question satisfactorily, and all present varying degrees of unlikelihood.[12]

---

[5] The impetus to include these details may also be ultimately derived from the example of Servius, who named the cities where Virgil studied, also with little elaboration (ad *Aen.* 1.*praef.* 5–7).

[6] Through Ausonius, Burdigala was famous for its universities, and likewise at Narbo after the tenth century there was a famous Jewish university, but there never was a reputable university at Tolosa. However, the *vita* of Virgilius Maro, the *grammaticus*, provides some further evidence for an associaton of Tolosa with learning. Virgilius Maro suggests that he himself came from Gaul (e.g., *Ep.* 3.8.4.203), and, according to Abbo Floracensis, he came from Tolosa. (As the passage that Abbo cites is not part of Virgilius' extant works, its validity is difficult to prove [see A. Mai, *Classicorum auctorum e uaticinis codicibus editorum tomus V* (Vaticano, 1833), 349]). Virgilius' works flourished mostly in Aquitania and England (see A. Ernault, *De Virgilio Marone*, Thesis facultati litterarum Parisiensi [Paris, 1886], 11), making his *vita* a distant but plausible source for the association.

[7] This provides us with no problem. In several traditions, Statius' name Papinius (with various spelling variants) is explained as being derived from his father.

[8] The actual name of Statius' mother is not transmitted, and this has led several scholars, among whom Pomponius Laetus (whose commentary is in Vaticano, Vat. lat. 3279), to preserve *Agillina*. In one instance (Durham, N.C., Special Collections Library, Duke University, Latin ms. no. 90 [XV s. ex.]), we find the note: "Plerique matrem eius Aulam Gellinam fuisse peribent." This likely stems from a confusion with *Agilina*, which the author, on the grounds of its unfamiliarity, sought to correct (Aulus Gellius is often written "Agellius" in manuscripts).

[9] *Agyllinus* (the adjectival form of *Agylla*, the ancient name for Caere) occurs in the *Aeneid* (7.652 and 8.478, *inter al.*), Martianus Capella (6.642), Silius Italicus (5.17, although the *Punica* was mostly unknown before Poggio's rediscovery), *et al.*

[10] *Agillina* as a variant for *Agylla* is attested in one manuscript of Servius, Vaticano, Reg. lat. 1674 (ad *Aen.* 10.183).

[11] Cf. *genere Aquitanus* in the Freiburg *accessus* (below, p. 46).

[12] I lean against the first two possibilities because Agilina is such an uncommon name, occurring neither in the *PRR*, the *PRE*, nor the *CIL*. The possibility that scholars had some inscription or short biography is also unlikely, as I can find no instance of a similar inscription or biography in medieval literature.

The fifth, and most likely possibility, is that the name arises from a confusion with *Acilia*, Lucan's mother. A likely source for this confusion is the shorter version of the so-called Xicchonian Life:[13]

> *Lucanus patre Mella uiro non ignobili, matre uero Acilia*
> *uiragine natus est*

which bears a marked similarity to the *In principio accessus* (15–16):

> *nobili patre, scilicet Papinio, matre uero Agilina.*[14]

Still, whatever the source of these new details may be, it is important to note that they remain markedly sparse and undeveloped, and suggest that, in the case of Statius, the work was much more important than the man.

The *In principio accessus*

The most widely transmitted *accessus* to the *Thebaid* in the thirteenth century (transmitted in six manuscripts, three of which are of French or English origin) is the lengthy *In principio accessus* that precedes a commentary extant in various forms in at least 15 manuscripts.[15] The Berlin and Leipzig witnesses provide us with possible authors. The former manuscript contains Anselm of Laon's commentaries to Lucan and Virgil's *opera*, and the library catalog attributes all of the commentaries to Anselm;[16] but as there is no attribution at the beginning of the Statius commentary, it could simply be the case that a scribe added a different Statius commentary in an attempt to collect commentaries to the Latin epics. In the Leipzig manuscript, the title of the commentary reads, *Glose Statii Thebaidos Alberti.*[17] In any case, the commentary is mostly a glossary to the *Thebaid* filled in with centos and extracts taken from the Lucan and Ovid commentaries of Arnulf of Orléans.

The *accessus* (Incipitarium 126) and the commentary that accompanies it are extant in a longer and a shorter version. Since the two differ only in wording and not in sources or interpretation, it seems to be the case that the shorter version is a recension of the longer one and not that the longer one is an expansion of the shorter. Since our oldest witness of the commentary, the Leipzig witness (end of the twelfth century), transmits the shorter version, this recension was made at an early age. Further, the earliest witness of the *accessus*, that in København (twelfth century), transmits a heavily abbreviated text and preserves readings found in both the longer and the shorter versions; for example in lines 63–67, the longer version (BFN) reads:[18]

---

[13] Weber 3.117

[14] This relationship was first noted by Sabbadini 1910.846; cf. Sabbadini 1914.55. De Angelis (1997.102) is uncomfortable with this explanation and notes, "la fonte di queste affermazioni mi è ancora ignota." The texts are so similar, that I have no doubt as to its origin. In two possibly XIII s. French manuscripts (one of Barth formerly at Sellerhausen bei Leipzig and the other Cambridge, Trinity College, Ms. O.9.12), Statius is called *Aquilinus*, which may be related to this, although it may also be related to *Aquitanus* (see below, p. 45).

[15] On the commentary, see D. Anderson 1988 and 1994 and de Angelis 1997. Although its earliest witness dates to the twelfth century, I date it to the thirteenth century as the twelfth century witness is much shorter, while the expansions provided in the later witnesses are much more typical of this century.

[16] V. Rose, *Verzeichnis der lateinischen Handschriften*, vol. 2.3, Die Handschriften-Verzeichnisse der Königlichen Bibliothek zu Berlin, 13 (Berlin, 1905), 1304–308 [1306–308]

[17] There is a mark between *Thebaidos* and *Alberti* that D. Anderson interpreted as an *et*. I believe that the mark is the remnant of an initial-stroke from the parent manuscript, since I can find no parallel title in any other commentary. The identity of this *Albertus* is still a question. A guess is that it refers to *Albericus*, the third Vatican mythographer (see Landi 1914)— it is possible that a scholar made the attribution after noting the relationship between the two texts (I owe this insight to Rainer Jakobi).

[18] The words in common with the København witness are not italicized.

> quid contigerit *illis* duobus *pessimis* fratribus, *scilicet Ethiocli et Polinici, qui tanta regni cupiditate exarserunt quod se mutuis uulneribus interfecerunt,* isti *a consimili scelere desistant* (abstineant F)

and the shorter (LU):

> *huius rei exitu,* isti a simili *scelere se* abstineant.

In the København witness (𝕶), we find:

> quid *inde* duobus fratribus contigerit, *fratres* isti a simili *errore* abstineant.

However, 𝕶 also preserves several readings that are not transmitted in either version, such as *cuiuslibet* for *uniuscuiusque* (1), and as such provides us with an interesting problem. Many of the variants in 𝕶 that are not found in the other manuscripts are attested in later rewritings of this *accessus* (for example, the fifteenth-century manuscript Vaticano, Reg. lat. 1375, 140r–141r, which begins "In principio cuiuslibet auctoris et maxime hystoriographi, quinque sunt inquirenda... "). 𝕶, then, appears to be both an intermediary between the two versions and also a rewriting of the *accessus* with affinities to the parents of F and B.[19] The testimony of 𝕶 is thus at best ancillary, and cannot be used as more than a support for readings found in the other manuscripts.

The *In principio accessus* itself adheres to Servius in form, and expands his catalog to ten *circumstantiae*: *uita poete, titulus operis, qualitas carminis, intentio scribentis, modus tractandi, materia, finalis causa, quo genere stili utatur, quem actorem imitetur,* and *cui parti philosophie supponatur.* The *vita* is then subdivided to include questions about Statius' character, origin, and education (*a quibus originem duxerit, quibus extiterit moribus, vnde sit natus, quando et ubi studuerit,* 11–14).[20]

The details given as to Statius' *origo, natio,* and *educatio* are scanty, as I noted above. What receives the greatest weight are the unexpressed question, *quando* and a lengthy catalog of Statius' *mores.* The *circumstantia quando* is answered by the sentence, *studuit autem tempore Vespasiani et Titi filii eius, peruenitque ad imperium Domitiani, qui minor Titus dictus est* (18–19), which is only slightly modified from the *Quaeritur accessus* (q.v., 2–4), the only noteworthy alteration being *studuit* in the place of *fuit/fuisse.*

The catalog of *mores* provides us with a succinct view of the judgment to Statius in the thirteenth century (19–24):

> *Fuit autem morum honestate preditus, acris intelligentie, tenacis memorie, clarus ingenio, doctus eloquio, liberalium artium scientia feliciter eruditus. Fuit adeo nimie facundie ut de eo meminerit Iuuenalis....*

The parallels with the *Quaeritur accessus* are apparent, both in the repetition of the assessments, *clarus ingenio* and *doctus eloquio,* and in the rephrasing of the line, *cuius Iuuenalis sic meminit dicens,* (*Quaeritur accessus,* 8), but we also see a continued emphasis on Statius as *doctus* and *doctor.* Here, he is endowed with a strong moral character (he is *firmus contra uicia et fortune bifformes euentus,* 40–41), as well as with wisdom and a keen memory; he is modest, and, most importantly, he is well versed in the liberal arts. Juvenal's assessment is then repeated, here with some variants unattested in the standard editions of Juvenal.

---

[19] It is for this reason that I use a fracture letter to designate it.

[20] We find the same expanded catalog in the fifteenth-century *accessus* to Ovid's *Ars* in Napoli, BNC, V.D.52, which begins similarly: "In principio huius auctoris, cuius fama propter operum diuersitatem late circumuulgata est, quatuor inquirenda sunt, scilicet unde duxit originem, quibus parentibus ortum habuerit, ubi et quando studuit et quomodo uixerit... " (Ghisalberti 1946.58–59).

The *accessus* goes on to tell us, after a discussion of Statius' popularity, that he was the most popular and favorite poet, second to Virgil.[21] This is followed by a confusing etymology of his name that has some textual problems.[22] In the shorter recension, the text reads (28–37):

> *Vnde et dictus est Cursulus quia secundum inter poetas locum tenuit et fauorem populi obtinuit et ultimus apud Romam declamauit. Satira enim non solebat recitari.*

The longer recension reads (28–37):

> *Vnde etiam sortitus est hoc nomen Sursulus quasi Surculus, id est, sursum canens, eo quod post Virgilium inter ceteros poetas principatum obtinuit et popularem adeptus est fauorem. Nemo enim post eum declamauit,* sed opponitur quod Iuuenalis et multi alii post eum fuerunt. Ergo multi post eum declamauerunt. Non sequitur. *Satira enim non solebat recitari.*

Based on the shorter recension and on its contradictory nature, the passage *sed opponitur* through *non sequitur* is likely an interpolation, and I have thus italicized it. However, if we remove this passage, we are left with the verbs *declamare* and *recitari* linked by *enim*. Grammatically, this would suggest an equation between the two verbs, which is unparalleled and stylistically awkward. Further, it is only the last phrase, *Satira... recitari*, that has parallels in other *accessus*; but based on these parallels, there must be a lacuna before the phrase. The *accessus* in London, BL, Royal 15.A.XXIX, for example,[23] notes that Statius is one of the *Simplicium poetarum* (39). An interpolated note explains this (39–40):

> *Quod autem simpliciter sit poeta patet. Non enim est satiricus, nec historiographus, nec comicus et cetera.*

In a similar vein, one *accessus* to Lucan (Huygens 1970.39–44) claims that Lucan "est etiam historicus et tamen satyricus" (146–47). Arnulf of Orléans counters this last opinion and gives us a better view of the concept (*Accessus in Lucanum* 4.6):[24]

> *Sicut Iuuenalis purus est satiricus, Terencius purus comedus, Horacius in odis purus liricus, non est iste poeta purus, sed poeta et historiographicus. Nam historiam suam prosequitur et nichil fingit, unde poeta non simpliciter dicitur, sed poeta et historiographicus. Nam si aliquid ficticii inducit, non ex sua parte sed ex aliorum hoc inducit, apponit enim uel ut perhibent, uel ut dicunt, uel ut memorant.*

Both of these interpretations of Lucan are rare in the *accessus* to Lucan; most of the scholars argued that Lucan was not *poeticus*, but *historicus*.[25] This idea may be behind the assignation *historiographi* (1) here in our *accessus*.

What I suspect is occurring in our passage is that with the phrase *nemo... declamauit*, the scribe wished to explain Statius' rhetorical abilities; this may originally have been a marginal note to *docuit* (17) or to *historiographi* (1). The last phrase, *satira... recitari*, is probably part of a discussion of his *popularem fauorem*, and is likely dependent on some lacuna after *fauorem*

---

[21] The K version reads *preter Virgilium*. This may actually be a misunderstanding of the abbreviation $\widetilde{pt}$ (*post*) resulting in $\overline{pt}$.

[22] This passage is not transmitted in the K witness.

[23] I treat this *accessus* further below.

[24] This *accessus* is discussed in depth in B. Marti, *Arnulfi aurelianensis Glosule super Lucanum*, Papers and Monographs of the American Academy in Rome, 18 (Rome, 1958), XXXVII–XXVIII.

[25] See E.M. Sanford, "Lucan and his Roman critics," *CP* 26 (1931), 233–57. The *locus classicus* of the debate is in Isidore, *Etymologiae* 8.7.10: "Officium autem poetae in eo est ut ea, quae vere gesta sunt, in alias species obliquis figurationibus cum decore aliquo conversa transducat. Vnde et Lucanus ideo in numero poetarum non ponitur, quia videtur historias composuisse, non poema."

(32). We should remember, however, that in medieval traditions, Juvenal first delivered speeches (*declamauit*) and then moved to writing satire.[26]

The interpretation of the *Thebaid* begins at line 56 with a discussion of the *intentio*. The first *intentio* is a typical of the *intentio* that we commonly saw in the twelfth century, that Statius wished to keep the imperial brothers from squabbling. But here, the author advances on his predecessors and explains why this cannot be the case. First, Titus was already dead when Statius began his epic (ll. 79–80); second, there is no point at which Statius directly advises or chastises the brothers (l. 80).

The second *intentio* is that Statius, after hearing of the rewards poets were receiving at Rome, came to the city and, after long considering a theme,[27] decided that he would bring back the long-forgotten myth of Thebes.[28] This is an important step in interpretation, as the poem takes on a less political and rather a more individual context, that is, Statius does not write so much for the emperor, but for all readers; likewise, the work takes on a relevance for the "modern" reader.[29]

There are, later in the *accessus*, two *intentiones* (labeled *fines*), the first of which is "Ethioclis et Polinicis bellum describere" (94), that is, to tell the story. The second *intentio*, here labeled the *finis ad quem tendit* or *finalis causa* (103), is again more geared toward the private reader, "ne tale aggrediamur officium per quod simile incurramus periculum" (104–106). These are essentially the same as the first *intentio*, in which Titus and Domitian were urged not to engage in fraternal warfare, but here intended as an *exemplum* for the reader.[30]

The final noteworthy aspect of this *accessus* is the attribution of the poem to political philosophy, not just the usual ethical genre. As political philosophy is explained as "scientia que ad regnum ciuitatum est necessaria" (114), it is likely that the author had some sort of "mirror for princes" in mind, but that is difficult to prove, as this is the only instance of such an attribution.

The manuscripts of this *accessus* are divided into three families, the first, which is descended from the α hyperarchetype, preserves the order of the *questiones* (for the most part), throughout the text.[31] The β family, on the other hand, places the *quo genere stili utatur* after the *qualitas carminis*. This second family is the poorer and seems to represent attempts at rewriting or, in the case of the archetype γ, heavy abbreviation. The third family, κ, is either the result of a third copy of the original manuscript or is the result of a collation of the α and β families. I lean toward the first explanation.

---

[26] *Vita Juvenalis* (in Wessner 1931.1.3–4): "... ad mediam fere aetatem declamavit... ."

[27] This detail may be partially based on *Thebaid* 1.3–4: "Pierius menti calor incidit. unde iubetis ire, deae" or on 12.811, "o mihi bissenos multum uigilata per annos."

[28] Cf. the twelfth-century Bern-Burney *accessus* (above, p. 11), ll. 19–20.

[29] Another version of a poet coming to Rome is found in the *accessus* in the P commentary to Juvenal (Löfstedt 1995.217.7–13): "Iuuenalis iste natus de Aquitane opido tempore Neronis Romam venit, vidensque Paridem panthomimum ita familiarem imperatori, ut nihil unquam nisi eius nutu ageret... ad satiram scribendam se transtulit."

[30] Cf. the *accessus* fragment in Zürich, Rh. 53 (XII s.), "Intentio eius dissuadere fraternum odium ne tale incurramus periculum"; cf. as well Arnulf of Orléans, *Glosule super Lucanum*, 3.15–18: "uiso quid contigerit utrique de ciuili bello,... caueamus nobis a bello consimili."

[31] The *circumstantiae* are listed in the order *vita, titulus, qualitas, intentio, modus, materia, finalis causa, stilus, imitatio,* and *philosophia*. They are answered in the order *vita, titulus, qualitas, intentio, materia, finalis causa* (note that it is the shorter version that preserves this reading; the longer reads *finis*), *stilus, philosophia,* and *imitatio*.

Figure 4. Stemma of the *In principio accessus*

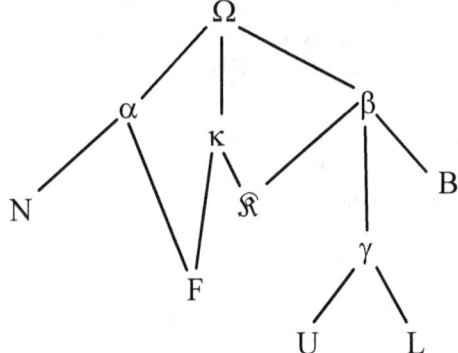

Text 7. The *In principio accessus* to the *Thebaid*

B = Berlin, Statsbibliothek - Preußischer Kulturbesitz, Haus 2, lat. fol. 34 (XIII s.), 86ra
F = Firenze, Biblioteca Riccardiana e Moreniana, Ricc. 842 (XV s.), 1ra–b
L = Leiden, Bibliotheek der Rijksuniversiteit, BPL 191A (XIII s.), 214r
N = London, British Library, Add. 16380 (XIII s.), 144ra–va
U = Leipzig, Universitätsbibliothek, MS. 1607 (XII/XIII s.), 10r
Ƙ = København, Kongelige Bibliotek, Fabricius 29 2° (XII s.), 6r

Glose super Statium Thebaidos

BFNƘ	LU
In principio uniuscuiusque auctoris historiographi, ut Seruius testatur, hec inuestiganda diligenter iudicantur: uita poete, titulus operis, qualitas carminis, 5 intentio scribentis, modus tractandi, materia, finalis causa, quo genere stili utatur, quem auctorem imitetur, cui parti philosophie subponatur. Horum unumquodque eo ordine quo 10 proposuimus exequamur. Circa uitam poete hec queri digna perhibemus: a quibus originem duxerit, quibus extiterit moribus, unde sit natus, quando et ubi studuerit.	Que uita poete, titulus operis, qualitas carminis, intentio scribentis, modus tractandi, materia, finalis causa, cui parti philosophie supponatur uideamus

15   Legitur itaque auctor iste ciuis Tholosanus extitisse, nobili patre, scilicet
Papinio, matre uero Agilina. Burdegali et Nerbone studuit et in Gallia
rethoricam celeberrime docuit. Tandem Romam se transtulit, ubi hoc opus
composuit. Studuit autem tempore Uespasiani et Titi filii eius, peruenitque
usque ad imperium Domitiani, qui minor Titus dictus est. Fuit

BFNƘ	LU
20 igitur morum honestate preditus,	autem uite honeste

acris intelligentie, tenacis memorie, clarus ingenio, doctus eloquio,

BFNƘ	LU
liberalium artium scientia feliciter eruditus. Fuit adeo nimie facundie ut de eo meminerit Iuuenalis, dicens <*Sat.* 7.82–84>:	adeo ut cuius meminerit Iuuenalis:

25   Curritur ad uocem iocundam et carmen amice
Thebaidos letam Stacius cum fecerit urbem,
promisitque diem.

BFNℜ

Vnde etiam sortitus est hoc nomen Sursulus
quasi Surculus, id est sursum canens,
30 eo quod post Uirgilium inter ceteros poetas
principatum obtinuit et popularem
adeptus est fauorem. Nemo enim post
eum declamauit, *sed opponitur quia*
Iuuenalis et multi alii post eum fuerunt.
35 *Ergo multi post eum declamauerunt.*
Non sequitur.

U

Vnde et dictus est
Cursulus quia secundum inter
poetas locum
tenuit et fauorem populi obtinuit

LU

et ultimus apud Romam declamauit.

Satira enim non solebat recitari.

Huius libri talis est titulus: Surculi Papinii Stacii Thebaidos liber primus
incipit. Surculus ut prediximus dictus est quasi sursum canens, et est agnomen.
40 Papinius dictus est a patre et est cognomen, Stacius uero proprium nomen a
statu uite sue sic dictus est. Erat enim firmus contra uicia et fortune biformes
euentus, neque enim ea blandiente efferebatur uel contumacius tonante tristis
habebatur. Thebais Thebaidos femininum est patronomicum nomen Thebane
historie. Bene dicitur primus quia sequitur secundus. Sunt enim duodecim libri.
45 Liber dicitur quasi liberans a curis, uel liberum et expertem curarum expetens,
vnde Iuuenalis <*Sat.* 7.63–65>:

Quis locus ingenio nisi cum se carmine solo
Vexauit et dominis Cirre Niseque feruntur
Pectora nostra duas non admitencia curas?

50 *Unde finxerunt philosophi duos deos esse poetarum, Bacum et Apollinem.*
Per Apollinem sapientia per Bacum innueretur temporalium sufficiencia.
"Incipit" et<iam> dicit quia nichil premiserat. Queritur quare tot
nomina in titulo apponantur. Respondemus ut per ea auctore commendato
opus reddatur autenticum.

55 Qualitas carminis est metrum heroicum, et est metrum continens tam
diuinas quam humanas personas, uera falsis admiscens.

Intentio Stacii in hoc opere est Thebanam describere historiam,
cuius intentionis diuerse a diuersis cause assignantur. Quidam enim dicunt
quod mortuo Uespasiano, filii eius Titus et Domitianus in tantam regni
60 cupiditatem exarserunt ut fraternale odium incurrerent. Ad quorum
dehortationem auctor iste Thebanam proposuit describere historiam et
secundum hanc causam talis erit huius intentionis utilitas, ut uiso

BFNℜ

quid contigerit illis duobus pessimis
fratribus, scilicet Ethiocli et Polinici,
65 qui tanta regni cupiditate exarserunt
quod se mutuis uulneribus interfecerunt,
isti a consimili scelere desistant. Verum
qui hoc dicunt ex Suetonio hoc habere
uidentur, qui in libro De duodecim
70 Cesaribus inter cetera de Tito dicit,

LU

huius rei exitu,

isti a
simili scelere se abstineant. Et qui
hoc dicunt ex Suetonio De duodecim Cesaribus hoc habere uidentur, qui de Tito dicit

fratrem suum Domicianum insidiari uite sue desistere nolentem, exercitus aduersus se excitantem, tamen noluisse, cum posset occidere, neque seponere, neque in minori honore quam cepisset habere; sepe autem rogare ut apud se mutua dilectione teneretur, seque succesorem suum in regno promittere.	quod ei frater suus insidias moliri solebat.
Alii uero considerantes	Et similiter alii dicunt

quia Tito iam mortuo et Domiciano iam regnum adepto, Stacius hoc opus incepit, et ita nullum esse dehortationis locum, hanc premisse causam intentionis assignant, dicentes quia cum tempore Domiciani

BFNℜ	LU
Romam vndique poetas confluere Stacius audierat, ibique ad maximos honores prouehi, tandem Romam uenit et qualiter populo Romano et imperatori placere posset diu apud se excogitauit. Denique animum suum aplicuit ut Thebanam historiam prenimia annorum uetustate iam pene deperditam describendo ad memoriam reuocaret, sicque imperatori et populo Romano placeret.	poetas undique uideret Romam confluere et ab eo habunde remunerari, idem expectens ut etiam fauorem princi- pis acquireret et famam ampliaret, animum suum ad scribendam applicuit hanc his- toriam que iam uetustate fere erat deperdita

Intentio auctoris est Ethioclis et Polinicis bellum describere cum utriusque partis fautoribus. Modus tractandi tripartitus est: quia nunc historiam tangit, nunc figmento subseruit poetico, nunc scripto utitur allegorico.

Materia est Ethiocles et Polinices et acies utriusque confecte, vel, ut uerbis auctoris utamur, "Oedipode confusa domus," scilicet crudelis Edippus, matris Iocaste corruptor, Laii patris interfector; Ethiocles et Polinices, ceci patris contemptores, qui regni cupiditate cecati <se> mutuis uulneribus ceciderunt.

BFN	LU
Finis ad quem tendit talis est, ut uisis utriusque partis incommodis ne tale aggrediamur officium per quod simile incurramus periculum.	Finalis causa est ut uiso utriusque partis exitio, a consimili scelere nobis caueamus.

Nota tria esse genera scribendi, humile, mediocre, grandilocum, quibus omnibus utitur Uirgilius. Que alii caracteres uocant, alii stilos. In Bucolicis utitur humili, in Geogicis mediocri, in Eneide alto. Hic autem auctor grandiloquo genere stili utitur.

Ethice supponitur per politicam, quia nobis informat morum doctrinam. Ethice autem due sunt partes, economica, qua proprie dispensamus familie (economicus enim dispensator interpretatur),

<et politica>. Politica est scientia que ad regnum ciuitatum est necessaria (polis enim ciuitas interpretatur).

BFNUℜ	L
115 Quem auctorem imitetur ipse docet in fine, vbi dicit, "Vive precor nec tu diuinam Eneida tempta, sed longe sequere et uestigia semper adora." Per hoc innuens se imitari Virgilium, optimum 120 Latinorum. Scribit autem ad laudem Domiciani imperatoris, non quia Thebana historia ad eum quicquam pertineat, sed dicit se in hoc opere suum preacuere ingenium ut postmodum ad 125 fortia eius facta describenda ualeat sufficere. Dicit itaque, "Tempus erit cum laurigero tua fortior oesto facta canam."	Imitatur autem Uirgilium, unde in fine, "precor uiue" et cetera. Scribit autem ad laudem Domitiani non quia hec ad eum pertinet historia, sed ut ingenium suum peracuat et acutius reddat in sua facta describenda vnde "Tempus erit" et cetera.

Item in opere Achilleidos ad ipsum promisit dicens, "Magnusque tibi 130 preludit Achilles." Sed quod et hic et ibi promiserat morte preuentus exibere non potuit.

Auctor iste Thebanam scripturus historiam more aliorum recte scribentium proponit, inuocat, narrat. Proponit ubi dicit "Fraternas acies" et cetera. Invocat ubi diuinum implorat auxilium, ut ibi, "Unde iubetis ire 135 dee." Narrat ubi lectionem suam inchoat ibi scilicet, "Impia iam merita scrutatus lumina dextra" et cetera.

His iam decursis que extrinsecus erant dicenda, ad litteram exponendam accedamus.

---

2 Seruius] ad *Aen.* 1.*praef.* 1–3

15 nobili... Agilina (16)] cf. vitam Lucani Xicchonianam contractam, *Lucanus patre Mella uiro non ignobili, matre uero Acilia uiragine natus est* (ed. Hummel, *Nova bibliotheca* 1.153–56; et C. F. Weber, *Vitae M. Annaei Lucani collectae* III, Indices lectionum... in Academia Marburgensi [Marburg, 1858], 17)

16 Burdegaldi... studuit] cf. Servius *ad Aen.* 1.*praef.* 6–7: *nam et Cremonae et Mediolani et Neapoli studuit.*

30 post... obtinuit (31)] cf. Huguccio Pisanus, s.v. *sursum*

50–51 cf. schol. B in Juv. (ed. Löfstedt 1995.110), ad 7.63: *In Cirra colitur Apollo, per quem designatur sapiencia; in Nisa Bachum, per quem notatur sufficiencia.*

62 uiso... consimili (63)] cf. Arnulfi Aurelianensis accessum in Lucanum, 3.15–18: *uiso quid contigerit utrique de ciuili bello, uidelicet et Pompeio capite truncari, Cesari... perforari, caueamus nobis a bello consimili.*

71–78 Suet. *Titus* 9.3, *rectius*

98 *Theb.* 1.17

102 uisis... periculum (105)] cf. Zürich, Rh. 53: "intentio eius dissuadere fraternum odium ne tale incurramus periculum."

102 uiso... caueamus (104)] cf. Arnulfi Aurelianensis Glosule, *loc. cit.*

106 tria... grandiloquum] Servius *ad Aen.*1.*praef.* 82–83

116–18 *Theb.* 12.816–17
126–28 *Theb.* 1.32–33
129–30 *Ach.* 1.19
133 *Theb.* 1.1
134 *Theb.* 1.3–4
135 *Theb.* 1.46

---

65 intentio] uel nutrire ingenium suum in hac (?) nostra ut fortior sit ad facta Domitiani describenda. *add. marg.* N (cf. accessum in Vaticano, Reg. lat. 1375, 21–22)
68 materia] uel Thebana historia. Utilitas est notitia (fabularum, *del.*) ystorie; ethice supponitur
uel morali scientie. Omnes enim auctores spectant ad mores. *add. marg.* N (cf. accessum in Vaticano, Reg. lat. 1375, 23–25)
133 proponit²] ubi materiam suam prelibat *add. sup. lin.* N (cf. inter al., Vat. lat. 1663, ll. 18–
19)
134 narrat] ubi materiam suam incipit explanare *add. sup. lin.* N (cf. ibid.)

Inscr. L : super stacium thebaidos N : glose statii thebaidos alberti liber primus incipit L :
Stacius thebaidos 𝕽 : *om.* BF   **1** cuiuslibet 𝕽   **2** ut... testatur *om.* 𝕽   hec... iudicantur (3) ista
sunt inquirenda 𝕽   **3** dilligenter inuestiganda (inquirenda B) BF   iudicantur] sunt F   operis]
auctoris U   **4** qualitas carminis *om.* B𝕽   **5** tractandi] materiei F   **6** materia *om.* U   uideamus *om.* U   **7** utitur... imitatur B   **9** unumquodque] quodlibet 𝕽   eo... exequamur (10) pro
posse suo ordine prosequamur 𝕽   circa... studuerit (14) *om.* 𝕽   **11** digna queri F   **12** duxit
FN   **13** moribus extiterit BF   vnde... natus *post* perhibemus (11) *dist.* F   quando] quid N
quando... studuerit (14)] vbi et quando studuerit *post* duxerit (12) *dist.* F   studuit N
15 itaque *om.* BLU   quod *post* itaque *add.* F   tolosensis F : tolonensis 𝕽 : tolosanus B : tole-
tanus U   extitisse] BLU : extitit F   nobili... scilicet] natus est a patre   nobili *om.* LU
scilicet *post* nobili *dist.* F : *om.* LU   **16** papino N𝕽   uero *om.* FLU   burdegali... et] qui 𝕽
narbone L : urbene U   studuit *post* burdegali *dist.* LU   et *post* studuit *om.* LU   galliam FU :
gallias N   **17** rethoram L   celeberrime rethoricam NB   edocuit NB   tandem] sed postea 𝕽
se Romam LU   **18** composuit] constituit U   studens LU   autem] que U : *om.* L   eius filii
𝕽   peruenitque] peruenit *post* est (19) *posuit* L : *om.* U𝕽   usque *om.* BN   ad *om.* U
19 imperium] tempus L𝕽 : *om.* U   iunior U   tito N   dictus est] dicebatur U : erat uel est
dictus N   **20** igitur morum] itaque stacius 𝕽   uite *ex* et iste L   **22** scientia *om.* B   **23** adeo]
etiam B : autem F𝕽   nimie] tante 𝕽   usque adeo *ante* ut *add.* BF   ut] quod 𝕽   cuius] eis
U   **24** meminit N : memoriauerit 𝕽   **25** iocundam... diem (27) *om.* L   et... diem (27)] et
cetera U   **26** fecit cum stacius F𝕽 : cum fecit stacius B   **28** et B   sortitus est *post* nomen
dist. B   vnde... obtinuit (31) *om.* L   vnde... canens (30) *om.* 𝕽   thebais... patronomicum]
thebaidos patronomicum est femininum B : thebais est femininum patronomicum U
29 sursulus] surculus F   surculus... est *om.* FN   **30** eo... obtinuit (31) *post* canens (39) *dist.* 𝕽
post uirgilium] preter (!) virgilium *post* poetas (31) *dist.* 𝕽   quia F   **31** obtinet 𝕽   et... recitari (37) *om.* 𝕽   **33** rome *post* enim *dist.* B : *post* eum *dist.* N   **34** quod F   actores *post* multi
add. B : *post* alii *add.* F   et... declamauit] declamauit autem ultimus apud romam L   ultimus
ante declamauit *dist.* U   **35** multi *post* eum *dist.* F   **37** satira... recitari] quia satira declamari
non solet L   enim] nam *ante* satira *dist.* U   **38** huius... titulus] titulus talis L : titulus est U
titulus] inscriptio FN   sursuli 𝕽 : sursulii N : suruli B   primus liber BU   **39** sursulus B   ut
prediximus *om.* 𝕽   ut... canens et *om.* BLU   prediximus] supra dixi F   *post* canens *add.* 𝕽:
eo quod inter ceteros poetas preter virgilium principatum optinet   agnomen est B   **40** dictus
est *post* patre *dist.* B   dictus... et est *om.* U   uero] est N : *om.* FL𝕽   est *post* uero *add.* U
nomen proprium L   nomen *om.* F   est *post* nomen *add.* BF (eius est 𝕽)   a... habebatur (43)
om. BLU   **41** sue... est] dictum F𝕽   est *post* proprium (40) *dist.* F   biformes fortune F   **42**

non ℜ   enim *om.* F : *add. sup. lin.* ℜ   efferente blandiebatur F   uel... tonante] neque ea intonante ℜ   contumacitus intonante F   **43** thebaydos thebais F   thebais *om.* B   thebaidos
om. LU   patronomicum est feminimum B : formam habet patronomici feminini   est *ante*
femininum *dist.* U : *om.* L   nomen] uoce L   nomen... historie (44) *om.* B   est *post* nomen
add. N (id est ℜ)   thebane... curas (49) *om.* L   **44** bene... libri *om.* U   bene dicitur *om.* F
dicit ℜ   liber *post* primus *add.* F   quia *om.* B   enim *post* sequitur *add.* B   etenim ℜ   libri
om. Bℜ   **45** liber... autenticum (54) *om.* ℜ   liber dicitur *om.* F   quasi] id est B : quia U
liberat U   a curis liberans BF   et... expetens] exigit U   **46** vnde... curas (49) *om.* F   **47**
nisi... curas (49)] et cetera U   **48** vexant N   **49** uel quia antiqui in libro id est cortice scribe-
bant *post* curas *add.* U   **50** vnde... sufficienciam (51) L : *om.* BFLU   **51** sapientiam...
sufiicienciam (*ex* sufficiencie) N   **52** incipit... autenticum (54) *om.* LU   et *om.* F   nil B
53 titulis BF   **55** qualitas] Scd (?) ℜ   metrum[1] est N   hoc *post* est[2] *add.* FN   heroicum]
homericum U   et... metrum *om.* LU   et... admiscens] quod conuenit historiagraphis ℜ
heroicum *post* metrum *repet.* F   **56** etiam *post* quam *add.* F   **57** etiam *post* intencio *add.* ℜ
Stacii] sua LU : eius ℜ   in... opere *om.* LU   est *post* Stacii *dist.* F : *om.* N   **58** intentionis
om. ℜ   a diuersis *om.* LU   ac uarie *post* diuerse *add.* ℜ   assignantur cause BLUℜ
quidam... quod (44) *om.* LU   dicunt enim quidam ℜ   enim *om.* B   **59** enim *post* mortuo
add. U   filius ℜ   filii *post* domitianus *dist.* L   eius *om.* L   titus et domitius *post* uespasiano *dist.* L   regni] imperii F : uel imperii *add. sup. lin.* ℜ   **60** cupiditatem *post* tantam
(59) *dist.* B   exarserunt cupiditatem LU   ut] quod N   iam *post* ut *add.* F   fraternale] ferale
F : etiam horribile ℜ   quorum] cuius LUℜ : quam rem N   **61** actor... thebanam] hanc LU
proposuit] proponit BFL : *om.* ℜ   describere *om.* BFLU : scripsit ℜ   et... utilitas (62) *om.*
LUℜ   **62** erit] est *post* utilitas *dist.* B   **63** qui B   contigerit... desistant (67)] inde duobus
fratribus contigerit, fratres isti a simili errore abstineant ℜ   pessimis *om.* B   **64** scilicet...
Polinici *om.* B   Ethiocli scilicet F   ex *post* qui *add.* F   **65** imperii BF   exarserunt cupiditate B   exarserunt quod *om.* F   **66** sese BF   uulneribus *post* interfecerunt (interfecere F)
dist. BF   et *post* interfecerunt *add.* N   **67** scelere *post* desistant *dist.* F : *om.* U   desistant]
abstineant F   verum... promittere (78) *om.* ℜ   se abstineant] absterreantur U   **68** hoc[2] *om.*
BF   uidentur habere FN   **69** scripto *post* cesaribus *add.* U   hec U   uidentur] dicere L
70 de... dicit] de tito et domiciano agit, de tito B   **71** domicianum *ante* fratrem *dist.* B   in-
sidiari *post* sue (72) *dist.* B   **72** nolentem desistere B   exercitum B   **73** excitantem susci-
tantem F   noluisse tamen BF   **74** com N   cum posset] eum post se F   neque... neque
(75)] nec... nec B   **76** se *om.* N   mutua apud se B   **77** dellectacione F   **78** successorem
suum] suum fore successorem BF   **79** alii aliter dicunt ℜ   similia LU   **80** quia... assignant
(82) *om.* ℜ   iam[1] *om.* BFLU   et *om.* U   regnum] imperium BF   regnum adepto] regnante
LU   opus hoc F   **81** incohauit LU : composuit B   et ita] itaque BF   et... assignant (82)]
nota quod non stat prima sentencia U : sed quod Statius prima sentencia L   dehortacionis locum esse B   premissam B   **82** intencionis causam F   dicentes] dicunt ergo LU : dicunt
etiam ℜ   cum] in BFN   imperatoris *post* domiciani *add.* BF   **83** romam... audierat (84)]
stacius uidens poetas romam vndique confluentes ℜ : romam undique confluere poetas audierat
Stacius B   Rome U   confluere *om.* L   stacius *om.* F (*add. marg. man. rec.*)   **84** et ibi ℜ :
itaque B   eos *post* ibique *add.* F   maximas prouehi dignitates ℜ   **85** eos *post* honores *add.*
N   ipse *post* tandem *add.* BF (et ipse ℜ)   fauorem] habundum L   **86** quomodo B   romano
populo ℜ   et | et N   et imperatori : *om.* Bℜ   principis] populi U   expetens L   **87** possit F
diu *om.* ℜ   excogitatum N   demum ℜ   **88** animum... deperditam (90)] ad thebanam historiam describendam per vetustatem pene disperditam animum applicuit ℜ   appulit BF
suum... hanc (90)] et ad hanc precipue appulit U   **89** pro(*uel* per)nimia F   scribendum L
90 iam *ante* prenimia (89) *dist.* B   vt eam *ante* describendo *add.* ℜ   describendo *om.* B
populo *post* describendo *add.* ℜ   et (?) *ante* ad *add.* N   **91** sicque] et   **92** et... romano *om.* ℜ
93 auctoris] sua ℜ   igitur (itaque B) *post* intentio *add.* BF   intentio... est] intendit itaque LU
in hoc opere *post* est *add.* B   bellum polinicis et ethioclis LU   describere *post* fautoribus

(95) *dist.* LU   **94** cum... fautoribus] et utriusque partis fautores N : cum fautoribus partis utriusque B : cum fauctoribus utriusque partis F   fauoribus L   tractandi] materiei FN : tractande materie B   talis est et *post* tractandi *add.* U   est tripertitus BFU   **95** quia] quod B : *om.* LU   poetico *om.* L   figmento... poetico] poeticum figmentum interserit ℜ   poetico subseruit U   nunc² | nunc *repet.* N   enim *post* nunc² *add.* U   **96** scripto... allegorico] allegorice scribit LU : allegoria (*ex* aulegoria) utitur B   aulegoria utitur *subpunct.* B   undique B   **97** sua *post* materia *add.* ℜ   polinices et ethiocles Lℜ   polinix (*et passim*) F   et... confecte] cum suis U : *om.* ℜ   et acies... utamur (98)] cum suis uerbis autem actoris utamur U : *om.* L   conserte F   **98** vel] et U   actoris] anactoris U   edipodis confusa domus *post* est (97) *dist.* L   edipodis U   scilicet... ceciderunt (101) *om.* BLUℜ   **100** cupidine F   **101** ceciderunt] cecidere *ante* mutuis (100) *dist.* F   **102** finis... alto (108) *om.* ℜ   talis *om.* FN   est *om.* N   uiso... exitio (103) *om.* L   **103** partis utriusque F   incomodum F   ne tale] tale n̄ B   a] de U   **105** periculum] incomodum F   **106** nota... alto (108) *om.* LU   nota... utitur *post* admiscens (56) *dist.* B   scribendi genera BF   **107** que] quod F   uocant] (appellant B) *post* stilos *dist.* BF   in... alto (108) *om.* BF   **108** hic... utitur (109) (et utitur... stili L) *post* admiscens (56) *dist.* LU   hic... utitur] gradiloquo vtitur stilo quia de magnis agit personis ℜ   hic... auctor (109)] et L : *om.* U   hic autem *om.* F   **109** utitur (nititur U) *post* auctor *dist.* BLU   grandidiloco *subpunc.* N   autem *post* grandiloquo *dist.* F   stili genere utitur F   **110** ethice... interpretatur (114)] *post* potuit (131) *dist.* B : *post* cetera (128) *dist.* LU   hetice N   per... interpretatur (114)] quia de moribus loquitur ℜ   polinicam U   quia... politica (113) *om.* LU   morum informat BF   **111** sunt *om.* B   **112** disponimus F   **113** politica est] et est politica LU   uero *post* politica *add.* BF   ciuitatis BL   et morum (mores U) *post* ciuitatum *add.* LU   est *post* necessarium *add.* L   polis... interpretatur (114) *om.* LU   **114** dicitur BF   **115** ipse docet *om.* B   docet] intimat (ostendit ℜ) *ante* vbi (116) *dist.* Uℜ   **116** operis *post* fine *add.* Bℜ   vbi dicit] dicens FUℜ : ipsemet insiuat dicens B   **117** sed... adora (118)] et cetera BU   **118** per... latinorum (120) *om.* BU   **119** innuit ℜ   imitari] sequi ℜ   optimum... potuit (131) *om.* ℜ   **120** domitus L   autem *om.* L   quod U   **122** de *ante* thebana *add.* F   eum] domicianum BF   quicquam *post* historia (122) *dist.* F   **123** pertineat] spectet L   suum *om.* B   ingenium preacuere B   **124** preexercat U   **125** eius] domiciani BF   describenda *post* sufficere (126) *dist.* B   possit B   **129** item... ipsum] in achilleide U   item... potuit (131) *om.* L   idem N   opere] libro F   ad... dicens *om.* B   promittit F   **130** preludit achilles] et cetera U   et¹ *om.* BF   et¹... ibi *om.* U   ibi] illic B   promiserat] promisit F : promisit *post* quod *dist.* B   morte preuentus *post* sed *dist.* U   exibere *post* potuit *dist.* B   **131** exibere non potuit] non potuit exibere B : non exhibuit U   **132** auctor... scribentium (133)] more aliorum historiagraphorum incipit quia ℜ   auctor... historiam *om.* LU   Thebanam *om.* LNU   scric|turus N   recte] bene F   recte scribentium *om.* U   recte... narrat (135) *om.* L   **133** ubi dicit] dicens LU   et *post* invocat *add.* Uℜ   ait ℜ   acies *om.* L   **134** et cetera *om.* LNU   ubi... ut *om.* LU   diuinum... ibi] dicit Bℜ   ibi] dicens U   ire dee *om.* LU   **135** ubi... inchoat *om.* LU   lectionem... scilicet] ait ℜ   suam lectionem F   inchoat] explanat B   ibi] dicens U   scilicet *om.* FLU   iam... dextra (136) *om.* LU   merita *om.* N   **136** scrutatus... dextra *om.* BF   scrutatus lumina *om.* N   et... accedamus (138) *om.* LU   et cetera *om.* B   cetera] cum N   **137** iam *om.* Bℜ   decisis F : expeditis ℜ   que... dicenda *om.* ℜ   extrinsecus] exterius(?) B : *om.* F   predicenda erant BF   **138** exponendam *om.* F

The Freiburg *accessus*

With the exception of the *In principio accessus*, the remaining *accessus* of the thirteenth century are extant in one or two manuscripts only, but represent the same interest in Statius' origin that I mentioned above.

One of the more interesting and problematic of these *accessus* is that found in Freiburg, Universitätsbibliothek, HS 375 (Incipitarium 274). Here the biography is essentially the same as we saw in the *In principio accessus*: as a child, Statius was well-versed in all of the arts (*omnium arcium peritus industria*, 3–4). He then decided to go to Rome, here in the hope of furthering his education. Once he noted the fame that the poets receive, he decided to study poetry and was then either asked or persuaded by the emperor to write the *Thebaid*. The problem with this *accessus* lies in its explanation of Statius' origin.

Statius, the *accessus* informs us, is Aquitanian (*genere Aquitanus*, 1), born into the noble ranks of the city of Tolosa, which is a city on the west coast of *Lugdunensis Gallie* (2–3). Again, this confusion might suggest the presence of a second, poorly represented tradition, but I believe that that is not the case. Tolosa was certainly not in Aquitania during Statius' life (although Burdigala was), but both Tolosa and Burdigala were in Aquitania after the tenth century AD. However, neither of these cities, and certainly not Narbo, was in Gallia Lugdunensis.

I suspect that the scribe made a series of geographical mistakes. The *accessus* is labeled *Vita Stacii Tolonensis*, which may suggest that the author confused Tolosa with Tullum (modern Toul). During the thirteenth century, Toul was in the Kingdom of the Lotharii, but during Statius' lifetime, was a part of Gallia Lugdunensis.[32] It is unclear how the scribe, who was French, made this error; we have, however, seen similar confusion before, namely in the twelfth-century Bern-Burney *accessus*.

There are two likely explanations for the placement of Tolosa *ad occidentalem plagam sita*. The author either made the error of adding Burdigala's geographical position to the muddle, or made the massive error of confusing Tolosa and Tullum with Telo (modern Toulon on the Côte d'Azur) and then, thinking Telo was in Gallia Lugdunensis, placed it on the Atlantic.[33] Whatever the case may be, I believe that the author simply tried to adapt what little information about Statius there was to a confused view of historical Gaul.[34]

---

[32] Alternately, it may be the case that the scribe confused Tolosa's vicinity to Lugdunum Convenarum (modern Saint-Bertrand) with the provence of Gallia Lugdunensis.

[33] This error is not as unlikely as it may appear. In the *accessus* in Soest, Stadtarchiv und wissenschaftliche Stadtbibliothek, Cod. 34 (dated 1406–12), the scribe (Jacob de Susato) first describes Statius as *Theloseus*, which he corrected. We might compare as well the title to the *Thebaid* in Firenze, Biblioteca Nazionale Centrale, II.II.55 (XIV s.), *Papinii Surculi Statii Thelosensis uel Nerbonensis liber primus incipit*. In his commentary to the *Purgatorio*, Christoforo Landini also placed Tolosa in neighboring Gascogne: "perche fu da Toloso, la quale citta e ne confini di guascogna verso Brettagne" (ed. P. da Figino 1491 [repr. 1507], 191v).

[34] A similar confusion can be found in the *accessus* in Paris, BnF, lat. 8055 (XII s.), p. 1b: "Iste poeta Statius nomine, Pampinus cognomine, Surculus agnomine, Tolosensis genere, hoc est de gente *Bauosa*, temporibus Domiciani fratris Titi iunioris filii Uespasiani fuit." A similar confusion occurs in the beginning of the unedited *vita* of Sidonius Apollinaris in London, BL, Royal 4.B.IV (England, XII s.): "Sidonius Narbonensis [*ex* Lugdunensis] genere, cuius ciuitas ipse facit mentionem...."

Text 8. The Freiburg *accessus* to the *Thebaid*

F = Freiburg im Breisgau, Universitätsbibliothek, HS 375 (XIII s.), 106v

Vita Stacii Tolonensis

Stacius Papinius Surculus genere Aquitanus nobili exortus prosapia inter primos
ciuium Tolosane vrbis. Est autem hec ciuitas Lugdunensis Gallie ad occidentalem
plagam sita. Hic itaque ab ipsis ut ita dicam puerilibus annis omnium arcium
peritus industria, apud plurimas eiusdem prouincie urbes rethoricam celeberrime
5   docuit. Postea uero (nisi modicus) aptus desiderio uisendi studia, Romanorum
urbem adire maturauit; ea namque tempestate Uespasianum Romani imperii
monarchiam regere videbat. Dicitur autem iste philosophus tam diu inter
Romam annos commorari, vsque ad imperium Domiciani fratris Tyti, qui etiam
10 Tytus iunior dictus est. Considerans enim Romanorum proceres poetarum ad
primum delec<t>ari carminibus, sese omnino ad poetriam transtulit. Iussus ergo
uel pocius crebris supra taxati imperatoris precibus exoratus, Thebanorum
Grecorumque bella duodecim libellis per totidem annos describere studuit, quem
codicem de Thebanorum gestis Thebais feminino genere, sicut Eneis et Theseis,
15 nominan[s] insticuit. Hunc etiam fuisse clarum ingenio, doctum eloquio
Iuvenalis famosissimus poeta carmine suo testatur dicens <*Sat.* 7.82–86>:

> Curritur ad uocem iocundam et carmen amice
> Thebaidos letam Stacius cum fecerit urbem
> Promisitque diem tanta dulcedine captos
20 > Afficit ille animos, tantaque libidine uulgi
> Auditur, sed cum fregit subsellia uersum
> Esurit intactam Paridi in [*sic*] uendat Agauem.

Stacius autem dictus est nomine, Papinius uero cognomine, Surculus quippe
quasi sursum canens.

15–24 cf. *Quaeritur* accessum, 7–18

22 *in uendat*] cf. Kraków, Muzeum Narodowe, Biblioteka Czartoryskich, 1876 II (XII–XIII s.),
         p. 215

---

6 uespasianus F   **11** prime F   **24** q̣ịạ quasi *subp.* F

The *accessus* in London, BL, Royal 15.A.XXIX

The *In principio accessus* presented us with the picture of Statius as a man of proper morals and of outstanding education. Both of these ideas achieve their widest expansion in the thirteenth century in an *accessus* that is found on a small scrap of parchment that forms the fourth folio of London, BL, Royal 15.A.XXIX (Incipitarium 265).

In this *accessus*, Statius is first and foremost described as a *uir scientie* (5); the name *Surculus*, likewise, is explained as "quasi surgulus a surgendo, quia surgebat et crescebat in sua sapientia" (11–12). The allegory of his name continues, further explaining *Surculus* as some sort of a root on which one stubs one's toe,[35] which the author explains as meaning that he is difficult to imitate ("ita iste erat offendiculum emulari," 13). The name Papinius is next explained as being derived from a supposedly Greek word, *pape*.[36] Finally, the name Statius is explained as "quasi stans dictus est... stando enim in summo cacumine philosophie fuit" (23–24). This is a common allegory that we first saw in the early–twelfth century Oxford, Lincoln College 27 *accessus* (ll. 18–20). We also find it briefly mentioned in London, BL, Add. 17408[37] and Sankt Florian, XI.587.[38]

Two *intentiones* for the *Thebaid* are given, one more intrinsic and textually based, the other extrinsic and based on an interpretation of the text. In the first instance, Statius "intendit... comouere homines ad castitatem et concordiam in probando eorum incesta scelera" (24–26); in the second, Statius sought to describe "bellum quod Ethiocles et Polinices inter se gesserunt" (32–33). That is, Statius intended to write a specific story, and also had a moral motivation.

---

[35] The definition of *surculus* as a sort of root is a stretch from any of the standard lexical entries, and I have been unable to find a parallel etymology. Although no *accessus* makes the comparison, an epithet in the 1496?, Poitiers edition of Bouyer and Bouchet includes the comparison "alter Virgilius de virga Surculus exit" (Incipitarium 46; see Appendix III, text IV).

[36] The etymology is also found in the Bern-Burney *accessus*, l. 46–47.

[37] "Stacius dictus est a stando nam stetit in sciencia maxima."

[38] "Dicitur Stacius quasi stans in bonis moribus quia bene morigatus fuerat."

Text 9. The Royal 15.A.XXIX *accessus* to the *Thebaid*

L = London, British Library, Royal 15.A.XXIX (XIII s.), 4v

Stacius iste tempore Uespasiani imperatoris dicitur fuisse, qui cum
duos filios haberet, Titum scilicet et Domicianum, cum altero eorum
Iudeam euertit. Dicitur etiam peruenisse usque ad imperium iunioris
fratris, Domiciani scilicet, qui etiam Titus dictus est. Fuit equidem
5   uir scientie, nobilis genere, Tolosensis, quae ciuitas est Gallie, et in
Gallia celeberrime didicit et docuit retoricam. A Domiciano quippe
rogatus est ut de se scriberet, sed cum nichil dignum scriptu uideret,
transtulit se ad aliam materiam, scilicet Thebanam historiam, faciens
prologum excusatorium in quo honeste se excusat. Titulus talis est:
10   Surculi Papinii Stacii Thebaidos liber incipit. Surculus dicitur
quasi surgulus a surgendo, quia surgebat et crescebat in sua
sapientia. Surculus pars trunci que super terram eminet ubi pes
alicuius offenditur. Ita iste erat offendiculum emulari. Papinus
dicitur a Greco quod est pape, quasi admirabilis in sapientia.
15   Statius proprio nomine. Uel si uoluimus Surculus potest ei esse
prenomen et nomen Papinius agnomen ab euentu, quod per euentum
contigit sibi ut tantum sapientie haberet quod admirabilis inde fieret.
Statius est cognomen ei quod euenit sibi tam ex cognitione sapientie
quam ex carnis cognatione quia aliquis ex parentela sua sic
20   uocatus est. Uel quasi quosdam gradus sapientie eius possumus
notare quia dum puer erat et crescebat in eo sapientia, Surculus
dicebatur. Postquam autem adulte etatis fuit, tam sapiens fuit quod
Papinus id est admirabilis fieret. Stacius autem quasi stans dictus
est, stando enim in summo cacumine philosophie fuit. Intendit autem
25   comouere homines ad castitatem et concordiam in probando eorum
incesta scelera—scilicet incestum quod contrarium est castitati, et <quod>
paci opositum scilicet discordiam. Incestum in Edippo habemus
quia cum matre cocubuit; in Ethiocle et Polinice discordiam.
Incestum est enim concubere cum sorore, uel matre, uel monialibus;
30   fornicare, cum meretricibus; adulterium, cum uxoratis. Debemus autem
notare quod peccatum est pena peccati, sic ex oraculo Edippi fuit
pena incestus illius. Intentio Stacii est scribere illud bellum quod
Ethiocles et Polinices inter se gesserunt et illi qui causa istorum inducti
sunt ibi. Materia est Ethiocles et Polinices principaliter eorumque
35   secundario auxiliatores. Finalis causa ostendere quanta pena et quam grauis
exitus humanum defectum comitetur. Titulus huius libri talis est:
incipit Stacius Thebaidos in qua ostendit principaliter atentionem et
secundario docilitatem. Hoc enim debet fieri in omni titulo. Facit
etiam more simplicium poetarum (*quod autem simpliciter sit poeta*
40   *patet. Non enim est satiricus, nec historiographus, nec comicus et*
cetera) *** in propositi[one] uero ostendit docilitatem principaliter,
secundario atentionem, licet ubicumque unum at aliud. Invocatione autem
reddit nos beniuolos, ubi dicit, "Unde iubetis" et cetera. Quicumque enim
invocat se humiliat. Ex humilitate autem ipsa beneuolentia procedit.
45   Ad quam partem philosophie liber iste spectet satis patet, id est ad
ethicam.

12 Surculus... trunci] cf. Huguccio Pisanus, s.v. sursum: *unde hic surus, -ri, truncus qui remanet post abscisionem arboris.*

14 pape... mirabilis] cf. Remigius, *Expositionem de celebratione misse* (Migne, *PL* 101, col. 1257^d; Bernensis-Burneius *accessus*, 46–47 (supra, p. 11)

39 simpliciter... historiographus (40)] cf. Prisciani *Partitiones Aeneidos* 1.3 (*GLK* 3.459.23–24); cf. Arnulfi Aurelianensis *Accessum in Lucanum*, 4.4

41 docilitatem... beniuolos (43)] cf. accessum in *Disticha Catonis* quem ed. Huygens (p. 21–22, ll. 16–17): *premittit itaque prologum in quo nos attentos, dociles, benivolos fieri desiderat.*

43 *Theb.* 1.3

---

15 statius *ex* suaitus L   **18** cognatione L   **27** pacis L   **41** *ante* in *lacuna, continens* tria facit, proponit, inuocat, et narrat *uel simile*   **45** spectet *ex* spectat

The *Achilleid*

The Gronov. 66 *accessus*

In contrast to the small number of *accessus* to the *Thebaid* transmitted in thirteenth-century manuscripts, a large number of ones to the *Achilleid* are extant, including three that are well transmitted. Still, in spite of this abundance, none of these *accessus* equals the broad advances made by the scholars on the *Thebaid* during the same century, and while rewritings and adaptations abound, the actual biography and interpretation make no advancement over the scholarship of the twelfth century. What we do find in these *accessus* is a growing distinction between the audiences of the *Thebaid* and *Achilleid*. In the *In principio accessus*, the author (in three of the manuscripts) referred to Statius as *historiographus*.[39] In contrast, our first *accessus* to the *Achilleid* refers to Statius as *precipuus*—or *primus et principalis*—*inter libros scolasticos*. The driving force behind scholarship to the *Achilleid* in this century is not so much the interpretation of the poem—that was cemented in the previous century—but an increasing emphasis on the *Achilleid* as a school text. What we find, then, are more general *accessus* that include more scholastic information. Unfortunately, this results in longer *accessus* that have more to do with literature in general than they do with the *Achilleid* itself. A good example of this type is the *accessus* found in El Escorial, Real Biblioteca, f.III.11, Leiden, Gronov. 66, and Wolfenbüttel, 292.2 Gud. lat., which I shall refer to as the Gronov. 66 *accessus* (Incipitarium 117).

The beginning of this *accessus* bears a marked similarity to that of the *In principio accessus*:

> *In principio huius auctoris, qui est precipuus inter libros scolasticos, plura sunt inquirenda, scilicet titulus operis, materia carminis, qualitas metri, quo stilo auctor utatur, cui parti philosophye supponatur.*

The major difference between the two *accessus*, aside from the immediate change from *historiographus* to *precipuus inter libros scolasticos*, is the absence of the rubrics *uita poete* and *intentio scribentis* that played so prominent a role in the *In principio accessus*; the adaptation of the list of *circumstantiae* reflects this more general approach to the *Achilleid*.

The Gronov. 66 *accessus* is, at heart, a very brief discussion of the text, filled in and rounded out by a lengthy series of literary lists: in 7–12, the author lists the *tres stili scribendi* (6–12); tells of Achilles' genealogy (within a discussion of the myth of Peleus, combined with a lengthy discussion of the names *Amphitrides* and *Thetis*—14–25); he then continues with a discussion of the *titulus* (26–32; cf. 13), which is followed by an explanation of the *duo ordines scribendi* (33–44). These lists are all only loosely connected to the text at hand, and seem more to reflect an introduction to literature in general than an introduction to the text of the *Achilleid*.

The most worthwhile development in this *accessus* occurs in the *pars philosophiae*. As we see in other *accessus*, fictional literature is usually relegated to the *ethica pars philosophiae*.[40] There are, of course, occasional instances where a scholar will find some other reason why the poem is labeled *ethica*;[41] in this case, the scholar applies the *Achilleid* to the *ethica pars* because of its implied didactic nature (69–72):

> *Ethice id est morali scientie subponitur, nam intentio sua est ut nos per uirtutes Achillis informet ad uirtutes et doceat nos uitare desidiam et torporem.*

---

[39] In addition to the late–twelfth century *In principio accessus* and *accessus* directly related to it, he is also referred to as *istoriografus* in Kraków, Muzeum Narodowe, Biblioteka Czartoryskich, 1876 II (XII–XIII s.), p. 216.

[40] See Clogan 1968.9 and Allen 1982.67–178.

[41] Cf. the early–twelfth century *accessus* in Oxford, Lincoln College, lat. 27 (above, p. 22), ll. 56 ff..

There is one more feature of this *accessus* that is worth noting. When we peel the grammatical lists and the other superfluous information away, the *accessus* is rather thin. As a result, an interpolating hand in the Escorial witness has expanded the *accessus*, taking material from the twelfth-century *Universitatis bruxellensis accessus* (above, p. 27), from the parent of the *accessus* in Vaticano, Pal. lat. 1695,[42] and from common *periochae*[43] to fill out the information. As we shall see below, rewriting and borrowing will be an important aspect of *accessus* to the *Achilleid* in this and later centuries.

---

[42] See above, p. 28. The Pal. lat. 1695 *accessus* itself is based on the original version of the Gronov. 66 *accessus* (cf. its incipit, "Domicianus quidam Romanus imperator," with line 47), as well as on the *Universitatis bruxellensis accessus*, from which it preserves many passages that are not transmitted in the Gronov. 66 *accessus*. It is difficult to say, then, whether the Escorial witness of our text influenced the author of the Pal. lat. 1695 *accessus* or *vice versa*.

[43] These periochae are found in an *accessus* in Paris, BnF, lat. 8559 (XIII s.), the KP *accessus* (XII s. ex.), Leiden, Lips. 36 (XIII/XIV s.), and Düsseldorf, K2: F.50 (XIV s.), *inter al.*

Text 10. The Gronov. 66 *accessus* to the *Achilleid*

E = Escorial, El, Real Biblioteca, ms. f.III.11 (XIV s.), 151v
L = Leiden, Bibliotheek der Rijksuniversiteit, Gronov. lat. 66 (XIII s.), 1r
W = Wolfenbüttel, Herzog-August-Bibliothek, Cod. 292.2 Gud. lat. 8° (XIII–XIV s.), 6r

 In principio huius auctoris, qui est precipuus inter libros scolasticos,
plura sunt inquirenda, scilicet titulus operis, materia carminis, qualitas
metri, quo stilo auctor utatur, cui parti philosophye supponatur. Titulus
operis talis est: Incipit Statius Achilleidos, id est Stacius de historia
5 Achillis. Nomen itaque istius autoris Statius est. Qui Statius doctissimus
poetarum in libris suis ita solebat uti grandiloquo stilo, id est, difficili modo
scribendi. Nam tres sunt stili, id est modi scribendi, scilicet humilis,
mediocris, grandiloquus. Humili stilo utitur Virgilius in Bucolicis, mediocri
in Georgicis, grandiloquo in Eneide. Hoc itaque stilo usus est autor iste.
10 Et dicitur grandiloquus quasi grandia loquens, siue pro eo quod
habet difficilem modum scribendi; siue quod de grandibus
personis, id est, de personatis tractatum habeat. Sic itaque
intelligendum est hoc nomen Statius Achilleydos.

 Achilles filius fuit Pelei et Thetidis. Peleus filius fuit Eaci regis et
15 frater fuit Thelamonis et Phoci. Hunc Phocum idem Peleus in uenatione
ignoranter interfecit, vnde et compulsus est exulare. Deinde duxit in
coniugium Thetidem filiam magne Thetis et Occeani, qui est deus
magni maris qui alio nomine dicitur Amphitrides, id est circumterens,
ab amfi, quod est circum, et tero et dicitur Amphitrides quia totum
20 circumterat mundum, id est, circumeat. Hoc nomen Amphytrides inuenies
in primo folio Ouidii magni. Hoc nomen Thetis quando ponitur pro nomine
magne dee, post primam sillabam producit et declinatur hec Thetis,
huius Thetis, vnde in Ouidio magno dixit, "ad canam descendit in
equora Thetim." Quando autem signat Thetis filiam, declinatur
25 hec Thetis, huius Thetidis, et tunc primam sillibam corripit.
De hoc nomine Achilles uenit patronomicum femini generis,
hec Achilleis, huius Achilleidis uel -dos. Et sicut hoc nomen hic
Achileides, huius Achilleyde signat proprie filium uel nepotem
Achillis, ita hoc patronomicum facimus. Hec Achilleis, huius
30 Achilleydis, proprie signat filiam uel neptem Achillis, sed in hoc
loco ponitur Achilleydos pro historia Achillis et dicitur liber iste
Stacius Achilleydos, id est Stacius qui descripsit facta Achillis.

 Et notandum quod in hoc libro utitur Statius ordine artificiali. Nam
duo sunt ordines scribendi, videlicet naturalis et artificialis. Naturalis
35 ordo scribendi est cum eo ordine historia describitur quo
facta est, ut in Statio Thebaidos et in Sedulio et in Aratore.
Artificialis autem ordo est quando ea que primo describi
deberent ad tempus differuntur, et postmodum apte
introducuntur, ut in Eneide et in hoc libro Stacii, nam in hoc
40 libro primo describitur qualiter Achilles a matre deliberato
consilio translatus sit timore Troiani belli in insulam Chiros
in aulam Licomedis. Postea in fine apte et competenter
aduertitur de infantia ipsius Achillis, ipso Achille per ordinem
referente Vlixi et sociis suis uirtutes et facta sue infantie. Et
45 sciendum ipsum Statium morte preuentum hoc opus consumare
non potuisse. Causa quare Statius hunc librum conscripsit talis

est: Domitianus quidam imperator Romanus uidens hunc Statium
doctum esse poetam, rogauit ipsum sua facta uelle describere,
sciens quod librum Thebaidos bene scripserit. Sed quia idem

50 Domitianus nichil dignum memoria exercuerat, iste Statius
callide se excusauit, dicens se non presumere facta tanti principis
describere, *necque suo ingenio confidens*, rogauitque ipsum
Domitianum ut licentiam sibi daret describere prius facta Achillis
ut in tali preludio suum animum acueret et sic ingenio suo in

55 hoc opere preceptato dicebat se postmodum laudes Domitiani
describere, sicut in hoc uersiculo demonstratur: "Magnusque tibi
preludat Achilles." *Et sic Statius hunc librum nomine
Achilleidos componere cepit, vnde historie facte sunt de
Achille.*

60   Materia carminis est uirtus Achillis *et Thetidis.* Qualitas
metri est sicut solet fieri in heroico carmine, uersus tantum
exametri. Stilo utitur ut iam diximus grandiloquo. *Intentio sua est
dehortari quemlibet ne contraire uelit dispositioni fatorum, cui
nitebatur Thetis contrahire. Vel intentio eius est animum suum ad*

65 *exercitia reddere in hoc libro ut facta Domitiani regis, sicut rogatus
fuit ab eo, digne possit describere. Domitianus et Titus filii erant
Vespasiani. Mortuo vero Domitiano, facta eius inscripta manserunt.
Utilitas est ne diuine dispositioni contrahire nitamur, uel utilitas puerilis
est eruditio et bone discipline exercitatio.* Ethice id est

70 morali scientie subponitur, nam intentio sua est ut nos per uirtutes
Achillis informet ad uirtutes et doceat nos uitare desidiam et
torporem.

    Pandet itaque istis premissis, nunc ad prologum libri
transeamus. *Prologum facit in hoc in quo proponit de quo tractaturus*

75 *sit; inuocat suam Musam et Apollinem; excusat se erga Domitianum
quare facta sua non inceperit scribere. Liber iste in V uolumina
distinguitur. In primo legitur de sollicitudine Thetidis, in secundo de
absconsione Achillis, in tertio de adquisitione Grecorum, in quarto de
inuentione Achillis, in quinto de eductione eius in Troiam ubi periit.*

80 *His uisis ad litteram accedamus.* Iste itaque auctor more aliorum
poetarum primo proponit, postea inuocat, deinde narrat. *Proponit ubi
dicit "Magnanimum," inuocat ubi dicit "Tu modo," narrat ubi dicit
"Soluerat" et cetera.*

---

7 nam... Eneide (9)] cf. Servius *ad Aen.*1.*praef.* 81–83
20–21 Ovid, *Met.* 1.14
23–24 *Met.* 2.509
49 sciens... scripserit] *accessus* in Pal. lat. 1695, l. 3
52 non... ingenio] *ibid.*, 1. 3
57 *Ach.* 1.19
62 intentio... contrahire (64)] *accessus universitatis bruxellensis*, ll. 2–4
64 vel... manserunt (67)] *ibid.*, ll. 19–23
68 utilitas... exercitatio (69)] *cf. ibid.*, ll. 25–26
76–79 cf. periochas in Paris, BnF, lat. 8559 (XIII s.); KP *accessu*; Leiden, Bibliotheek der
     Rijksuniversiteit, Lips. 36 (XIII/XIV s.); Düsseldorf, Landes- und Stadtbibliothek, K2:
     F.50 (XIV s.) *inter al.*

1 precipuus] primus et principalis E   **2** scilicet *om.* L   S (*?*) *post* operis *habet* E   **3** stilo] titulo W   **4** stacius *post* id est *om.* E   id... achillis (5) *om.* W   **5** istius] huius L : *om.* W est statius W   statius (*post* qui) *om.* W   in *post* qui statius *subpunx.* E   **6** ita *om.* E   uti *om.* L   **7** stili... modi] modi et stili W   scribentium L   scilicet *om.* EL   **8** stilo *om.* W **9** autem *post* grandiloquo *add.* L   **10** quod *post* siue *add.* E   **11** habet] habeat *post* modum *dist.* W   difficilem habet L   loquendi uel scribendi E   **12** id est] seu W   uiris *post* personatis *add.* L   **13** id est *post* achilleydos *add.* E   fuit filius EW   **14** fuit filius EW   fuit *post* frater *om.* W   **14** thetidem in coniugium (15) W   **16** compultus L   **17** magni EL   **18** amphitrites L   id... ab (19)] et dicitur W   **19** amfi] an L   -ris *post* tero *add.* L   et... amphitrides *om.* W   **20** circumterit... circumit W   mundum *om.* EL   id est] uel W   hoc... amphytrides] et W   hoc... achillis (32) *om.* E   **21** autem *post* hoc *add.* W   ponitur *om.* L   **22** post] ponitur L *om.* W   sillabam *om.* W   hec Thetis *om.* W   **23** dixit... canam *om.* W **24** filiam thetis EW   **25** hec thetis *om.* W   primam... coripit] prima corripitur W   **27** hic E : hoc *subpunx.* L : *om.* W   et... achilleyde (28) *om.* W   **28** proprie significat W   **29** ita... achillis (30) *om.* W   **31** iste liber W   **32** con|scripsit L   **33** statius *om.* W   artificiali ordine W   **34** videlicet W : scilicet E : *om.* L   **35** scribendi ordo L : *om.* W   eo] quo L : in E historie W   describitur *om.* W   **36** et in aratore] et maratone E : *om.* W   **37** autem *om.* W ^{de} scribi E   scribi primo W   **39** statii] narii L   nam *om.* EL   **40** quomodo W   **41** troia̅ L in insula *om.* E   chiros insulam W   chiron EL   **42** apte *om.* E   **43** adnectitur L : addicitur? W   ipso] ipse L   achille *om.* W   **44** suis sociis E   **46** stacius *post* librum *dist.* L   composuisset W   **47** quidam *om.* LW   imperator *om.* W   romanus *om.* LW   **48** esse] et L ipsum... uelle] ut facta sua uellet W   facta] gesta E   **49** sciens... scripsit *om.* LW   idem *om.* W   domitianus idem E   **50** digni E   **51** se callide excusans W   principis] uiri E*ac*   **52** nec... confidens *om.* LW   -que² *om.* W   ipsum *om.* W   **53** sibi licentiam W   primo L   **54** ut... acueret E   et] quod W   **55** preceptato] prece precando E   dicebat *om.* E   se *om.* W **56** ut W   **57** et... achille (59) *om.* LW   **60** et thetidis *om.* LW   **62** iam *om.* W   intentio... exercitatio (69) *om.* LW   **69** ethyce... est] ethicus est quia honeste et E   **70** nos *post* achillis (*l.* 71) *dist.* W   **71** nos *om.* W   deuitare E   **73** pandet iamque *om.* EW   istis] paucis W **74** accedamus E   prologum... accedamus (80) *om.* LW   **81** primo... narrat] recte scribentium tria facit proponit inuocat narrat E   postea] deinde W   deinde] inde L : postea W   proponit ubi... et cetera (83) *om.* LW

Rewritings of the KP *accessus*

Although the *Universitatis bruxellensis accessus* shows indirect evidence of wide influence, the major source for interpretation of the *Achilleid* between the thirteenth and fifteenth centuries was the twelfth-century KP *accessus*. The difference between the usage of the two traditions is an important one. The Bruxelles tradition, as is the case in the example we have just seen, tends to be present more through interpolation; the KP *accessus*, on the other hand, was much more prominent, and tends to be either transmitted whole (or in large portions) or rewritten. The *accessus* in Vaticano, Vat. lat. 1663 (Incipitarium 125), and that in Vaticano, Reg. lat. 1556 (Incipitarium 119),[44] represent this second aspect of the reception of the KP *accessus*. The verbal similarities among the three *accessus* show this interrelation, as demonstrated in the table on the next page.

The Vaticano, Vat. lat. 1663 *accessus* is actually a great deal more complicated than this collation shows. Vaticano, Reg. lat. 1556 contains three *accessus*, the first beginning *Actor iste Stacius de Tolosa ciuitate extitit...* ,[45] the second beginning *In principio huius libri considerandum est...* (which is the rewriting of the KP *accessus* that we have just treated), and the third beginning *In principio huius actoris quattuor sunt inquirenda...* (the KP *accessus*). Vaticano, Vat. lat. 1663 contains two *accessus*, the same *Actor iste...* , and then one beginning *In principio huius libri...* (which is collated in Table 1 on p. 56). This second *accessus* is actually a medley of the last two *accessus* in Vaticano, Reg. lat. 1556 (or its parent). It seems likely to me that the scribe of Vaticano, Vat. lat. 1663 saw the two *accessus* in Vat. lat. 1556 and, noting similarities, tried to make one "pure" *accessus* out of them.

---

[44] The *accessus* is also transmitted in Oxford, Bodleian Library, Ms. Canon Class. Lat. 72 (dated 1274), 19v; and Paris, BnF, lat. 8207 (XIV s.), 83ra.

[45] This *accessus* bears some relation to the third *accessus* to the *Thebaid* in Bern, Cod. 528 (XII s.— Incipitarium 277).

Table 1. Derivatives of the KP *accessus*

Reg. lat. 1556	Vat. lat. 1663	KP
1: in principio huius libri	1: In principio huius libri	1: in principio huius auctoris
1–2: que sit materia operis, que sit auctoris intentio in hoc opere, que sit libri utilitas, quis sit titulus.	1–2: que sit materia huius operis, que sit actoris intentio in hoc opere, que sit libri utilitas.	1–2: intentio scribentis, materia, vtilitas, titulus
3–5: materia huius operis est Achilles... Achillis facta uirtuosa describere,	2–3: Achillis facta virtuosa describere,	5: materia eius est Achilles et eius forcia facta
supplendo que minus dicta sunt ab Homero	supplendo ea que minus dicta sunt ab Homero	4: supplendo ea que minus ab eo dicta sunt
5–9: Vtilitas est ne fatis amplius inutiliter obuiare temptemus, cum Thetidem eis obuiando nichil profecisse nouimus. Titulus talis est: Stacii liber Achilleidos primus incipit, et bene dicitur primus quia sequitur secundus. Sunt enim IIII, secundum quosdam, secundum alios V.	4–7: Vtilitas est ne fatis amplius inutiliter obuiare temptemus, cum Thetidem eis obuiando nichil profecisse nouimus. Titulus talis est, Stacii liber Achilleydos primus incipit. Bene dicit primus quia sequitur secundus. Sunt enim quinque.	16–19: Vtilitas est ne fatis obuiare temptemus, cum Thetidem eis obuiantem nichil profecisse nouerimus. Titulus talis est: Stacii Achilleidos liber primus incipit. Bene dicitur primus quia sequitur secundus. Sunt enim quattuor, secundum alios quinque.
	7–10: In primo matris sollicitudinem et causam sollicitudinis describit. In secundo filii absconsionem. In tertio Grecorum inquisicionem. In quarto invencionem. In quinto adduccionem ad Troiam	13–16: In primo matris sollicitudinem et causam sollicitudinis describit. In secundo filii absconsionem. In tercio Grecorum inquisitionem. In quarto inuentionem. In quinto adductionem ad Troiam
9–10: Actor iste tractaturus Achilleidem, id est historiam de Achille.	14: Actor iste tractaturus Achilleydem, i.e. historiam de Achille.	
10: more aliorum poetarum, tria facit	14–15: more aliorum poetarum, tria facit	21: more aliorum poetarum
13–16: Est autem proponere materiam de qua tractandum est breuiter explicare. Inuocare est diuinum auxilium implorare, narrare est materiam suam explanare. His dictis, ad litteram accedendum est	16–19: Est autem proponere materiam de qua tractandum est breuiter explicare. Inuocare est diuinum auxilium implorare, narrare est materiam suam explanare. Hiis visis, ad litteram accedendum est.	

Text 11. The Reg. lat. 1556 *accessus* to the *Achilleid*

O = Oxford, Bodleian Library, Ms. Canon. Class. Lat. 72 (dated 1274), 19v
P = Paris, Bibliothèque nationale de France, lat. 8207 (XIV s.), 83ra
R = Vaticano, Città del, Biblioteca Apostolica Vaticana, Reg. lat. 1556 (XIII s. med.), 74v

Glose Stacii parui

In principio huius libri considerandum est que sit materia operis, que
sit auctoris intentio in hoc opere, que sit libri utilitas, quis sit titulus.
Materia huius operis est Achilles. Intentio auctoris est in hoc opere
Achillis facta uirtuosa describere, supplendo que minus dicta sunt
5   ab Homero. Vtilitas est ne fatis amplius inutiliter obuiare temptemus,
cum Thetidem eis obuiando nichil profecisse nouimus.
Titulus talis est: Stacii liber Achilleidos primus incipit, et bene dicitur
primus quia sequitur secundus. Sunt enim IIII, secundum quosdam,
secundum alios V. Actor iste tractaturus Achilleidem, id est
10   historiam de Achille, more aliorum actorum, tria facit:
proponit, dicens "Magnaninum Eacidem," inuocat
his uerbis, "Tu modo si ueterem," narrat dicens, "Soluerat
Oebalio." Est autem proponere materiam de qua tractandum est
breuiter explicare. Inuocare est diuinum auxilium implorare.
15   Narrare est materiam suam explanare. His dictis, ad litteram
accedendum est.

Inscr. add. man. rec. P : glossa in Statii Achilleidem *add. man. recentius* P : *om.* OR   **2** quis...
opere (3) *om.* R   **3** est *post* opere *dist.* O   **5** inutiliter *om.* O   **6** cognouerimus P   **7** et *om.*
P   **9** secundum alios *om.* OR   id est]... (*subpunct.*) P   **10** tria facit *om.* P   primum *post*
facit *add.* P   **11** et cetera postea *post* Eacidem *add.* P   postea *om.* OR   **12** his uerbis *om.* R
si ueterem] et cetera OR   deinde *post* ueterem *add.* P   explicare] prelibare P   **15** his] de
hiis O

Text 12. The Vat. lat. 1663 *accessus* to the *Achilleid*

V = Vaticano, Città del, Biblioteca Apostolica Vaticana, Vat. lat. 1663 (XIII s. ex.), 56v

In principio huius libri videndum est que sit materia huius operis, que
sit actoris intentio in hoc opere, que sit libri utilitas. <Materia est>
Achillis facta virtuosa describere, supplendo ea que minus dicta sunt
ab Homero. Vtilitas est ne fatis amplius inutiliter obuiare temptemus,
cum Thetidem eis obuiando nichil profecisse nouimus. Titulus talis
est, Stacii liber Achilleydos primus incipit. Bene dicit primus quia
sequitur secundus. Sunt enim quinque. In primo matris
sollicitudinem et causam sollicitudinis describit. In secundo filii
absconsionem. In tertio Grecorum inquisicionem. In quarto
invencionem. In quinto adduccionem ad Troiam. Uel titulus talis
est, Stacii Achilleydos primus liber incipit. Bene dicit etc. Sunt
enim quattuor, secundum alios quinque, qui vnum in duos diuidunt.
Achilleis patronomicum femininum est ab Achille, sicut Eneis ab Enea.
Actor iste tractaturus Achilleydem, id est historiam de Achille. More
aliorum tria facit. Proponit vbi dicit "Magnanimum Eacidem,"
inuocat "Tu modo" et cetera, narrat dicens "Soluerat Oebalio." Est autem
proponere materiam de qua tractandum est breuiter explicare;
inuocare est diuinum auxilium implorare; narrare est materiam suam
explanare. Hiis visis, ad litteram accedendum est. A proposicione
incipit dicens "Magnanimum."

---

3 Achillis... secundus (7)] Vaticano, Reg. lat. 1556, ll. 4–7

7 in... Troiam (10)] *ibid.*, ll. 13–16

10 titulus... Enea (13)] *ibid.*, ll. 17–21

14 Actor... Oebalio (16)] *ibid.*, ll. 9–13, *rectius*

16 Est... est (19)] *ibid.*, ll. 13–16

19 a... incipit (20)] cf. Arnulfi Aurelianensis Accessum in Lucanum 5.34

The *accessus* in Wolfenbüttel, cod. Guelf. 13.10 Aug. 4°

Only at the end of the thirteenth century do *accessus* to the *Achilleid* slowly begin to show advancement over their predecessors. We see this in two traditions: Paris, BNF, lat. 8559 (Incipitarium 115; cf. Text 20 below) and Wolfenbüttel, cod. Guelf. 13.10 Aug. 4° (Incipitarium 111). The former is heavily rooted in tradition, but also demonstrates a growing interest in reconciling Statius' disjunct social and political roles. Here, the scholar resolves the problem by introducing the *duplex utilitas*, that is, the *utilitas* that is both *communis* and *privata* (36–44):

> *Communis ne fatis obsistere temptemus, cum Thetis eis obsistere, que dea erat, non potuit. Priuata ut ingenium suum per hunc tractatum posset acuere ad nobilia facta Domiciani discribenda, ut posset per hoc fauorem ipsius impetrare.*

However, this concept, which will be further expanded in manuscripts of the fourteenth century, is the only advancement in this *accessus*.

A fuller example of the slow development of ideas at the end of the thirteenth century is the *accessus* found in Wolfenbüttel, cod. Guelf. 13.10 Aug. 4° (dated 1276), London, BL, Addit. 10090 (XIV s.), and Stuttgart, Poet. et phil. 4° 34 (XIV s.), here referred to as the Wolfenbüttel, cod. Guelf 13.10 Aug 4° *accessus*. This *accessus* begins with five *circumstantiae*: *quis actor*, *que materia*, *que scribentis intentio*, *que utilitas*, and *quis titulus* (2–3). The *circumstantiae* are similar to those of the roughly contemporary Gronov. lat. 66 *accessus*, with the important addition of the authorial element that was missing there.

This *vita* of the author provides us with the traditional life that we found in the *Achilleid* traditions up to this point. Statius, who was *in poetica scientia... commendatissimus* (4–5),[46] was asked by Domitian to write the emperor's achievements.[47] This *accessus* then breaks with the tradition and expands on an idea we saw in the previous century, that Statius wrote the *Achilleid* as a preparation for writing Domitian's *res gestae*.[48] Here, the scholar writes that Statius, after completing the *Thebaid*, ceased writing poetry ("cum iam quasi hebetare sciret suum ingenium, eoquod iamdiu post compilationem Thebaidos a studio cessauisset," 7–9). This last detail is most likely taken from a literal reading of *veterem* (*Ach.* 1.8) and *te longo necdum fidente paratu* (1.18). Thereafter, the manuscript conforms to earlier developments, including the typical *utilitas*, that we concede to fate.

The manuscripts are represented by two major families, based on other aspects of the texts, or three families, based on their readings. The Wolfenbüttel and London witnesses are both followed by the same mythological preface to the *Achilleid*, which is wanting in the Stuttgart witness. The textual differences among the manuscripts, which are not great, come as a result of stylistic changes by later hands. I have added a dotted line between λ and S, as it is not apparent whether the similarities between L and S (cf. lines 28 and 31) are a result of a single parent or whether the stylistic changes in the two manuscripts were made independently.

---

[46] Cf. the assessment *doctissimus poetarum* in Gronov. 66 (XIII s.), ll. 5–6.

[47] Cf. the interpolations in the fourteenth-century Escorial manuscript to the Gronov. 66 *accessus* (ll. 47–49): "Domitianus quidam imperator Romanus uidens hunc Statium doctum esse poetam, rogauit ipsum sua facta uelle describere, [sciens quod librum Thebaidos bene scripsit]."

[48] Cf. the late–twelfth century *Universitatis bruxellensis accessus* (above, p. 27), ll. 19–21: "Altera intentio sua est animum suum exercere ut facta Domitiani imperatoris, sicut rogauerat, posset digne describere."

Vitae and Accessus

Figure 5. Stemma of the Guelf. 13.10 Aug. 4° *accessus*

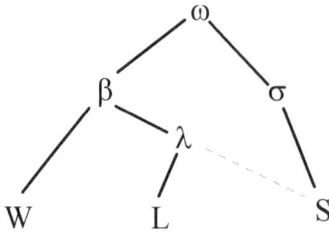

Text 13. The Guelf. 13.10 Aug. 4° *accessus* to the *Achilleid*

L = London, British Library, Addit. 10090 (XIV s.), 8rb
S = Stuttgart, Wurttembergische Landesbibliothek, Poet. et phil. 4° 34 (XIV s.), 101v
W = Wolfenbüttel, Herzog-August-Bibliothek, Cod. 13.10 Aug. 4° (dated 1270), 142r

In presentis libri primordio sunt hec quinque specialiter inquirenda,
scilicet quis actor, que materia, que scribentis intentio, que utilitas,
quis titulus. Actor siquidem istius operis fuit Stacius, qui in
tempore Domiciani Romanorum principis in poetica scientia fuit
5 commendatissimus, vnde post commendabilem Thebaidos
editionem rogauit eum Domicianus ut ipsius gesta describeret.
Ipse uero se diffidens tante materie posse sufficere cum iam
quasi hebetatum sciret suum ingenium, eo quod iamdiu post
compilationem Thebaidos a studio cessauisset, et ne tum tanti
10 domini uideretur preces contempnere, presens opus suscepit
agendum, suum in hoc opere preacuere uolens ingenium, ut
sic ad ulteriorem materiam, que erat describere Domiciani gesta
egregia, consequenter facilius se transferret, quod ipse testatur in
prohemio petens a Domiciano ueniam dicens "At tu quem" et cetera.
15 Sequitur ibi:

te longo necdum fidente paratu
Molimur magnusque tibi preludit Achilles.

Patet itaque quod Achilles et ipsius egregia gesta sunt
subiectum siue materia actoris in hoc opere. Intentio uersatur
20 circa materiam. Intendit enim actor Achillis gesta describere
et supplere quicquid Homerus de illo dimisit intactum, quod
ostendit in prologo dicens:

quamquam acta uiri multum inclita cantu
Meonio sed plura uacant nos ire per omnem,
25 Sic amor est, heroa uelis...
nec in Hectore tracto
Sistere sed tota iuuenem deducere Troia.

Sed sciendum est quod morte preuentus propositum non inpleuit,
sed opus suum dimisit incompletum. Vtilitas huius operis est ut
30 uiso quod uelle fatis resistere nichil Thetidi profuit, contra fata
nichil attemptemus. Est enim fatum diuina dispositio temporalium
euentuum.

Titulus libri talis est: Stacii Achilleidos primus liber incipit.
Bene dicit primus, sunt enim quattuor distinctiones in hoc opere, uel
35 ut plerisque placet, sunt quinque et sic vnam in duas diuidunt, et
notandum quod Achilles est proprium nomen illius de quo hic agitur.
Achilleis uero dicitur historia de ipso facta et est patronomicum
femininum a genitiuo isto, Achillis, formatum per interposicionem -e-.
Ut uero se conformet actor ceteris poetis, morem poeticum obseruando
40 opus suum in tria diuidit; proponit enim cum de quo tractaturus
est ostendit, ut ibi, "Magnanimum Eacidem" et cetera. Inuocat ibi, "Tu
modo" et cetera. Narrat materiam suam persequens in hec uerba,
"Soluerat" et cetera. A propositio ergo incipiens per prosopopeiam Musam
suam alloquitur ita dicens "diua refer" et cetera.

14 *Ach.* 1.14
16–17 *Ach.* 1.18–19
23–27 *Ach.* 1.3–5, 6–7
41 *Ach.* 1.1
41–42 *Ach.* 1.8
43 *Ach.* 1.20
44 *Ach.* 1.3

1 principio L   **2** quis *om.* S   **7** et *post* sufficere *add.* W   **8** quasi] quod L   hebetare L
9 et *om.* LS   tum] tamen S   **12** alteriorem *mss.*   gesta domiciani W *fort. rectius*   **14** ut *post*
ueniam *add.* L   dicens *om.* S   **17** achilles... actoris (19)] toris S   **18** gesta egregia W
20 conscribere L   **21** quidquid W   **23** uiri multum *om.* W   **25** heroa *om.* S   **27** troia] cuius
L   **29** ut *om.* L   **30** in *post* fatis *del.* W   resistere *om.* S   profuit thetidi W   profuerit S
31 attemptemus] accipit tenuis L   **33** liber primus LS   **34** dicit *om.* LS   sunt *post* opere
dist. W   **36** achille S   **37** uero] autem LS   **38** genitiuo] g͞co (*pro* Greco?) W   achilles S
39 morem L   **40** suum opus LS   cum *om.* L   tractatus L : tractaturus *ex* tractatus W   **41** ut
post inuocat *add.* W   **42** prosequens S   **43** et cetera *om.* L   ergo] igitur W   **44** allotur W
ita *om.* L   diua refer *om.* L

Conclusion

In this century, we saw the beginnings of a new critical approach to the *Thebaid*. The poem takes on a more moral and individual, and a less political aspect. We see a greater emphasis on *Statius doctor*, that is, Statius the teacher seeking to instruct the reader, and not the emperor.[49] If it is right to interpret the note *offendiculum emulari* (in the London, BL, Royal 15.A.XXIX *accessus*, line 13) and the earlier note that Statius was *tenacis memorie* (in the *In principio accessus*, l. 21) in this regard, we also see an increasing emphasis on Statius' works as texts to be imitated.

What we see in the approaches to the *Achilleid* in this century is less interesting than what we see in the *accessus* to the *Thebaid*. In the *Achilleid*, instead of focusing on Statius the author, we see that the *accessus* themselves tend to be rewritings of earlier *accessus*, mostly of the *Universitatis bruxellensis* and KP *accessus*. Those *accessus* that provide degrees of development reflect more Statius' role in the school-room.

The reason for the difference between the two approaches likely has something to do with the different audiences of Statius' texts. The *accessus* to the *Thebaid* often refer to him as an *auctor historiographus*, while those to the *Achilleid* treat him as a (morally) didactic poet (*poeta doctor*). Now, the roots for Statius as a didactic poet were present from the very beginning, when the Firenze, BML, Plut. 24 sin. 12 *accessus* noted that Statius wrote his poem to solve an academic or philosophical debate. Thus, little adaptation to the previously existing criticism was needed. The historiographical approach to the *Thebaid*, however, was new, and scholars wrote new *accessus* with this interpretation as a focal point; influenced by the other *accessus* of their age, these scholars felt at liberty to expand on aspects of the *accessus*, including the author's biography.

---

[49] In this latter regard, *accessus* of the previous centuries saw Statius emphatically as the *poeta doctus*.

FROM THE FOURTEENTH CENTURY TO THE REDISCOVERY OF THE *SILVAE*

In the fourteenth and fifteenth centuries, *accessus* to Statius show a dramatic change from those of the previous centuries and began to reach their most advanced state. In addition to some 40 individual *accessus* transmitted from these centuries, we have at least twenty mythological introductions, prologs, and compendia, all of which reflect keener scholastic attitudes than we have seen in the previous centuries. These newer attitudes, which were likely influenced by the scholarly attitudes of Petrarch and Dante, provided greater freedom to expand on the previous traditions. Of course, this "break" must be taken in context.[1] *Accessus* to Statius (perhaps owing to the dearth of information available), were always more conservative and much less prone to typological and tropological allegory than the *accessus* to other poets.[2] What we see, then, is that while the core information about Statius' biography and works remains the same, *accessus* pay much more attention to interpretation of the texts, possibly with an eye toward the school student. These new aspects are centered about two key developments: detailed plot summaries[3] and conscious criticism of other interpretations.

The *Thebaid*

Whether or not I am correct in connecting these new approaches to Dante and Petrarch, it was certainly Dante who played the greatest and most puzzling role in the history of Statian biography. In *Purgatorio* 21–22, Dante and Virgil meet Statius, who has just been freed from a thousand years of punishment and is about to ascend into Paradise; in recounting his life, Statius explains that he was a Christian, but for fear of punishment kept his religion a secret. Since the rediscovery of the *Silvae*, scholars have noted Dante's error,[4] but there is little early evidence as to why Dante made this claim.[5] The earliest explanation that we have is that of Politian

---

[1] Dante and Petrarch, despite their new attitudes towards scholarship, held closely to the *accessus* scheme. See Curtius 1954.357.

[2] Compare, for example, the lengthy discussions that occasionally accompanied etymologies to Ovid's and Virgil's names (among others, *ouum diuidens* and *uirga*, respectively). See Ghisalberti 1946 and Suerbaum 1981.

[3] We also find several lengthy *compendia* to Statius' works in this century, the most famous of which is that of Laurentius Campanus (Laurent de Premierfait). See Jeudy-Riou and Jeudy-Bozzolo 1979.

[4] This often with great vehemence. Gevartius (*Statii Opera*, Leiden, 1616) stresses what he calls "gravissimus doctorum error" (p. 3), including the "error Danthis" (pp. 9–10).

[5] There is little explanation, even in the early scholia to Dante. J. de Seravalle's commentary to the *Divina commedia* (in London, BL, Egerton 2629, [XIV s.], 214r–v) notes that Titus and Vespasian "fuerunt ultores de morte Christi," but they are not included in the list of Christian emperors that follows. The passage identifying Statius only tells us "in cuius imperii tempore iste Statius oriundus de Tholosana ciuitate, qui fuit poeta magnus... propter sua opera coronatus," which is derived from the *Quaeritur accessus*. The commentary on the passage in London, BL, Egerton 943 (XIV s.) (101r–v) reads: "Titus fuit filius Vespasiani imperatoris, qui cum liberatus fuisset, iussit Iudeos dispergi in uindictam mortis Christi... [Statius] poeta fuit et fuit de Tholosa et uenit Romam et ibi meruit coronari mirto... . Ornabantur enim capita poetarum antiquitus ex mortella et ista talis umbra fuit Stacius poeta... Dicit Stacius quod tractauit de gestibus Thebe et postea de Achille, set obiit ante quam expleret tractare de Achille. Ideo dicit 'macadi in uia cola seconda soma,' id est obiit tractando de Achille."

Benvenuto da Imola relates only that Statius "fu da Tolosa e fu nel tempo dello aduenimento di Cristo e fu un grande poeta" (*Comentum super D. Aldighierii Comoediam*, ed. G.F. Lacaita [Firenze, 1887], *ad loc.*). It is only in the mid–thirteenth century commentary of Filippo Villani (ed. G. Cognoni, *Il commento al primo canto dell' 'Inferno'* [Città di Castello, 1896], 41) that we find acceptance of Dante's claim: "Statium Christianum poetam symiamque Virgilii," but again without explanation (on Statius as the *simia Virgilii*, see de Angelis 1983.167–68 and nn. 119 and 121).

This question has seen many explanations in recent scholarship. However, as this study is focused on the medieval interpretation, these will not be discussed in-depth here. See Sante Bastiani, *La Matelda e lo Stazio nella Divina Commedia* (Napoli, 1865); G. Schiavo, *Stazio nel Purgatorio: Contributo agli studi danteschi* (Firenze, 1902); A.W. Verrall, "'To Follow the Fisherman': A Historical Problem in Dante," *Independent Review* 1 (1903), 246–64; P.A. Isola, *L'incontro di Dante e Virgilio con Sordello e Stazio* (Alatri, 1906); A.W. Verrall, "Dante on the Baptism of Statius," *Albany Review*, n.s. 3 (1908), 499–514; Zabughin 1909.1.216; Landi 1913 (rev. E.G. Parodi, *Boll. della Soc. Dantesca*

in his commentary on the *Silvae* that he used for his lectures in Florence (1480–81),[6] now Firenze, BNC, Magl. Cl.VII. 973:[7]

> *Nam et in patriae ratione rhetoris ipsius nomine deceptus est et ad relligionem Christianam ipsi applicandam versiculo, ut arbitror, quodam ex Thebaide Statii adductus est, in quo Tiresias:* <4.516–17>
>
> > *"Et triplicis, inquit, mundi summum, quem scire nefandum est, Illum—sed taceo: prohibet tranquilla senectus."*

The equation of this passage from the *Thebaid* with the "unknowable God" of Judaism is also found in Pomponius Laetus' commentary to the *Thebaid* (now Vaticano, Vat. lat. 3279), *ad* 4.516–17:[8]

> *Hoc nomen sanctissimum et toti antiquitati nomen incognitum nobis aperuit Paulus apostolus cum ait* <Philipp. 2.10>, *"in nomine Iesu omne genu flectatur celestium, terrestrium et infernorum," hoc est* <Theb. 5.516> *"summum triplicis mundi".... In omnibus templis erat ara in medio sine simulachro, in quo sacrificabatur tanto numini licet incognito. Hoc est et illud quod erat in arcanis Iudeorum, quod nemi<ni> licebat scire.*

Most modern scholars, without knowing of Politian's argument, also draw our attention to Christian or Christianizing elements and ideals in Statius' poems[9] or in his life and attitudes.[10]

Ital. 20 [1913], 184–93); M. Scherillo, *Lectura Dantis: Stazio nella 'Divina Commedia,'* estratto dalla *Miscellanea di Studi*, pubblicata per il cinquantenario della R. Accademia scientifica letteraria di Milano (Milano, 1913) (rev. E. Parodi, *Bulletino della Società Dantesca Italiana* 20 [1913], 184–93); W.R. Hardie 1916; Landi 1921; W.P. Mustard, "Note on Dante and Statius," *MLN* 39 (1924), 120; M. Pastore Stocchi, "Il cristanesimo di Stazio (Purgat. XXII) e un'ipotesi del Poliziano," *Misc. di studi offerta a A. Balduino e B. Bianchi per le loro nozze* (Padova, 1962), 41–45; Brugnoli 1965; A. Nolte, "De figuur van Statius in de Divina Commedia," *Hermeneus* 40 (1968), 21–36; Brugnoli 1969; P. Th. R. Mestron, "Dante-Statius," *Hermeneus* 41 (1969), 29–30; Mariotti 1975; and Heil 2002. See also the bibliography of E. Paratore (in U. Bosco, *at al.*, ed., *Enciclopedia Dantesca*, vol. 5 [Roma, 1976], 425).

[6] The commentary is edited in Cesarini Martinelli 1978. See A. Perosa, *Mostra del Poliziano* (Firenze, 1954), 16, nr. 2; Wasserstein 1956; Iter 1.129; Cesarini Martinelli 1975 and 1982; E.B. Fryde, *Greek Manuscripts in the Private Library of the Medici*, 2 voll. (Aberystwyth, 1996), 229–30 and *passim*. Two commentaries to Ovid by Politian have been edited, that to the *Epistola Sapphus* (E. Lazzeri, *Angelo Poliziano, Commento inedito all'Epistola Ouidiana di Saffo a Faone* [Firenze, 1973]; Coulson-Roy 68) and to the *Fasti* (F. Lo Monaco, *Angelo Poliziano, Commento inedito ai Fasti di Ovidio* [Firenze, 1991]; Coulson-Roy 462).

[7] See Cesarini Martinelli 1978.7.28–33. I have chosen to eliminate the phrases crossed out in the manuscript, which are themselves of peripheral nature.

[8] The transcription is that of Zabughin 1909.1.216, as corrected by S. Mariotti, "Il cristianesimo di Stazio in Dante secondo il Poliziano," in *Letteratura e critica, Studi in onore di N. Sapegno*, vol. 2 (Roma, 1975), 152 (repr. in *Scritti medievali e umanisti*, Storia e letteratura, 137 [Rome, 1976], 75).

[9] W.R. Hardie 1916 argues that because of the Christian outlook of his poem, it was easy to assume that Statius was a Christian, much as Virgil, because of the magical (or at least clairvoyant) aspect of his works, could be assumed to have been a magician. Hardie then searches Statius' epics for any details that could appear Christian, and as such is largely fantastic and badly flawed, not least because the ideals that permeate Statius' epic are by no means different from those of his contemporaries and do not explain why Statius alone was seen as Christian. Mariotti 1975 finds Christian motives in Capaneus' impiety (especially his proclamation at 3.661: "Primus in orbe deos fecit timor"), Apollo's lament of his own impotence against Destiny (9.653 ff.), and the Altar of Mercy (12.481 ff.). R.L. Martinez (*Dante, Statius, and the Earthly City*, Dissertation, Univ. California Santa Cruz, 1977, cf. *DA* 38 [1978], 6707a–6708a) sees a Christian cosmography in Statius' works, mostly influenced by *Theb.* 4.514, which he argues might have influenced the medieval mind. B. Kytzler ("Die Darstellung von Ehe und Familie in den epischen und lyrischen Dictungen des Statius," *VoxP* 5 [1985], 63–74) argues that Dante was influenced by the way Statius depicts domestic and family issues, but this argument rests entirely on passages from the *Silvae* which Dante could not have known.

[10] "Dante invece rappresenta qui la fede armata della Ragione che move alla conquista delle verità eterne, la fede illuminata doposecoli di lotte del pensiero, la fede affermata dal discorso della mente non più soltanto dall' impulso del cuore" (G. Schiavo, *Stazio nel Purgatorio: Contributo agli studi danteschi* [Firenze, 1902], 41). That is, it is *sapientia*

Still others find his love of Virgil as a key.[11] As attractive and widespread these interpretations are, we should note that they are all achieved by fallacious logic. It is not difficult to search through a text looking for a specific interpretation; that is, after all, what allegory is.[12] The only sure evidence we can have is external evidence for a popular belief in Statius' Christianity. Unfortunately, outside of Dante, there is very litttle, and scholars have come to argue for some lost medieval tradition that proclaimed (or at least suggested) Statius' Christianity. So, V. Zabughin (1909.1.216) and (later) S. Mariotti argue that Pomponius Laetus' note "dipenda da precedente tradizione scoliastica" (1975.153), which has not been transmitted to us. However, the problem with this argument is how an interpretive belief that was widely held in thirteenth- and fourteenth-century Florence would not be transmitted to us.[13]

One solution to this is that of L. Constans, who argues that there was a lay tradition in which Statius was a Christian, but it was ignored by the more serious (clerical) scholars.[14] I find this unlikely, since, in *accessus* to other authors it is common to mix serious scholarship with preposterous vulgar interpretations.[15] Further, we often find prominent scholars (or clerics)

(exemplified by Statius), when bound with faith, that brings us to "eternal truth." Likewise, L.A. MacKay ("Statius in Purgatory," *C&M* 26 [1965 (1967)], 293–305) argues that Statius embodies poetic intuition, which is secondary to revelation; however, Statius shows this inspiration only in the *Silvae*—in the *Thebaid*, he depicts his creative process only indirectly and then as a result of toil (cf. 12.797–819). There is also the suggestion of W.W. Vernon (*Readings of the Purgatorio of Dante, Chiefly Based on the Commentary of Benvenuto da Imola* [London, 1897], 2.188; this interpretation is Vernon's own and is not found in Benvenuto's commentary), that Dante chose Statius because "it is known that he lived in the greatest poverty and want; which one would not think would happen to a man of such distinction in the city (Naples) in which he taught rhetoric, unless he had fallen into the fault of great extravagance." This is unlikely not least because of the confusion between Naples and Toulouse but also because this poverty (which is attested only in the *Silvae*) was not widely in medieval criticism (our only source is Petrus de Caneffis de Parma's *Proehemium* to the *Achilleid* [transmitted in Berkeley, CA, MS UCB 145 (XIV s. ex.)]: "Statius fuit pauperrimus, vnde Juuenalis, 'Exurit intactam Paridi nisi uendat Agauen.'") There is also the view of A. Grafa (*Roma nella memoria* [Torino, 1882], 318–20) that "il Tolosano surebbe stato un santo, un martire sotto il grande persecutore Domiziano," but any hint of Domitian having persecuted Statius is absent from the medieval tradition. The only mention we have of Domitian bringing about Statius' death is in the *vitae* of Statius by Sicco Polenton (Incipitarium 93) and Petrus Crinitus (ed. 1515, Strasbourg: M. Schürer). The former, after mentioning Domitian's preoccupation with killing flies (Suet. *Dom.* 3.1), notes, "poeta etat eodem ipso transfixus insano ac tyrannino [*sic*] ac crudeliter interfectus." Crinitus denies this assertion: "Neque inclinat animus ut verum esse existimem, quod a quibusdam scribitur, fuisse illum stylo praeacuto occisum a Caesare Domitiano."

[11] D. A. Slater (*The Silvae of Statius* [Oxford, 1908], 14), suggested that the medieval student may have imagined a meeting between Paul and Statius at Virgil's tomb (that Paul was in Rome in the early spring of 61 was deduced by J.B. Lightfoot, *St. Paul's Epistle to the Philippians* [London, 1879²], 2. This is of course unlikely as a source for Statius' Christianity, as the association between Statius and Naples was not made before the rediscovery of the *Silvae*. We also might compare Secundianus, Marcellianus, and Verianus, all of whom were converted after reading the fourth *Eclogue* (see Mariotti 1975.155), which Dante himself suggests ("Tu prima m'inviasti," *Purg.* 22.64–66).

[12] Cf. J. Allen, *The Friar as Critic* (Nashville, 1971), 1. L.E.M. Alexis demonstrates the problem with such an approach in his study, *School of Nero: Europe's First Christian Ruler Identified* (Aberdeen, 1975), where he finds Christianizing and Biblical elements in Silius Italicus' descriptions of Hannibal (*Pun.* 7.276–380) and Scipio (13.762–894) and in Valerius Flaccus' treatment of Hylas (*Arg.* 3.459–597, 726–40; 4.1–57). In Statius' works, he discovers parallels between Oedipus and Tisiphone and Ankhnaten and a UFO (*Theb.* 1.46–164), and Christian elements in the funeral of Archemorus (6.54–248, 760–825), the Altar of Mercy (12.481–518), and in *Silv.* 2.3. H. Usher, in his review of the study (*CR* 27 [1977], 279–81) ignores Alexis' approach, perhaps diplomatically, and criticizes only the edited texts and exegetical notes.

[13] We can dismiss confusion with the Greek novelist Achilles Tatius (*Statios*, mss.)—who, according to a discredited tradition (*Suda* Adler α 4695), converted to Christianity and became a bishop—as a potential source. The *Suda* was probably unknown in Italy at this time.

[14] Constans 1881.135 (cf. also pp. 143–55).

[15] An abundance of apocryphal stories about Virgil have been transmitted to us, including Alexander Neckham's palace, the *Virgilius Dolopathos*, and Virgil's imprisonment in the tower. See Comparetti 1941.70–119.

agreeing with even the most absurd beliefs.[16] Still, as the scholars of Statius were always more conservative, it is possible that this was one cause for the separation.

Two other medieval sources for Statius' Christianity were put forth in the last century as evidence of this lost scholarly tradition: Giovanni Colonna's *De viris illustribus*[17] and Francisco de Fiano's defence of the Classics, *Contra ridiculos oblocutores et fellitos detractores poetarum.*[18] Taking Colonna first, the *vita* of Statius in his *De viris illustribus* only dubiously relates to our problem. The *vita* itself is largely related to the *In principio accessus* and nowhere alleges Statius' Christianity directly.

There are two versions of the *De viris illustribus.* In one family, including the Vatican witness, the authors are listed alphabeticaly and there is no mention of Statius' conversion. However, in the other family, represented by the Venetian witness, the text is divided into two sections, Christian and pagan, with Statius being included among the Christians. Although the Venetian witness gives no reason for Statius' inclusion, Sabbadini claims to find evidence implicit in the description of Statius' character:

> *Mirum honestate preditus, viciis instanter restitit coluitque indefesse virtutes.*

But these virtues are hardly original to this text—they are taken from ll. 20 and 40–41 of the *In principio accessus*—and are not particularly Christianizing.

Colonna's testimony for Statius' Christianity is further weakened when we compare the *vita* of Statius with that of Seneca (whom Colonna calls "Seneca noster"). In the latter life, Colonna goes to great lengths to cite as many Christianizing lines in Seneca's works as he can, assembling some ten quotations that have some verbal or moral similarity to the *VT* or *OT*,[19] and he is careful to properly cite and critically judge his sources (including the apocryphical correspondance with Paul, which he discounts somewhat).[20] We find neither of these aspects in the *vita* of Statius, and I conclude that Colonna probably did not consider Statius a Christian, and the inclusion of Statius among the Christian authors seems to have been made by a later source, probably only on the basis of Dante.

The second source for Statius' Christianity, Franciscus de Fiano, is a bit more specific. The passage on Statius reads (141r):

> *Quid Statius natione Tolosanus quem aliqui Narbonensem uolunt? Siquidem Domitiano, Titi Vespasiani germano fratre imperante, qui Christianorum inexorabilis persecutor fuit; eum clam, metu principis in Christianos omnium suppliciorum generibus seuientis, Christi tenentem fidem et, si non aque uel sanguinis, baptismo quidem flaminis legimus fuisse respersum.*

On the basis of the word "legimus," Sabbadini argues for a written tradition that has not been transmitted,[21] but the lack of specific details in the passage leads me to believe that Franciscus

---

[16] For example, Roger Bacon (1214–c. 1291) noted in his *Opus maius* that he was very happy to discover that the pagan Ovid had been converted to Christianity. See Robathan 1968.1 and n. 4.

[17] Incipitarium 285

[18] Incipitarium 235. See A. Altamura, "Una testimonianza medievale sul criptocristianesimo di Stazio e di Claudiano," *GIF* 3 (1950), 81–82 (with transcriptional errors). The text is transmitted in Vaticano, Ottob. lat. 1438 (XV s. in.), 132r–47r.

[19] See Ross 1970.542–43.

[20] *ibid.*

[21] Sabbadini 1910.268: "Sicché la notizia della Cristianità di Stazio gli dev'essere venuta da una tradizione allora viva."

did not actually have a source at hand. A comparison of this passage with Franciscus' treatment of Ovid will demonstrate this point (139v–140r):

> *Quid Naso in libello a posteris ut quorundam fide dignorum tradit auctoritas in ipsius inuento sepulchro, cui Vetula titulum dedit? Ibi enim Christum precernens futurum, tempusque magnalium ac mirificorum ipsius instare, que se auidum describere innuit, fatetur tanta misteria* [cf. 3.756 R; 3.755 K] *suo non esse ingenio peruia* <3.757–58 R; 3.756–57 K>:

> > *nisi postquam uenerit ille*
> > *De celo celi plene secreta reuol\uens.*

> *Ipsius Nasonis uersiculum posui, deinde subicit* <3.759–62 R; 3.758–61 K>:

> > *Tunc et enim credam si tantum diceret ipse*
> > *Et quia uenturum dicunt hunc modo credo.*
> > *Christum*[22] *uenturum iam diligo, iamque paratus*
> > *Credere.*[23]

Here, in contrast to the Statius passage, Franciscus gives us specific evidence and quotes his source; in the Statius passage, he does not, and we can argue that if he had a source for Statius' baptism, he would have quoted it.[24] The word "legimus," then, is either a deliberate falsification on his part or a historical note as to how baptism was performed in the early church.[25]

What Sabbadini and Altamura missed in discussing this text is Franciscus' aim: he sought to justify the Classics not as being good literature, but as being harbingers of and witnesses to Christ; it was in his interest, then, to emphasize the Christian aspects of his subjects.[26] Where he had data, he happily provided it; where he did not, he seems purely to have invented it or to have stretched it.[27] The immediate source of his data, then, appears to be Dante again.

More recent scholarship has turned up a third source. In a discussion of the Altar of Mercy (*Theb.* 12.481 ff.), the scholiast of the *In principio* commentary cites Paul's conversion of Dionysius the Areopagite (cf. *Acts* 17:34). The note reads:[28]

> 12.497 *FAMA EST: Determinat qui fuerunt illius templi positores. Hylus, Deianire et Herculis filius et reliqui ex eodem nati, postquam Hercules interiit, pulsi ab Ericteo Athenas confugerunt. A quibus facile impetrantes auxilium hanc aram consecrauerunt, asserentes apud Athenas tum miseram sedem posuisse, ad eam igitur aram quicumque supplice accedebant misericordiam impetrabant. Cum beatus Paulus Athenas predicaturus aduenisset, inuenit Dionisium Ariopagitam uirum prudentissimum. Quem cum non potuisset conuincere, duxit eum per singulas aras deorum inquirendo cuius esset. Tandem ad hanc aram peruenit et inquisiuit cuius esset. Cui Dionisius, "Ara est ignoti dei." Tunc beatus Paulus, "Quem ignotus appellas, solus ille notus est." Et sermonem suum sic incepit, "Notus in Iudea deus" et cetera.*

---

[22] The manuscripts edited by Robathan 1968 and P. Klopsch (*Pseudo-Ovidius de Vetula*, Mittellateinische Studien und Texte, 2 [Leiden, 1967]) all read *Illum*; *Christum* is likely an interpolated gloss.

[23] On Christianity in the *De Vetula*, see Robathan, *ibid.*, 5. On the attribution of the poem to Ovid, see her pp. 1–3.

[24] We should note, however, that all of the passages from Ovid are quotations from Ovid's own works, whereas there are no passages from Statius' works that Franciscus could have quoted.

[25] Sabbadini (268) tries to make a connection between *flaminis* and πνεύματος (which he suggests might be "lo Spirito Santo"), but this is purely speculation.

[26] On this aspect of medieval biography, especially in Giovanni Colonna's writings, see Ross 1970.540 and 542–43.

[27] Franciscus also claims the Christianity of Virgil (the source being the fourth *Eclogue*) and Claudian (following Petrarch).

[28] The note is transcribed from Berlin, Staatsbibliothek—Preußischer Kulturbesitz, Ms. lat. 2° 34.

While it is certainly possible that scholars could have confused the *ara ignoti dei* with Statius' *ignotae tantum felicibus arae* (12.496), there is no evidence for that in this note. Rather, the note uses *Acts* as testimony for the existence of the altar and does not suggest any specific connection between Statius and the altar or between Statius and the early Church,[29] and if there was a tradition that Statius was Christianity, we would expect to find some connection between the *ignotus deus* here and the unnamable god at *Theb.* 4.516, but I have not found an exegesis of the latter passage that includes Christian elements. In short, this note seems interested only in discussing *realia*—that is, providing external testimony for a real object mentioned in the passage.

We are left then where we began. There are several possible explanations as to why Dante saw Statius as a "closet" Christian, but no specific evidence. What evidence we do have seems to contradict the claim of many scholars that there was a now lost tradition: had there been such a tradition, either Franciscus or Colonna would have mentioned or cited it.

The *accessus* in Firenze, BNC, II.II.55

Before the end of the fifteenth century,[30] Dante appears in two *accessus* to Statius: Firenze, BNC, II.II.55 and Genova, BU, E.II.8. I shall discuss each of these in turn.

The Florence *accessus* (Incipitarium 39) is unique among Statian scholarship, in that it is the only *accessus* that follows the Aristotelian schema for the work, that is, it indicates the four *causae—efficiens*, *materialis*, *formalis*, and *finalis*.[31] Under the rubric of the *causa efficiens* is the author. Here, as we saw in the *accessus* in London, Royal 15.A.XXIX (XIII s.; see above, p. 35), Statius' name is derived from the verb *sto* ("quia bene in scientia stetit" [2–3]), and it is perhaps on the basis of this *scientia* that the *accessus* then notes Statius' Christianity (3–6):

> *et est dictus inter poetas Christicolas et ita est causa: quia Dantes ipsum ponit in Purgatorio, quia erat antiquus et multa uiderat et erat vir bonus et optimus et ideo Cristicola[32] appellabatur.*

This is an interesting statement. The author of the *accessus* tells us that Statius is considered a Christian poet—on Dante's authority—and then gives the reasons why Dante (fallaciously) thought he was a Christian: simply because of age and experience,[33] and, moreover, because he was a "good" and "best" man.[34] Still, Dante is expressly stated as the authority behind Statius' Christianity. The author gives no indication of a lost tradition outside of Dante. That the author impugns this attestation suggests that he saw Dante as the ultimate source for Statius' Christian-

---

[29] The only other text that I have found that cites Statius in connection with the passage from *Acts* is in the *vita* of Dionysius in Bruxelles, Bibliothèque Royale Albert 1ᵉʳ, 21891 (XV s.). On fol. 143r, after quoting the passage from *Acts* on Dionysius' conversion, the author writes, "De ista ara ignoti dei scribit Statius XII libro Thebaidis." Here again, the citation is merely testimonial.

[30] Sicco Polenton mentions the attribution without comment: "Locat hunc Statium inter prodigos Florentinus poeta Dantes." In the end of the sixteenth century, the annotator of Karlsruhe, Badische Landesbibliothek, Augiense 159 (dated 1614), 189r, labelled *Thebaid* 1.582–86 as "De Christo nato" and followed them with the note , "qn̄ i.iv. pag. 138." I have been unable to find out to what this citation refers (it does not refer to any texts on f. 138 of the manuscript).

[31] The *accessus* in Wrocław, BU, IV.Q.64 (dated 1374) also divides the *circumstantiae* into *causae*, but then rejects this in favor of a more Servian scheme.

[32] The manuscript reads here *Cristicolas*. I believe this stems from a repetition from line 3. It could also be *Cristicolans*, from an otherwise unattested verb, *cristicolo, -are*; or a *faux* Graecism.

[33] The meaning of *multa uiderat* here is unclear. Two possibilities are that Statius saw much and was thus wise, or that he saw much and, thereby, witnessed the infancy of Christianity.

[34] *Optimus* is equally puzzling. The word could mean noble (for *optimus* as *optimates*, see Gregory of Tours, *Hist*, 4.9), or it could mean that he was most excellent (of character) (cf. Martianus Capella 4: "Optimitas... summa bonitas"), but this redundancy is awkward; alternatively, it could reflect some influence from Augustine (*Conv.* 1.2.14): *bonus... melior... optimus.*

ity. Up to this point, this *accessus* seems to support Schiavo's theory that Statius represented Christian ideals; but before we jump to a conclusion, we need to look at this *accessus* in context.

In other *accessus*, the catalogue of Statius' virtues is admittedly vague, but not as vague as it is here. Instead of citing Statius' *scientia, boni mores*,[35] or even the moral *utilitas* and *intentio* usually given to his works, the author of this *accessus* gives four qualities (*antiquus, multum uiderat, bonus*, and *optimus*), none of which is particularly concrete and none of which is particularly Christian or was used to distinguish pagans from Christians.[36] The author of the *accessus* seems to have had no idea whatsoever as to why Dante included Statius in his *Purgatorio*.

After discussing Statius' Christianity, this *accessus* continues the explanation of Statius' names in a way similar to what we saw in the London, BL, Royal 15.A.XXIX *accessus*: he was named Papinius because of his father and Surculus is derived from the verb *surgo*, with further reference to Huguccio of Pisa.[37] The *causa formalis* is not expanded upon in the *accessus* (an interpolating hand has added the note "forma tractatus est d..."[38]).

The author of the *accessus* then discusses the *intentiones* of the poem. Now, it is not uncommon in this century to divide the rubric *intentio* into *privata* and *communis*,[39] but here, the *intentio* is divided into three parts: *propria* (which is akin to *priuata*), *specialis*, and *communis*, all of which serve the same goal, "ut sibi gloriam aquireret" (13).[40] The author then explains this by means of a quote from Dante,[41] demonstrating a link between the quest for fame and the desire to help others.[42] Next, the *accessus* gives the *modus tractandi* of the work, "est in stilo trayco, quia in illo stilo includuntur autores" (15). The note is tantalizingly brief, and the meaning of the second clause is not quite clear, and it may be the case that the author's thought is broken off by a lacuna. If it is not, then the author had in mind some sort of separation between *autores* and *tragoedi*.[43]

---

[35] Cf. the catalog of *circumstantiae* in the *In principio accessus* (ll. 20–24): "morum honestate preditus, acris intelligentie, tenacis memorie, clarus ingenio, doctus eloquio, liberalium artium scientia feliciter eruditus."

[36] No modern lexicon suggests particularly Christian aspects of these traits. We might compare the unnamed poem of Reinfrit von Braunschweig (see Comparetti 1941.95), in which a Virgil's Christianity is argued on the basis of his having been *plenus virtute*. An anecdote in the life of St. Cadoc provides us with two other "Christianizing virtues." While speaking with St. Gildas, Cadoc expresses his distress that Virgil, "the author of this book that I love so well and that brings me such great pleasure, is perhaps in pain and suffering." Later, Cadoc meditates on "how God deals with those who sing in this world as the angels sing in heaven." See W.J. Rees, ed., *Lives of Cambro-British Saints* (London, 1853), 8; and B. M. Peebles, "The *Ad Maronis Mausoleum*: Petrarch's Virgil and Two Fifteenth-Century Manuscripts," in C. Henderson, Jr., ed., *Classical, Medieval, and Renaissance Studies in Honour of B.L. Ullman*, vol. 2 (Roma, 1964), 197–98.

[37] The passage in Huguccio reads, "Surculus ille dictus est quasi sursum canens, quia post Virgilium inter ceteros poetas principatum obtinuit" (transcribed from München, Clm. 14056).

[38] The end of the note has been worn away; it likely read something like "diuisio libri."

[39] Cf. the *accessus* in Firenze, BML, Plut. 38.10 (below).

[40] This is a common motif in *accessus* in the fourteenth century. Cf. the *accessus* to Sallust, *BC* in Berkeley, CA, MS UCB 85 (XIV s. ex.) (35r): "Communis intentio omnium auctorum est acquirere gloriam et famam" and the Carpentras *accessus* (discussed below), which uses a quotation from Ovid (*AA* 3.403) to prove the same point.

[41] The citation appears to be a paraphrasis of *Monarchia* 3.2.1: "nam sine prefixo principio... laborare quid prodest?"

[42] Although this is potentially a Christianizing virtue, the author makes no attempts to show it as evidence for Statius' Christianity.

[43] There is an indirect precedent for this. Isidore (*Etymologiae* 8.7) defines tragedy as "Tragici... res publicas et regum historias" and then goes on to argue that Lucan is not a poet, "quia videtur historiam composuisse." It is possible that this *accessus* had an equation between *poeta* and *author* in mind that was contrary to Isidore's critical exclusion, but that is by no means sure.

The *accessus* ends with an abbreviation of the typical division of the text into *propositio*, *invocatio*, and *narratio*, with the addition of a syncopation of the *attentos*, *beniuolos*, and *dociles* motif that we saw in London, BL, Royal 15.A.XXIX, and in several other *accessus*.

The *accessus* in Genova, BU, E.II.8

The second text, the Genovese *accessus* (Incipitarium 33), displays a similar perplexity with the attribution but provides us with a better view of the currency of Statius' putative Christianity. This *accessus* is divided into four parts. The first, lines 1–16, is a paraphrasis of the *Quaeritur accessus*, which is followed by a brief discussion of the *titulus*, *materia* and *metrum* (lines 17–23). Lines 24–36 contain a discussion of Statius' reputed Christianity, whereafter the *accessus* discusses the choice of material.[44] The third part is the most important part of the *accessus* for our purposes.

The discussion of Statius' Christianity begins with the strong denial: "vero religione paganus fuit" (24). The text then moves on to discuss the reasons why "quidam" suppose that he was Christian:[45]

> *Quod satis mirum est putare tantum virum hortodoxe fidei preceptis imbutum, que tot martirum confirmatur exemplis, mortem uel iram Cesaris timuisse, quamuis et minime consonum uideatur, virum in quo tanti ingenii uena prodierit donum sane diuinum, Christi nomen illis precipue temporibus ignorasse, quod refragante Romano imperio et euntis pene mundi principibus nec legibus tolli, nec innumerabilium Christianorum suppliciis potuit occultari, quin in dies fides illa adolesceret et Christi virtus clarius eluceret* (25–33).

In essence, the commentator attributes Statius' putative Christianity to two factors. First, Statius was endowed with great wisdom. Second, Statius could not have ignored the goings-on of the time, specifically that Christians were being increasingly persecuted as their religion grew. The commentator states that these two factors are assumptions on his part ("quid de hoc uerum fuerit satis certum non habeo," l. 33) and that he cannot be sure of the rationale behind Dante's statement. Contrary to Dante's claim, he continues, Statius' poetry clearly shows that he was a pagan:

> *Palam autem est eum quanquam fuisse paganum, quamuis et ipse dicere suisque inserere libris non dubitauerit: "Primus in orbe deos fecit timor"* (34–36).[46]

This *accessus* provides us with three important pieces of evidence. First, as the details of Statius' Christianity are only those that are found in Dante, Dante seems to have been the only source for the attribution.[47] Second, on the basis of *quorundam* (24), we can argue that the belief took on some currency (although I believe it to be an allusive plural).[48] Lastly, the insistence upon Statius' paganism with evidence derived from Statius' works shows that the author did not see Dante's claim as a viable construct within which Statius could be read.

From an academic standpoint, the most important aspect of this *accessus* is its vehemence. The author approaches the theme of Statius' Christianity as if it were a heated academic debate.

---

[44] This last portion is in the common dialogue style of commentary, in which the commentator imagines a dialogue between Statius and his detractors or audience.

[45] Dante is mentioned in the *accessus* at line 39: "uates Etruscus" and line 66: "Dantes."

[46] In some *florilegia*, e.g. that in Venezia, BNM, Lat. XIII.114 (XV s.), *Theb.* 3.661 is rewritten as "primus in orbe deos fecit amor [timor, mss.]," but I have not seen this *varia lectio* in any witnesses of the poem.

[47] I should add that this text was written in Tuscany and, in all likelihood, would have been familiar with any popular traditions there.

[48] Dante is the only other scholar mentioned in the *accessus*, either directly or indirectly.

However, this attitude deflated by the author's admission that the "quorundam opinio" is actually held by only one person, and the author has to go to great lengths to explain (and even defend) the reasons behind the assignation. This would not be the case were this an actual academic debate. As we will see in the next chapter this topic—the fallability of the great medieval scholars—would bring life to an otherwise stagnant academic climate in the end of the fifteenth century. Strangely, Dante's error would be one of the most important catalysts in the development of early modern scholarship—at least vis-à-vis Statius.

Why did Dante claim that Statius was a Christian? As Verrall points out,[49] there are three possibile sources of the attribution: first, that there was a medieval tradition that Statius was a Christian; second, that Dante realized from Statius' poems that he was a Christian; and third, that Dante made the story up. The data I have presented show that the first two of these are very unlikely, since no extant text links Statius with Christianity and even Dante's contemporaries were bluffed by the claim. The solution to the problem must then rest in Dante, and the studies that approach the truth in this matter will not focus on Statius' texts, but rather on the concept of Christianity in Dante's time and works and on the literary role Statius as a character plays within the *Purgatorio*.[50]

---

[49] A.W. Verrall, "'To Follow the Fisherman': A Historical Problem in Dante," *Independent Review* 1 (1903), 246–47

[50] Heil 2002 has recently argued that it was Statius' intertextual role as *imitator, inter alia*, that was the catalyst that led Dante to make the assertion. There are certainly several unexplored aspects of Statius' role in the poem, including his genuflection, which may be compared to that of Dante two cantos earlier, whereafter Adrian V tells him, effectively, that all distinctions between men ends with death (*Pg* 19.133–45).

Text 14. The Firenze, BNC, II.II.55 *accessus* to the *Thebaid*

F = Firenze, Biblioteca Nazionale Centrale, II.II.55 (XIV s. med.), 123r

Causa efficiens fuit Statius Surculus Papirius Tolosanus siue
Narbonensis, de quo scribit Iuuenalis. Statius potest dici a sto quia
bene in scientia stetit, et est dictus inter poetas Cristicolas et ita est
causa: quia Dantes ipsum ponit in Purgatorio, quia erat antiquus et
5   multa uiderat et erat vir bonus et optimus et ideo Cristicola
appellabatur. Est vero dictus Papinius a predecessori; Surculus
dicitur a surgo, -is quia surculi sunt ramuli et secundum
Huguiccionem dicitur quasi sursum canens, quia post Virgilium ipse
fuit secundus in poetica describenda et Rome suum hoc opus
10   composuit. Causa materialis huius libri videlicet dicitur Thebais a Thebis,
quia Thebarum mat[eriam] dicit. Thebais est nomen patronom[i]cum.
Causa formalis est forma tr[ac]tatus et tractandi. Causa finalis potest
esse propria et specialis et [com]munis, ut sibi gloriam aquireret,
secundum quod dicit Dantes:

15   Omnium qui laborant est vt prosint aliis.

Et est in stilo trayco, quia in illo stil[o] includuntur autores ***.
Supponitur morali philosophie quia de moribus hominum dicit.

     Iste liber primus diuiditur in tria quia primo proponit, secundo
inuocat ipsius Musas, tertio narrat et exequitur. Secunda, "Unde iubetis,"
20   tertia "Impia." Proponens facit auditores dociles et intendit dicere de
bellis duorum fratrum.

---

2 Juv., *Sat.* 7.82–86

7 surgo] cf. *accessum* in London, Royal 15.A.XXIX, l. 11

8 dicitur... describenda (9)] Huguccio Pisanus, s.v. *sursum*

12 causa... tractandi] cf. *accessus* in *Achilleidem* in Wien, 3114, l. 25

15 cf. *Monarchia* 3.2.1: *nam sine prefixo principio... laborare quid prodest?* et *Convivio* 4.30.2:
       ciascuno buono fabricatore, ne la fine del suo lavoro, quello nobilitare e abbellire dee
       in quanto puote.

19 *Theb.* 1.3

20 *Theb.* 1.46

---

2 statius *add. sup. lin.* F   **5** cristicolas F   **9** in... describenda *add. sup. lin.* F   **12** forma tractatus est d<iuisio libri> *post* tractandi *add. man. alt.* F   **13** est *post* munus *eras.* F   **14** alii
post vt *eras.* F   ita cum tres sint stili *post* autores *add. man. alt.* F   **16** *lacuna post* autores
mihi videtur   **18–21** *in marg. sin.* F

Text 15. The Genova, BU, E.II.8 *accessus*

G = Genova, Biblioteca Universitaria, E.II.8 (XIV s.), 145ra–b

Avctor iste Statius Papirius Surculus origine Thelosensis, que ciuitas
in com<i>t<i>a Gallia, Rome se transtulit tempore Uespasiani et usque in
tempora Domitiani peruenit, inque urbe rethoricam dicitur docuisse.
Qui primum aduertens inter imperatorem Domitianum et Titum
5   germanos seditionem et simultatem, ad illorum instructionem
Thebanam scripsit historiam a Latinis poetis intactam, et librum
illum in duodecim diuisit ad imitationem Uirgilii, quem nedum in
librorum numero se pene in omnibus adeo imitatus est ut non inmerito
Maronis scimia vocitetur, et sicuti a uirga Uirgilius dictus est, ita iste
10   Surculus a surco quod idem sonat est appellatus. Laudes autem
illiusce libri Iuuenalis Satira septima perstringit dicens <*Sat.* 7.82–83>:

Curritur ad uocem iocundam et carmen amice
Thebaidos, letam cum fecit Statius urbem et cetera.

Vixit tamen cum summa paupertate et rerum inopia ut idem satiricus
15   testatur vbi supra, sic inquiens:

Esurit intactam Paridi nisi <uendat> Agauen.

Fecit etiam librum paruum post predictum qui Achilleidos dictus
est, quem in quinque libros distinxit, in quo Achillis infantiam et prima
uite adolescentie rudimenta eiusque latibula in insula Schiros sub
20   habitu muliebri et amorem eiusdem atque Ulixis astutiam in ipso
reperiendo et denique eius discessum de insula Schiros ut ad Troianum
bellum proficisceretur, felici stilo carmineque heroyco dactilo exametro
et cataletico scripsit.

Vero religione paganus fuit. Quorumdam oppinione
25   clandestinus Christianus, scilicet timore Domitiani. Quod satis mirum
est putare tantum virum hortodoxe fidei preceptis imbutum, que tot
martirum confirmatur exemplis, mortem uel iram Cesaris timuisse,
quamuis et minime consonum uideatur, virum in quo tanti ingenii
uena prodierit donum sane diuinum, Christi nomen illis precipue
30   temporibus ignorasse, quod refragante Romano imperio et euntis pene
mundi principibus nec legibus tolli, nec innumerabilium Christianorum
suppliciis potuit occultari, quin in dies fides illa adolesceret et Christi
virtus clarius eluceret. Quid de hoc uerum fuerit satis certum non habeo.
Palam autem est eum quanquam fuisse paganum, quamuis et ipse
35   dicere suisque inserere libris non dubitauerit <*Theb.* 3.661>:

Primus in orbe deos fecit timor   145rb
Oritur autem questio an secundus liber completus fuerit, et ille
uates Etruscus, cuius nomen uulgaribus etiam innotauit, librum
40   Achilleydos asserit incompletum, prout in secundo eius libro
Purgatorii repperitur, eoquod videtur in prohemio dicere <*Ach.* 1.3–4>:

Quamquam acta viri multum inclita cantu
Meonio, sed plura uacat, nos ire per omnem, et cetera

et ita "nec in Hectore tracto sistere" <1.6–7>, quod dicit "non finiam in
45   morte Hectoris librum sed ibo per omnem." Qui quamuis ita uideatur
dicere tamen alii in quorum numero fuit dominus Gerius de Aretio,
dicunt librum fore completum, ex eo quod ibidem dicit "Sed tota

iuuenem deducere Troia" <1.7>, quasi dicat "non dicam de hiis que
apud Troiam gessit sed de aliis." Et tum expone "nec in Hectore tracto
50   sistere (pro insistere)," et quod supra dixit, "nos ire per omnem," lege
interogatiue, quasi dicat "Homerus multa dimisit; nos dicemus de
omnibus eius gestis?" Certe non. Sed subaudi <1.5–6>,

> Sic amor est, heros uelis Schiroque latentem
> Dulichia proferre tuba.

55   Que omnia plene exequitur. Huiusque opinionis, cui maxime assentior,
argumentum est quod librum in paruos libellos distinxit. Quod si omnia
comprehendere voluisset, maiora profecto librorum uolumina ferrent,
cum proditum sit eundem vicisse Telaphum, domuisse Thebas, Lesbon,
Thenedon, Cillam, Crisem, Sirum, Lernam et denique ea que apud
60   Troiam gessit. Que omnia si prosequi concepisset, quod illi uolunt, non
tam leuiter hanc tam uberem materiam fuisset aggressus, nec de tot
dicendis solum vnicum in prohemio tetigisset. Quare oppinor librum fore
completum, cum claudat optime materiam propositam, dicens <2.166–67>:

> Hactenus armorum comites elementa meorum,
65   > Hec memini et meminisse iuuat, scit cetera mater.

Dantes que autem gesta Domitiani debuit attingere dixit ***

---

1 avctor] cf. accessum in Milano, BN Braidense, AG.XI.29 (XII–XIII s.), 2v.
1–13 cf. *Quaeritur* accessum.
39 etruscus] *notatur in margine*: i.e. Dantes.

---

23 acataletico G   **24** vero] .℞. G   **41** repperiture G*ac*   **45** ƚ librum G

The *accessus* in Vaticano, Reg. lat. 1375

The two *accessus* that I have just discussed are somewhat of an abberation in the fourteenth century, in that their style and content are original. More typically, *accessus* to Statius in this century tend to follow the pattern of scholarship that we saw in the previous century, in which the goal of scholarship is to adapt previous traditions rather than copying them or creating new ones. That is, *accessus* tend to transmit rewritten versions of *accessus* from much earlier and outmoded scholastic traditions or present a syncopation of several previous *accessus* (usually from the thirteenth century) with attempts at modernizing them. A good example of the second technique is the *accessus* in Vaticano, Reg. lat. 1375 (Incipitarium 113), which rewrites the *In principio accessus*. The following table shows the relationship between the two manuscripts.

Table 2. Comparison of the Reg. lat. 1375 and the *In principio accessus*

Reg. lat. 1375	*In principio*
1: In principio cuiuslibet autoris et maxime hystoriographi	1: In principio uniuscuiusque actoris historiographi
4–6: Tholosa oriundus, patre Papinio, matre Agelina genitus. Narbone et Burdegali diu studuit. Postea vero apud Galliam rethoricam docuit	15–17: Legitur auctor iste ciuis Tholosanus fuisse, nobili patre, scilicet Papinio, matre uero Agilina. Burdegali et Nerbone studuit et in Gallia rethoricam celeberrime docuit
6–7: Videns igitur poetas et hystoriographos per carmina sua Rome ad magnos honores prouehi Romam venit et animum suum studio applicuit...	83–88: Romam vndique poetas confluere Stacius audierat, ibique ad maximos honores prouehi, tandem Romam uenit et qualiter populo Romano et imperatori placere posset diu apud se excogitauit. Denique animum suum aplicuit...
12–18: nutrire ingenium suum et preacuere describendo Thebanum bellum, et eo descripto ingenioque suo in hoc subtiliato promisit se descripturum Domitiani gesta, vnde ait "Tempus erit cum laurigero tua fortior oestro facta canam, nunc tendo chelim." Id vero promittit in principio Achileydis vbi ait "Magnusque tibi promittat Achilles." Quod autem promisit morte preuentus non soluit, quia eo libro non pertractato obiit	124–31: preacuere ingenium ut postmodum ad fortia eius facta describenda ualeat sufficere. Dicit itaque, "Tempus erit cum laurigero tua fortior oestro facta canam." Item in opere Achilleidos ad ipsum promisit dicens, "Magnusque tibi preludit Achilles." Sed quod et hic et ibi promiserat morte preuentus exibere non potuit
20–21: Materia in hoc opere est "Oedipode confusa domus," siue Thebays	68–69: Materia est Ethiocles et Polinices et acies utriusque confecte, vel, ut uerbis actoris utamur, "Oedipode confusa domus"

What is noteworthy about this *accessus* is what it adds to its parent *accessus*. The first 22 lines of Reg. lat. 1375 are a syncopation of the *In principio accessus*, but thereafter, this *accessus* breaks away from its tradition, changing the *utilitas*, title, and the explanation of the *pars philosophiae*. A glance at the first and last of these shows us the differing approach that this *accessus* takes.

In the *In principio accessus*, the *utilitas* and *pars philosophiae* reflect the *accessus'* general view of Statius as a didactic poet. Here, however, the *utilitas* is changed to a more traditional approach, "actoris preacuatio ingenii, lectorisque Thebane hystorie notitia" (23–24), which is ultimately derived from the *In principio accessus* (ll. 56 and 89–92).

The difference between the two *accessus* is best demonstrated by the explanations of the *pars philosophiae*. Whereas the parent *accessus* again took the dogmatic view of the text,[51] here the *ethice parti* is rather simply and ignorantly stated: "quia omnes auctores finaliter tractant propter mores" (24–25). Another instance of this simplified approach is the treatment of Statius' name. While the *In principio accessus* went into great detail to give us allegories for Statius' name (ll. 38–42), here the number of names is simply attributed to Statius' nobility,[52] without explanation other than the traditional etymology of *surculus* < *sursum canens* (l. 27).

---

[51] "nobis *informat* morum doctrinam," 111

[52] The idea that the plurality of names reflected Roman nobility is also found in the *accessus* to Ovid's *Ex Ponto* attributed to Fulco of Orléans: "eiusdem sunt nomina quia antiquitus nobiles multa habebant nomina" (ed. R. Hexter, *Ovid and Medieval Schooling* [München, 1986], 226–27; Coulson-Roy 467). Similarly, in the *accessus* to the B commentary to Juvenal (Löfstedt 1995.4), we find the note, "persona clara et illustris multis vult denotari nominibus."

Text 16. The Reg. lat. 1375 *accessus* to the *Thebaid*

V = Vaticano, Città del, Biblioteca Apostolica Vaticana, Reg. lat. 1375 (XV s.), 140r–141r

<I>n principio cuiuslibet autoris et maxime hystoriographi, quinque
sunt inquirenda: materia, intentio, vtilitas, cui parti philosophie, et
quis sit titulus, sed tamen de vita actoris huius pauca sunt prelibanda.
Autor iste nomine Statius, Tholosa oriundus, patre Papinio, matre
5   Agelina genitus. Narbone et Burdegali diu studuit. Postea vero
apud Galliam rethoricam docuit. Videns igitur poetas et
hystoriographos per carmina sua Rome ad magnos honores prouehi,
Romam venit et animum suum studio applicuit. Et haud mora
familiaritatem Domitiani imperatoris Romani promeruit. Domitianus
10   vero sciens eum esse peritum et eloquentem rogauit eum vt gesta
sua scriberet. Statius autem diffidens de ingenio suo dixit se velle
nutrire ingenium suum et preacuere describendo | Thebanum bellum,   140v
et eo descripto ingenioque suo in hoc subtiliato promisit se
descripturum Domitiani gesta, vnde ait <*Theb.* 1.32–33>:

15   Tempus erit cum laurigero tua fortior oestro
         facta canam, nunc tendo chelim

Id vero promittit in principio Achileydis vbi ait <1.19>:

         Magnusque tibi promittat Achiles.
Quod autem promisit morte preuentus non soluit, quia eo libro non
20   pertractato obiit. Et hec de poete uita sufficiant.

    Materia in hoc opere est Oedipode confusa domus, siue
Thebays. Intentio sua est tractare de Thebano bello vt sic possit
nutrire ingenium suum ad facta Domitiani describenda. Vtilitas est
duplex: actoris preacuatio ingenii, lectorisque Thebane hystorie
25   notitia. Ethice supponitur, id est morali philosophie, quia omnes
auctores finaliter tractant propter mores. Titulus talis est: Statii
Papinii Surcani primus liber Thebaydis incipit. Papinius a patre
dictus, Surcanus quasi sursum canens, Statius <nomen> proprium
ipsius est, vel quia | nobilis erat, plura habebat nomina. Omnes   141r
30   enim nobiles polinomii erant, vt per nominum pluralitatem eorum
manifestaretur nobilitas. Primus dicit quia sequitur secundus.
Sunt enim duodecim libri. Thebaydis nomen est hystorie
Thebane. More aliorum hystoriographorum tria facit: proponit,
inuocat, et narrat. Proponit vbi materiam suam prelibat, dicens
35   "Fraternas acies." Inuocat vbi difficultatem materie ostendit,
dicens "Vnde iubetis ire dee." Narrat vbi aggreditur principale
propositum, dicens "Impia iam merita." Hiis tribus vtitur tria
adoptando: propositione docilitatem, inuocatione beniuolentiam,
narratione attentionem. A propositione incipit dicens,
40   "Fraternas acies."

---

1 in... hystoriographi] *In principio accessus*, 1
4 patre... docuit (6)] cf. *ibid.* 8–9
6 videns... applicuit (7)] cf. *ibid.* 60–63
12 ingenium... obiit (18)] cf. *ibid.* 87–91
17 *Ach.* 1.19, *rectius*
21 materia... domus] cf. *In principio accessum*, 68–69

21 oedipode... domus] *Theb.* 1.17

24 historie philosophie (25)] cf. nota marg. in N ad *In principio accessum*, 68

27 papinius... canens (28)] *In principio accessus*, 38–39

29 omnes... nobilitas (31)] cf. accessum ad Ovidii, *Ex Ponto*, forte Fulconis Orleanensis: *eiusdem sunt nomina quia antiquitus nobiles multa habebant nomina* (Coulson-Roy 467; ed. R. Hexter, *Ovid and Medieval Schooling* [München, 1986], 226–27)

39 a... incipit] cf. Arnulfi Aurelianensis Accessum in Lucanum, 5.34

---

9 imperatorum(?) V   **38** prepositione V

The Olomouc *accessus*

Another example of the readaptation of *accessus* is the short *accessus* in Olomouc, Státní vědecká knihovna, M.I.167 (Incipitarium 42), which is a rare instance of an *accessus* to one of Statius' poems rewriting an *accessus* to the other poem, in this case an *accessus* to the *Achilleid* in Wien, cod. 13685 (dated 1477–79; Incipitarium 41). Again, a table shows their relationship.

Table 3. Comparison of the Olomouc and Wien 13685 *accessus*

Olomouc	Wien 13685
1: Causa suscepti operis huius librorum duodecim est	15–16: Causa suscepti operis: qui ipsum conpulit hunc librum scribere est hoc
1–10: Domicianus frater Titi, filius Vespasiani. Mortuo enim patre, Titus Iudeam et Domicianus Romam obtinuit. Deinde defuncto Tito, Domicianus solus regnauit. Homo scelestus et ferox. Hic uidens Stacium et in numero poetarum nullum ei esse secundum, rogauit eum vt gesta sua describeret. Statius autem videns Domicianum paucum memoria dignum fecisse, facere noluit. Sed ne tanti principis precibus videretur contraire, simulans se velle eius consentire precibus, dixit se velle peracuere et preexercere ingenium in materia humiliori et faciliori, videlicet in materia prius de Achille	16–24: Titus et Domitianus filii Uespasiani fuerunt. Quo mortuo, Titus Iudeam, Domicianus uero Romam obtinuit. Mortuo autem Tito, solus Domicianus regnauit, qui malus et scelestus fuit. Hic videns Statium in numero poetarum eximium, rogauit eum ut gesta sua describeret. Stacius autem videns Domicianum nil memoria dignum fecisse, facere noluit. Sed ne uideretur eius precibus contraire, simulans se ei consentire, dixit se uelle ingenium peracuere in materia humiliori et faciliori, videlicet in materia de Achille.

The Olomouc *accessus* then adds the brief note (10–14):

> *Suscepit Achilleidem librum, scilicet de vita puericie Achillis, in cuius principio dicit, "Magnusque tibi preludit Achilles." Scripsit etiam Thebaidem †ea racens†[53] vbi similiter dixit, "Tempus erit cum laurigero tua fortior oestro facta canam" etc.*

These last lines are too similar to too many *accessus* to pinpoint a definite source, and were most likely appended to the *accessus* to adapt it to its new context.

---

[53] This phrase, which I have obelized, is probably a note indicating that the two poems have been listed out of order, but I am unable to arrive at a neat emendation.

Text 17. The Olomouc *accessus* to the *Thebaid*

O = Olomouc, Státní vědecká knihovna, M.I.167 (XV s. ex.)

Causa suscepti operis huius librorum 12 est Domicianus frater
Titi, filius Vespasiani. Mortuo enim patre, Titus Iudeam et
Domicianus Romam obtinuit. Demum defuncto Tito, Domicianus
solus regnauit. Homo scelestus et ferox, hic videns Stacium et in
5   numero poetarum nullum ei esse secundum, rogauit eum vt gesta sua
describeret. Statius autem videns Domicianum paucum memoria
dignum fecisse, facere noluit. Sed ne tanti principis precibus
videretur contraire, simulans se velle eius assentire precibus, dixit
se velle preacuere et preexercere ingenium in materia humiliori et
10   faciliori, videlicet in materia prius de Achille. Scripsit Achilleidem
librum, scilicet de vita puericie Achillis, in cuius principio dicit,
"Magnusque tibi preludit Achilles." Scripsit eciam Thebaidem
†ea racens† vbi similiter dixit, "Tempus erit cum laurigero tua
fortior oestro facta canam" et cetera.

1 causa... operis] *accessus* in Wien, ÖNB, cod. 13685, 15
2 mortuo... Achille (10)] *ibid.*, 17–24
12 *Ach.* 1.119
13–14 *Theb.* 1.32–33

1 Titus *post* est *eras.* O   **12** A (*pro* Achilleidem?) *post* eciam *eras.* O

Text 18. The Wien 13685 *accessus* to the *Achilleid*

W = Wien, Österreichische Nationalbibliothek, cod. 13685 (annis 1477-79), 1v

Hunc Stacium constat veraciter fuisse tempore Vespesiani imperatoris
et pervenisse vsque ad imperium Domiciani fratris Titi, qui quidam
Titus iunior dictus est. Si quis autem vnde fuerit querat, invenitur
fuisse Tolonensis, que ciuitas est Gallie. Ideoque in Gallia
5   celeberrime docuit rethoricam, sed postea veniens Romam ad
poetriam se transtulit. Fuit enim nobili prosapia ortus, clarus
ingenio, doctus eloquio cuius Iuuenalis sic meminit:

    Curritur ad vocem iocundam ad cure
    Thebaidos, leta vt ficit cum Stacius vrbem,
10   Promisitque diem tanta dulcedine captos
    Afficit ille animos, tantaque libidini vulgi
    Auditus, et cetera.

Est autem autor huius libri Statius nomine, Pampinus cognomine,
Sursulus vero agnomine, quasi sursum canens.

15   Causa suscepti operis que ipsum conpulit hunc librum
scribere est hoc: Titus et Domicianus filii Vespasiani fuerunt. Quo
mortuo Titus Iudeam, Domicianus vero Romam obtinuit. Mortuo
autem Tito solus Domicianus regnauit, qui malus et scelestus fuit.
Hic videns Statium in numero poetarum eximium, rogauit eum ut
20   gesta sua describeret. Stacius autem videns Domicianum nil

memoria dignum fecisse, facere noluit. Sed ne videretur eius
precibus contraire, simulans se ei consentire, dixit se velle ingenium
preacuere in materia humiliori et faciliori, videlicet in materia de
Achille. Hac igitur de causa scripsit Achilleidem, de qua ad presens.
25   Nota titulus istius libri talis est: Stacius Achilleidos vel
Achilleis Stacii. Intentio vero eius est ut describendo puericiam
Achillis doceat nos pueros nutrire et virtutibus imbui et ut hortemur
nos exemplo Tetidis ne velimus diuiune disposicioni contraire, nec
infringere illud quod a diis dispositum est.

8–12 Juvenal, *Sat.* 7.82–86, *rectius*
16 titus...preacuere (23)] cf. accessum in Kraków, Biblioteka Jagiellońska, 525 III

---

2 imperarium W   **25** nota] vnde(?) W

The *Achilleid*

The Carpentras *accessus*

The nonauthorial *accessus* to the *Achilleid* represent trends similar to what we have seen in the *Thebaid* so far, with, however, one difference. While the rewritings in the *accessus* to the *Thebaid* tend more toward syncopation (except for responses to Dante), those to the *Achilleid* tend much more toward expansion, seeming to react against the poverty of interpretation of the poem that we have seen in the previous centuries. A good example of this tendency is the late–fourteenth century *accessus* found in Carpentras, Bibliothèque municipale, 369 and in the *editio princeps* (Roma?, 1471?; Incipitarium 263).[54]

The *accessus*, as de Angelis pointed out,[55] is based to no small degree on the *accessus* in Firenze, BML, Plut. 24 sin. 12, but it is also heavily indebted to the *Hoc ex ordine compendium*[56] and to the *Quaeritur accessus*. How the *accessus* extracts from the two *accessus* will demonstrate an integral aspect of the composition of *accessus* to the *Achilleid* in the fourteenth century.

The bulk of the Carpentras *accessus* comes either directly or indirectly from the *accessus* in BML, Plut. 24 sin. 12—the text was possibly chosen because of its *mythos* or simply because of its antiquity. Now, from the perspective of the fourteenth-century scholar, there are several problems with that *accessus*: it discusses only the questions *unde, quid, ubi*, and *quare*; it places Statius' birth in Thebes; and, outside of the fiction of Domitian's *controversia*, it does not discuss the origin, style, or completeness of the poem, all of which had become important questions by this time.

The author of this *accessus* first corrected the central problem with the parent *accessus* by adding information from the *Quaeritur accessus* (1–4), correcting the answers to the questions *unde* et *quando*. He then added information from the *Hoc ex ordine compendium* to correct other earlier information as well as give answers to the more contemporary questions of *ubi* (1), *quem auctorem imitetur* (9–13), the *qualitas* (12–15), the *materia* (16–18), the *intentio* (21–25), and *cui parti philosophie supponatur* (29–31). Additional information is derived from other antique *accessus*, in particular the thirteenth-century *Hoc ex ordine*—the earliest *compendium* to the *Achilleid*.

The Carpentras *accessus* also rewrites the periocha that we find in its parent, with the result that the two texts seem to appear only loosely related, as the table on the next page illustrates.[57]

---

[54] The text in the *editio princeps* is transcribed in J.C. Dommerich, *Ad P. Papinii Statii Achilleida ex membraneis Bibliothecae suae anecdota* (Wolfenbüttel, 1758), who did know the source of the pages. The *ed. princ.* was copied from the Carpentras manuscript. See H. Anderson, "The *Editio Princeps* of Statius' Epics," forthcoming.

[55] de Angelis 1984.165

[56] Jeudy-Riou 161–68

[57] In the following table, italicized words are words shared by the two *accessus*.

Table 4. Comparison of the Carpentras and Plut. 24 sin. 12 *accessus*

Carpentras	Plut. 24 sin. 12
43–59 *Presagitum enim fuerat quod si aliquis deorum Thetidem in uxorem acciperet, ex* eo *filium nasciturum* eo maiorem patre. *Vnde dii perterriti eam accipere noluerunt*, sed Iupiter prouidit quod Pelleus eius nepos eam susciperet in uxorem, et sic *terreno homini* nupta fuit. Et in eius *nuptiis dii deaeque omnes* conuenerunt. *Discordia uero* dea, quia *ad* nuptias inuitata *non fuit, pomum aureum clam in nuptiis inter Iunonem, Palladem et Uenerem proiiecit,* cui in*scriptum erat "pulcriori debetur."* Ob quod *litigium inter eas* maximum exortum est. *Vates* quidam *Carphatius,* scilicet Protheus deus marinus, Thetidi dixit ex illo pomo maximum periculum *nasciturum* et quod filius qui ex ea nasciturus erat id malum *uindicaret, postremo inde uitam amitteret.* Vnde Thetis huius predictionis fatalis memor anxia semper fuit. Exactis quoque *nuptiis,* hoc litigium terminandum prolatum est ad *Paridem, qui* sententiam pro Venere tulit, quum ipsa amore omnium mulierum sibi despondit (Pallas sapientiam, Iuno potentiam et dominium, sed amorem quibus aliis promissis preposuit). 59–77 *Nato* itaque Achille ex Thetide, id timens quod Protheus dixit, filium suum ad Chyronem *detulit nutri*endum, obsecrando ut illum diligentissime enutriret. Cum itaque Paris in Greciam pergeret, Thetis sentiens illos per mare nauigare, timens predictionem Prothei, ad *Neptunum* porrexit, implorans ut naues illas mergeret, ne periret filius eius. Et *quia Neptunus* concedere non potuit, quia sic fatatum erat, Thetis ipsa ad Chyronem gemebunda porrexit et casum timoris expressit, et filium ab eo suscepit et ad regiam Licomedis in insulam Schiros perduxit et in habitu muliebri induit, asserens eundem sororem esse Achillis, et quod inter filias suas ipsum *custodiret.* Interim Paris rapuit in Citharea insula prope Amiclas, ciuitatem Menelai, Helenam Menelai uxorem, ex quo Menelaus et Agamemnon omnes Grecie principes conuocauerunt ut tale *dedecus* ulciscantur et collectis undequaque presidiis erga Troiam pergunt, et petentibus omnibus ut inueniatur Achilles, ad Apollinis mittunt oraculum, ubinam posset repperiri Achilles. Responsum est eum repperiri posse in Schiros insula inter filias Licomedis regis in habitu muliebri, prout Calcas augur predixit.	*Presagium enim fuerat quod si aliquis deorum Thetidem uxorem acciperet,* ex ea *filium nasciturum* qui eum de regno expelleret. *Vnde dii perterriti noluerunt eam accipere.* Ipsa uero uidens nullum deorum eam accipere uelle, *terreno homini* se coniunxit. Cuius *nuptiis omnes dii et dee* interfuerunt. *Discordia uero,* que *non affuit, pomum aureum inter Iunonem et Paladem et Uenerem proiecisse* dicitur, in quo *scriptum erat "pulcriori debetur."* Unde, quia *litigium* erat *inter illas, Carpatius uates* pro pomo magnum fore *nasciturum* Thetidi predestinauit, quod malum filius qui ex ea nasceretur *uindicaret, postremo inde uitam amitteret.* Quod Thetis minime tradidit obliuioni. *Nuptiis* peractis, adiuere *Paridem qui* Uenerem pulcriorem asseruit, quia Elenam uxorem Menelai sibi promiserat. Puero *nato,* Thetis fatis resistere cupiens illum Chironi *detulit,* deprecans ut eum nutriat atque studiose conseruet. Exinde Paris iuit pro Helena et rapuit eam. Thetis uero uidens illum eam deferentem adiuit *Neptunum* ut sibi licenciam daret obruendi nauim suam, quia mortis filii sui causa erat. Quod *quia Neptunus* non sibi concessit, filium suum Chironi abstulit, eumque femineo more uestiens ad Licomedem regem Sciros detulit ut inter filias suas illum nutriret atque *custodiret.* Interea Menelaus suum suique regni *dedecus* uindicare cupiens Troiam armata manu porrexit. Vaticinatum autem fuerat quod numquam sine Achille ciuitas caperetur. Quocirca omnes unanimiter preces ad Apolinem fuderunt ut eis quo in loco Achilles absconditus fuerat pateficeret. Qui ore Calcantis inter Licomedis filias illum muliebria indumenta deferentem esse patefecit.

The Carpentras *accessus* omits only one detail from the myth transmitted in the Plut. 24 sin. 12 version, the statement that it was fated that without Achilles, the war could not be won (26) and only substantially changes one detail, how Thetis' mate was chosen (in Plut. 24 sin. 12, she chooses him herself [10–11], in the Carpentras version, Jove chooses one for her [45–46]). The other details that are new in this *accessus* are only of a glossary nature (e.g. "scilicet Protheus deus marinus," 43).

The most substantial change made in the Carpentras *accessus* is its language. As we saw above, one of the reasons for the inclusion of the material from the *Hoc ex ordine compendium* was to accommodate the new *accessus* requirements, specifically the inclusion of the *materia* and *intentio*. He also included the actual words *materia* and *intentio*, and in so doing made the *accessus* more technically modern. Likewise, in the summary of the poem I have just discussed, we see the addition of terminology found in other contemporary *accessus*, the most prominent among these being *habitu muliebri* (27 [where the Carpentras *accessus* reads *habitu puellari*], 64 and 72). The *muliebria indumenta* that we find in the Plut. 24 sin. 12 *accessus* (29) is only found there among *accessus* to Statius;[58] *habitus*, however, whether accompanied by *muliebris* or (more commonly) *femineus*, is found in six other *accessus*, only one of which can be dated prior to the fourteenth century.[59] The case is the same with *insulam Schiros* (1. 63).[60]

The Carpentras *accessus* had a great deal of influence in the fifteenth century. As the *editio princeps* is copied from it, we may argue that the volume was at Rome then and, as the readings in the manuscript copy of the text seem to have been preferred to those in the edition,[61] the manuscript seems to have stayed in scholarly circles.[62]

---

[58] The word *indumenta* occurs in connection with Statius only in the plot summary in Assisi, 309 (XV s.).

[59] In the twelfth century, we have the *accessus* in Graz, Universitätsbibliothek, 1495. In the fourteenth, the *accessus* in Padova, Biblioteca del Seminario Vescovile, Ms. 56; and Venezia, Zan. Lat. 541 (which also occurs in two other witnesses). In the fifteenth century, we have the *accessus* in London, BL, Harley 2693; Assisi, 309; and Paris, BnF, n.a.l. 166 (dated 1477).

[60] This occurs in several periochae and in the *accessus* in El Escorial, ms. f.III.11 (XIV s.) (three witnesses). It also occurs in the *accessus* in Praha, Národní Knihovna, XXIII.D.180 (XV s.), but that *accessus* is a rewriting of the Carpentras *accessus*.

[61] E.g., in the *accessus* in Vaticano, Ottob. lat. 1261 (below, p. 116), line 139 reads *nasciturum maiorem* (see the present *accessus*, line 44).

[62] The manuscript bears annotations by several hands, one of which is as late as the end of the fifteenth century.

Text 19. The Carpentras *accessus* to the *Achilleid*

C = Carpentras, Bibliothèque municipale, 369 (XIV s.), 124v
W = *editio princeps* (Roma?, 1471?), 155r–v

Magnanimum Eacidem et cetera: Statius hic fuit de Tholosa ciuitate, que
in Gallia est, in qua rhetoricam celeberrime docuit. Floruit enim maximo
ingenio tempore inperatoris Vespasiani et peruenit ad tempora Domitiani,
fratris Titi, qui et minor Titus appellatus est. Qui Romam se transferens
5 et plurimos poetas intuens in arte poetica glorie et fame titulis
premiorum pollere muneribus, se ad artem poeticam transtulit, et
Thebanam historiam iam longeua temporis nube obductam et ab omnibus
iam elapsam memoria elegantissimo stilo sine inuentione nouauit, et fecit
iuuenescere senescentem. Imitatus Virgilium nobilem principem
10 poetarum et usque adeo eum imitatus est quod aliqui eum Virgilii simiam
uocent. Vnde ipse in fine operis opus Virgilii gloriose extollit, suum librum
alloquens <*Theb.* 12.811>, "O mihi bissenos" et cetera. Quantum autem
fuerit huius fulmen eloquentie Iuuenalis testatur <*Sat.* 7.82–83>:

  Curritur ad uocem iocundam et carmen amice
15   Thebaydos, letam dum fecit Stacius vrbem.

 Materia huius libri, scilicet Statii, Thetis et Achilles, quem usque ad
Troiam perducit, aliqua gesta eius in sue primordio iuuentutis enumerans
ut in fine libri patet. Sed gesta eius apud Troiam Homerus Grece
facundie elegantissimo carmine docuit, ut autor ipse narrat, ubi dicit in
20 principio <*Ach.* 1.3–4>:

  Quamquam acta uiri nimis inclita cantu
  Meonio, et cetera

 Intentio est ut in arte poetica se exercens, adeptam iam famam
libri Thebaidos eternam posteris faciat, que est potissima omnium
25 poetarum intentio, ut testatur Ouidius <*A.A.* 3.403–404>:

  Quid petitur sacris tantum nisi fama poetis?
  Hoc precium certe summa laboris habet.

Et sic intentio est tractare de historia Achillis, quomodo Thetis mater
Achillis eum a Chirone abstulit et ad regiam Licomedis in Schiros
30 insulam tulit in habitu puellari et in tractando hoc tale negotium
ostendit Thetidem resistere uolentem fatis. Causa intentionis autoris
est talis, quod nullus uoluntati deorum resistere presumat. Et sic
ethyce parti philosophie supponitur, quia loquitur de moribus et
subtiliter tractat quid honestum, quid utile sit.

35 Statii titulus est Statii Papinii Surculi Achilleydos liber primus.
Que causa mouerit autorem principaliter ad hoc opus: est sciendum
quod postquam Thebaydem composuit, in qua per annos XII
inuigilauit, Romam uenit et ibi coronatus est et ab imperatore
Domitiano honorificentissime susceptus. Demum in aula imperatoris
40 questio talis fuit proposita, utrum ea que predestinata sunt possint
euitari uel ne. Ad quam questionem soluendam, Statius a Domitiano
imperatore inuitatus est, et eam soluere uolens, hunc libellum
composuit, ostendendo qualiter Thetis fatis resistere uoluit et nequiuit.
Presagitum enim fuerat quod si aliquis deorum Thetidem in uxorem
45 acciperet, ex eo filium nasciturum eo maiorem patre. Vnde dii

perterriti eam accipere noluerunt. Sed Iupiter prouidit quod Pelleus
eius nepos eam susciperet in uxorem, et sic terreno homini nupta fuit.
Et in eius nuptiis dii deaeque omnes conuenerunt. Discordia uero
dea, quia ad nuptias inuitata non fuit, pomum aureum clam in nuptiis
50 inter Iunonem, Palladem et Uenerem proiiecit, cui inscriptum erat
"pulcriori debetur." Ob quod litigium inter eas maximum exortum
est. Vates quidam Carphatius, scilicet Protheus deus marinus,
Thetidi dixit ex illo pomo maximum periculum nasciturum et quod
filius qui ex ea nasciturus erat id malum uindicaret, postremo inde
55 uitam amitteret. Vnde Thetis huius predictionis fatalis memor anxia
semper fuit. Exactis quoque nuptiis, hoc litigium terminandum
prolatum est ad Paridem, qui sententiam pro Venere tulit, quoniam
ipsa amorem omnium mulierum sibi despondit. Pallas sapientiam,
Iuno potentiam et dominium, sed amorem quibus aliis promissis
60 preposuit. Nato itaque Achille ex Thetide, id timens quod
Protheus dixit, filium suum ad Chyronem detulit nutriendum,
obsecrando ut illum diligentissime enutriret. Cum itaque Paris in
Greciam pergeret, Thetis sentiens illos per mare nauigare, timens
predictionem Prothei, ad Neptunum porrexit, implorans ut naues
65 illas mergeret, ne periret filius eius. Et quia Neptunus concedere
non potuit, quia sic fatatum erat, Thetis ipsa ad Chyronem
gemebunda porrexit et casum timoris expressit, et filium ab eo
suscepit et ad regiam Licomedis in insulam Schiros perduxit et in
habitu muliebri induit, asserens eundem sororem esse Achillis, et
70 quod inter filias suas ipsum custodiret. Interim Paris rapuit in
Citharea insula prope Amiclas, ciuitatem Menelai, Helenam Menelai
uxorem. Ex quo Menelaus et Agamemnon omnes Grecie principes
conuocauerunt ut tale dedecus ulciscantur et collectis undequaque
presidiis erga Troiam pergunt, et petentibus omnibus ut inueniatur
75 Achilles, ad Apollinis mittunt oraculum, ubinam posset repperiri
Achilles. Responsum est eum repperiri posse in Schiros insula
inter filias Licomedis regis in habitu muliebri, prout Calcas augur
predixit.

---

1 Statius... est (4)] cf. *Queritur accessum*, ll. 1–4
4 Romam... poetarum (10)] *Hoc ex ordine compendium*, 161.8–13
10 aliqui... cetera (12)] *ibid.*, 15–18
12 quantum... vrbem (15)] *ibid.*, 22–25
23 est... habet (26)] *Hoc ex ordine compendium*, 162.6–12
28 intentio... historia] cf. Arnulfi Aurelianensis Accessum in Lucanum, 3.14
32 et sic... sit (33)] cf. *Hoc ex ordine compendium*, 162.17–19
38 Romam... susceptus (38)] cf. Plut. 24 sin. 12 *accessum*, ll. 2–3
39 demum... noluerunt (45)] *ibid.* 3–10
47 terreno... tulit (56)] *ibid.* 10–17
65 mergeret... fatatum (65)] cf. *Ach.* 1.80–81
73 dedecus] Plut. 24 sin. 12 *accessus*, l. 25

---

1 et cetera *om.* W   **2** gallea W   **3** domitiano C   **5** titulis *ex* titulos C   **6** poll^{i}ere C
7 longeui W   **8** elegantissimi stili CW   **10** eum^1] ipsum W   **12** michi W   et cetera *om.* W
16 scilicet] *duo subpunctus habet* W   **18** sed *scripsi* : ṣed C : nam W   **22** et cetera *om.* W

23 ietentio W **26** sanctis W **29** chillrone W **34** et *post* honestum *add.* W quid² *om.* C **40** vutrum W possunt W **42** est *om.* W **45** filium... maiorem] filius nasciturus esset maior W eo maior patre *add. sup. lin.* C **48** et (*post* fuit) ut W **52** quidam] quoque W **54** filia W et *post* uindicaret *add.* W **57** prelatum W **59** quibus] omnibus W **73** conuocauit C **74** contra W

The *accessus* in Firenze, BML, Plut. 38.10

A less intricate, but more detailed instance of the rewriting typical of this century is the *accessus* found in Firenze, BML, Plut. 38.10 (dated 1394) and London, BL, Addit. 10095 (XV s.—Incipitarium 115). This *accessus* is a combination of borrowing and rewriting of Paris, BnF, lat. 8559 (XIII s.).

The first eleven lines of the rewritten version copy directly from the parent and begin with a short explanation of why Statius chose his present material (corresponding to the unstated question, *quare*), which is likely related to the source for the *accessus* in Wolfenbüttel, cod. Guelf. 228 Gud. lat.,[63] and then poses the four *circumstantiae*accessus of the work: *que materia, que intentio, que utilitas,* and *quis libri titulus* (8–9). The *accessus* as it stands in the Paris example is likely original,[64] but as the three extant manuscripts represent three recensions,[65] any statement as to the original state of the text must be made cautiously. In any case, it is the manuscript in Firenze that is the most important at present.

The manuscript in Firenze makes three large rewritings and one lengthy addition to the text, all of which are descended from the (interpolated) KP *accessus*, particularly through the π family; still, it remains truer to the London witness than the Paris witness does. The only additions in the Florence witness that are not related to the KP tradition are lines 38–40 (which correct the claim of the Paris witness, that Homer's work was incomplete because of his own death) and lines 43–52 (which expand the notions of the *utilitas priuata*, and the *fama* aspect of authorship[66]). It appears, then, that the author of the Firenze witness sought only to add information or alternate points of view that were not present in the original,[67] and chose an older tradition of scholarship to the poem as a source.

---

[63] Verbal similarities include *consumasse* (3) = *consumauit* (W, 7) and *leuiori opusculo* (5) = *leuiori materia* (W, 24).

[64] In the Paris and London witnesses, it is followed by a commentary (albeit only fragmentary in the Paris witness) that has some 11 witnesses. The London witness, which omits such details as the *titulus*, is likely a partial syncopation.

[65] The manuscript in London, as I said, is likely a syncopation; that in Firenze is an expansion.

[66] Cf. the *accessus* in Vaticano, Reg. lat. 1556 (XIII s., extant in two witnesses; see above, p. 57) and the Carpentras *accessus* (XIV s.), ll. 22–26 (cf. above, p. 71). In Sankt Florian, XI.58 (XIII s.), the *accessus* states, "priuata [*sc.* utilitas], quia uoluit placere Romanis."

[67] He does not delete any information in the original (with the possible exception of the note on Homer's death), and all of the additions are introduced by *uel.*

Text 20. The Plut. 38.10 *accessus* to the *Achilleid*

F = Firenze, Biblioteca Medicea Laurenziana, Plut. 38.10 (anno 1394), 1r
L = London, British Library, Add. 10095 (XV s.), 200v
P = Paris, Bibliothèque nationale de France, lat. 8559 (XIII s.), 32ra

In principio huius auctoris notandum est quod Domitianus
imperator Romanus Vespasiani filius, uidens Statium opus Thebaidos
feliciter consumasse, ipsum rogauit Statium quatenus sua fortia
facta describeret. Statius uero de actis tanti ducis describendis se
5   diffidens sufficere, aliquo leuiori opusculo suum uoluit preacuere
ingenium et expiriri. Vnde datis sibi indutiis a Domitiano, hoc opus
Achilleidos aggressus est. In cuius principio quattuor sunt
inquirenda, scilicet que materia, que intentio, que utilitas, quis
libri titulus. De hiis ergo propositis ordinem uideamus.

10   Materia uero actoris est virtus Achillis et acta. Intentio est fortia
facta Achillis describere,

P	F
nec sistere in Hectore distracto, sicut ait in textu, "nec in Hectore tracto sistere, sed iuuenem tota de 15 ducere Troia."	in Hectore tracto more Omerico desistere, sed supplendo ea facta istius Achillis, quamuis ab Omero dicta sunt, preterea plene de omnibus factis eius tractare.
L	F
	Uel intentio eius est agere non de illis bellis tantum que egit Achilles circa Troiam, sed quomodo Chiron eum nutriuit et quo modo mater eius, scilicet Thetis, tulit eum in aula Licomedis regis et abscondit. Quod fecit auctor hac intentione, ut retrahat nos ab hac intentione, scilicet ne uelimus res<is>tere predestinacioni deorum, sicut Thetis uoluit facere. Quia cum cognouisset quod filium suum, scilicet Achilles, in bello Troiano fata predestinauissent moriturum, uolens predestinationem fatorum obuiare, filium suum frustra recondidit, qui postea a Grecis inuentus est et ad Troiam ductus interiit. Quod eius de nichil profuit, multo maius certe mortalibus proficeret. Que materia et intentio circa idem uersantur. Dico uirtutem et acta Achillis habet pro materia. Acta dico que pretermisit Omerus, qui quedam de ipso tractauit, quedam pretermisit.
In quo materiam habet ut Achillis uirtutem et acta describet, acta dico que pretermisit Homerus, qui quedam de ipso 35 tractauit, quedam autem pretermisit.	

Tractauit enim Homerus de gestis Achillis apud Troiam usque ad illud
quo Achilles traxit Ethorem circa muros Troianos.

P	FL
Ibi uero Homerus preuentus morte suum opus terminauit	Ibi uero stetit Omerus et suum tractatum terminauit, quod innuit Statius dicens <1.6–7>, "Nec in Hectore tracto sistere."

Vtilitas autem potest esse duplex, scilicet communis et priuata. Communis, ne fatis obsistere temptemus, cum

P	F
Thetis eis obsistere, que dea erat, non potuit.	Thetidem eis obuiare uolentem nihil profecisse uidemus. Priuata, ut fauorem Domitiani imperatoris Romani per nobilia sua scripta posset acquirere. Vel fuit priuata
Priuata ut ingenium suum per hunc tractatum posset acuere ad nobilia facta Domiciani describenda ut posset per hoc fauorem ipsius impetrare.	in hoc ut ingenium suum per hoc tractatum posset acuere ad uersificandum facta Domitiani nobiliter describenda et ut posset per hoc opus fauorem acquirere et impetrare.

PF	L
Titulus talis est: Statii Achilleidos liber primus incipit. Bene dicit primus quia sequitur secundus. Sunt enim quinque libri. In primo enim sollicitudinem matris de morte filii describit. In secundo filii absconsionem. In tertio inquisitionem Grecorum. In quarto inuentionem Achillis per Ulixem. In quinto adductionem eius ad Troiam	Notandum igitur quod hoc opus in quinque libris diuisum est. Prima diuisio constat ex matris sollicitudine de morte Achilis quam presciebat. Secunda de asconsione. Tertia de inquisitione Grecorum. Quarta de inuentione. Quinta de eius tractu, id est ductu apud Troiam per Ulixem

et in hoc opus istud terminatur, quia auctor morte preuentus non potuit quod uoluit adimplere. Proposuerat enim dicere ea que prelibata sunt et omnia que egerat ipse Achilles aput Troiam, unde id in prologo <1.7>, "Sed tota iuuenem deducere Troia." Secundum enim alios, quattuor sunt libri, sed duos ultimos in unum copulant et coniungunt. *Achilleis, Achilleidos declinatur, et capitur hic pro istoria et est pronomen femineum ab Achille, quemadmodum Eneidos ab Enea uiro et cetera.* More aliorum poetarum bene scribentium, tria facit: proponit, inuocat, et narrat. Proposicionem includit in inuocatione prima, quia ibi ostendit de quo tractatus sit. Est enim eius triplex inuocatio. Primo enim inuocat suam Musam, secundo Apollinem, tertio Domitianum, excusando se erga eum. Inuocat enim Musam ubi dicit <1.3> "Musa refer." Inuocat Apollinem ubi dicit <1.8> "Tu modo si ueteres" et cetera. Inuocat Domitianum ubi dicit <1.14> "At tu quem longe" et cetera. Narrat ubi dicit <1.20> "Soluerat Ebalio classem de littore pastor" et cetera. A propositione narrat ubi dicit <1.1> "Magnanimum Eacidem."

5 leuiori opusculo] cf. *accessum* in cod. Guelf. 228 gud. lat. 24: *leuiori materia*
16 (F) uel... proficeret (31)] KP *accessus*, ll. 5–12
31 (F) materia... pretermisit (35)] cf. Wolfenbüttel, cod. Guelf. 13.10 Aug. 4°, ll. 17–23
38 (F) ibi... sistere (40)] cf. KP accessum, ll. 3–4
36 (F) Thetidem... uidemus (37)] *ibid.* 17 (cf. ms. P)

1 In... auctoris *om.* L   2 romanorum imperator F   romanus *om.* L   opus statium F   statium *om.* L   3 rogabat L   quatenus] ut F *fort. rect.*   4 factis F   se *om.* L   5 in *post* sufficere *add.* L   6 et experiri *om.* P   7 est aggressus L   in cuius... describere (11)] *om.* L 8 et *post* materia *add.* F   et *post* utilitas *add.* F   9 libri *om.* P   propositis] per F 10 materia... acta] materiam siquidem habet auctor iste Achillis uirtutem et acta *ante* tractauit (*l.* 36) *dist.* F   auctoris *post* intentio *add.* F   achillis habet pro materia *post* acta *eras.* F   11 et bellicosa *post* facta *add.* F *fort. rect.*   24 obuiare] destinare F   36 enim] uero P   gestis] actis L   illud] illum locum L   37 traxit achilles hectora L   38 omerus *om.* L   39 statius] bona F   41 vtilitas... cum (42) *om.* L   duplex potest esse P   scilicet *om.* P   51 opus *post* hoc *subpunx.* P   53 achilleidos] achillis P   56 enim *om.* F   57 enim *om.* P   matris sollicitudinem P   58 filii] achillis F   quod iam presciebat *post* sui *add.* F   59 libro ponit *post* secundo *add.* F   64 istud] suum P   in hoc terminatur hoc opus L   auctor] autor *post* quod (*l.* 58) *dist.* L   65 quod uoluit non potuit P   66 etiam *post* et *add.* L   omnia] ea P   egerat] fecit P   ipse achilles *om.* L   aput troiam] troia durante P   iuxta illud quod *post* troiam *add.* L   67 id *om.* P   iuuenem tota P   68 secundum... et cetera (71) *om.* L   alios] animos F quattuor sunt] non sunt nisi quattuor F   tantum *post* libri *add.* P   69 achilleis... et cetera (71) *om.* P   70 pronomine F   71 More... narrat (72)] diuiditur ergo prologus in 3 quia primo proponit, secundo inuocat, tertio narrat L   72 bene scribentium *om.* P *fort. recte*   73 prima euocatione P   uero *post* proposicionem *add.* L   quia... sit (74)] *om.* LP   74 est... inuocatio] que triplex est L   76 erga] uersus F   eum] ipsum L   enim *om.* P   ubi] dum F   77 inuocat... et cetera (79) *om.* L   ubi] dum F   et cetera *om.* F   78 ubi... ubi] dum... dum F   etc. *om.* F narrat... et cetera (79) *om.* F   narrat ubi] ergo incipiendum est L   79–80 a propositione] preterea F   80 magnanimum... eacidem *om.* L   eacidem *om.* F

The *accessus* of Thomas Walsingham

Beginning in this century, we also begin to have *accessus* that are attributable or attributed to an identified individual.[68] Despite their authority, these *accessus* do not show us the major advancements we would hope for; they are, in effect, attempts at vast rewriting and reveal the same limitations as their nonauthorial counterparts. As we have seen since the beginning of our investigation, there simply was not enough information about Statius to allow a scholar to break from tradition. An example of one scholar's attempt is the collection of *accessus* in London, BL, Harley 2693, which is attributed to Thomas Walsingham.[69]

The manuscript contains quite a good deal of Statius material. On 1r–40v, there is a paraphrasis of Lactantius Placidus' commentary on *Thebaid* 1–8, which is followed (on 41r–45v) by a separate commentary on *Thebaid* 1–4.[70] Later in the manuscript, on 131r–202v, is Thomas Walsingham's *Prohemia poetarum*, which contains two *accessus* to the *Thebaid*, one to the *Achilleid*, and two mythological prologues to the *Thebaid*.[71]

The first *accessus* to Statius (Incipitarium 279) is to the *Achilleid* and demonstrates one important methodological difference: the number of sources used. Here, Walsingham used four sources: the late–thirteenth century *accessus* in Wolfenbüttel, cod. Guelf. 13.10 Aug. 4°, the fourteenth-century *Casualis euentus accessus*, the interpolations in the fourteenth-century Escorial witness of the Gronov. 66 *accessus*, and a prominent group of periochae,[72] but the citations from each source are extremely brief.[73]

---

[68] The absence of authoritative *accessus* before this century is something of an anomaly. The *accessus* traditions to Virgil and Ovid, on the contrary, are attributed to named scholars almost from the beginning. Among others, three of the earliest authors of *accessus* to Ovid's works are Arnulf, William, and Fulco of Orléans and Giovanni del Virgilio (twelfth to fourteenth centuries) (see W. Engelbrecht, "*Bursarii Ovidianorum*—ein Ovid-Kommentar des Wilhelm von Orléans [um 1200]," *Mittellateinisches Jahrbuch* 26 [1991], 357–58; F.T. Coulson, "New Manuscript Evidence for Sources of the Accessus of Arnoul d'Orléans to the *Metamorphoses* of Ovid," *Manuscripta* 30 [1986], 103–107; and F. Ghisalberti, "Arnolfo d'Orléans. Un cultore di Ovidio nel secolo XII," *Memorie del Reale Istituto Lombardo di Scienze e Lettere* 24 [1932], 157–234 and his "Giovanni del Virgilio espositore delle *Metamorfosi*," *Giornale dantesco* 34 [1933], 1–110. Giovanni di Virgilio was active in scholarship to Statius as well (see de Angelis 1984, *passim*), but apparently did not write an *accessus*. In the case of Virgil, outside of Donatus and Servius, there were *accessus* by Probus and Focas; see G. Brugnoli and R. Scarcia, "Osservazione sulla Vita Probiana di Virgilio," *StudUrb* 39 (1965), which discusses the relationships among the four.

The only names associated with pre-*Silvae accessus* are those of Petrus de Caneffis de Parma (Berkeley, CA, MS UCB 145), Thomas Walsingham, Francesco Filelfo (Modena, Est. lat. 331 [α.F.8.15] [XV s.]; see below, p. 97), Petrus Crinitus, and "Martinus a S. Benedicto" (Paris, BnF, lat. 5137 [XIII s.], which is a rewriting of the *In principio* commentary). The anomalous character of Statian *accessus* may be a result of the stagnant nature of Statian scholarship that I discuss in the conclusion to this chapter.

[69] Likely educated at the abbey of St. Albans and at Oxford, Thomas Walsingham, OSB, became a monk at St. Albans, where he was in charge of the scriptorium and wrote a *Historia Anglicana* (ed. H.T. Riley, *Rerum Britannicarum medii aeui scriptores* 28.1.2 [London, 1863–64]). He died there, ca. 1422. See R. Sharpe, *A Handlist of the Latin Writers of Great Britain and Ireland Before 1540*, Publications of the Journal of Medieval Latin 1 (1997), 688–90 nr. 1850.

[70] On both of these commentaries, see Sweeney 1969.21.

[71] While it could be that Walsingham wrote several treatises on Statius, I believe that only the first *accessus* to the *Achilleid* and *Thebaid* (145v–46v) are by him. The later *accessus* are too different in form and content to have been by the same author, and I imagine that they were added because of the thinness of the original *accessus* to the *Thebaid* or out of an interest in collecting Statius commentaries in the manuscript. The Statius *accessus* are not treated in the studies of F.T. Cabral (*The Prohemia Poetarum of Thomas Walsingham and the Accessus ad Auctores*, Dissertation, U. of Nebraska-Lincoln, 1974) or of A.G. Rigg ("Medieval Latin Poetic Anthologies [1]," *MS* 39 [1977], 281–330).

[72] Represented by Paris, BnF, lat. 8559, the KP *accessus*, the commentary in Escorial, El, Real Biblioteca, ms. f.III.11, the *accessus* in Düsseldorf, K2:F.50, and the *accessus* in Leiden, Lips. 36.

[73] The *accessus* to the *Thebaid* are not as well developed as those to the *Achilleid*. The first *Thebaid accessus* (146r–v) is simply a plot summary, as is the third (168r). The second *accessus* (168r) is an abbreviation of the

Walsingham hails back to an older estimation of Statius, calling him *commendatissimus* (*accessus* after the thirteenth century refrain from simple praise of this sort, although there are some exceptions[74]), and echoes the older tradition that Statius was earnest in his desire to write the *Achilleid* to sharpen his wits. What is novel in this *accessus* is the *circumstantiae* that Walsingham has chosen: *causa materialis* (12) and *ordo* (13). The bulk of the *accessus* is not spent answering these (only lines 13–17 do), but in explaining why Statius chose his material (1–11) and in summarizing the plot (18–32). As a whole, then, the *accessus* seems somewhat anachronistic. The only anomalous aspect of it is the note that Book 1 begins at 1.20. We find this separation in only a few other manuscripts,[75] and in such cases, we usually see the first nineteen lines of the poem labelled as the prologue.

Quaeritur accessus, and the fourth is simply a common historical note on Titus and Domitian, explaining why Statius chose his material.

[74] Kraków, Muzeum Narodowe, Biblioteka Czartoryskich, 1876 II, for example, contains a fifteenth-century note, "Venerandi magistri Stacii Pampinii et Sursuli, in omni facultate et scientia peritissimi."

[75] Kiel, Universitätabibliothek, KB B 45 (XV s.) and Kraków, Muzeum Narodowe, Biblioteka Czartoryskich, 1876 II (XII–XIII s.). Some manuscripts, such as Vaticano, Barb. lat. 33 (XIV s. ex./XV s. in.), have periochae that designate 1.20 as beginning the first chapter.

Text 21. *Accessus* to the *Achilleid*, from Thomas Walsingham, *Prohemium poetarum*

L = London, British Library, Harley 2693 (XV s.), 145v–146r

Stacius poeta commendatissimus, cuius nomen propter commendabilem
edicionem libri Thebaidos inter principum Thebanorum nomina litteris
aureis scriptum fuit, floruit temporibus Domiciani imperatoris. Iste
Domicianus rogauit Stacium vt componeret librum de gestis suis. Ipse
5   autem non audebat satisfacere voluntati Cesaris, donec ingenium suum
prius exercuisset in aliis quibusque gestis. Excusauitque se penes
Cesarem, quod oportuit eum primo experiri ingenium suum in gestis
Achillis, cuius probitatem extollere cupiebat. Scripsit ergo librum
Achilleidos, qui sic incipit: <1.1–2>

10   Magnanimum Eacidem, formidatamque tonanti
              Progeniem.

       Causa materialis igitur huius libri est vita Achillis. Causa
       formalis est modus et ordo tractandi. Ordo duplex est, ordo
       naturalis et ordo artificialis. Ordo naturalis est quando res narratur
15   sicut gesta fuit. Ordo artificialis est quando res narratur non sicut res
       est, sed per poemata.

       Primo suo capitulo presentis libri vtitur pro prologo in quo ponit
       ea de quibus intendit agere, scilicet de illis rebus vel factis que gessit
       Achilles antequam veniret ad Troiam, quomodo scilicet nutriuit eum
20   Chyron et qualiter mater sua eum abscondit in aula Lychomedis regis.

       Iste liber diuiditur in quinque libellis. In primo agit qualiter
       Chiron centaurus nutriuit Achillem. In secundo de sollicitudine
       matris sue Thetidis, qualiter filium suum transformare duxit et habitu
       suo | mutato in habitum femineum illum Lichomedi commendauit.   146r
25   Et ex post porrexit ad litus maris et ascendit excelsam rupem vt terram
       eligeret cui filium suum committeret, ne Greci ducerent eum ad
       Troiam. Iterum ostendit postea ludos puellarum quos fecera<n>t ad
       honorem Palladis, et decessum Thetidis ab illa patria. In tertio agit de
       absencia filii. In quarto de inquisicione Grecorum. In quinto de
30   induccione ad Troiam. In sexto debuit fecisse de induccione ad
       Capadociam, sed deficit propter mortem auctoris. Incipit autem primus
       liber sic <1.20–21>,

              Soluerat Ebalio classem de litore pastor
              Dardanus.

---

1 commendatissimus... Thebaidos (2)] *accessus* in Wolfenbüttel, 13.10 Aug. 4°, ll. 5–6
3 iste... suis (4)] cf. ibid., l. 7
12 causa²... tractandi (13)] *Casualis euentus accessus*, ll. 188–89
12 ordo¹... est (16)] cf. accessum in Escorial, ms. f.III.11 ll. 34–38
21 in... Troiam (30)] periocha quae inuenitur in Paris, BnF, lat. 8559 et al.

---

5 e *post* donec *eras.* L

The *accessus* attributed to Francesco Filelfo

We see a similarly broad adaptation of traditional texts in the *accessus* attributed to Francesco Filelfo[76] (preserved in Modena, Biblioteca Estense universitaria, Est. lat. 331 [α F.8.15] [XV s.]; Incipitarium 249), but we also find a wider interest in academic problems with the poem. Based on its incipit, for example, this *accessus* appears to embody a much more scholarly approach, harking back to Servius (1–4):

> *Sicud dicit Seruius in commentario Virgilii, in exponendis auctoribus non nulla prius consideranda esse, videlicet vita poete, titulus libri, scribentis intentio, qualitas carminis, numerus librorum, et poete materia.*

However, in spite of the scholarly tone, the *accessus* has little new information; indeed, outside of the many tangents that have very little to do with Statius, his *accessus* is at heart a careful rephrasing of the Carpentras *accessus*. A few selections will show the degree to which the author altered the original.

Table 5. Comparison of Ps.-Filelfo's and the Carpentras *accessus*

Filelfo	Carpentras
17–18: qui, uidens Romanos in uoluminibus summam poetarum delectationem habere, tunc cepit describere	5–6: plurimos poetas intuens in arte poetica glorie et fame titulis premiorum pollere muneribus, se ad artem poeticam transtulit
19–20: secundum aliquos, in illo simia Virgilii fuit	10–11: aliqui eum Virgilii simiam uocent
40–41: possit sicut docti uiri apud posteros phamam ac laudes sibi comparare	22–24: adeptam iam famam libri Thebaidos eternam posteris faciat, que est potissima omnium poetarum intentio

There are only a few details in the interpretation of the poem that cannot be derived from the Carpentras *accessus*. The first of these is the second *intentio* (ll. 41–42):

> *ut excitaret adolescentes alios laudibus Acchillis ad virtutem,*

which is, in turn, derived from the *accessus* in Escorial, El, Real Biblioteca, ms. f.III.11:

> *intentio sua est ut nos per uirtutes Achillis informet ad*
> *uirtutes, et doceat nos uitare desidiam et torporem.*

The second detail is the explanation of the *duplex inuocatio* to Apollo and Domitian at ll. 68–69:

> *inuocationem quoque duplicem facit Statius, unam*
> *ad deum Apollinem, alteram ad imperatorem Romanum*

which is related to the *accessus* in Düsseldorf, K2:F.50 (18–19):

---

[76] Tolentino 1398–Firenze 1481. A philologist and scholar of Greek, he was the most revered—if not the foremost—scholar of his day. On his scholarship, see *Francesco Filelfo nel quinto centenario della morte, atti del XVII convegno di studi maceratesi*, Medioevo e umanesimo 58 (1986) and D. Robin, *Filelfo in Milan* (Princeton, NJ, 1991). On his career, see G. Prezziner, *Storio del pubblico Studio e della Società scienttifiche e letteraria di Firenze*, vol. 1 (Firenze, 1819), 91–102 and G. Zippel, *Il Filelfo a Firenze (1429–1434)* (Roma, 1899). On his translations from Greek into Latin, see J. Hawkins, *Plato in the Italian Renaissance* (Leiden, 1990), 1.89–95.

> *sciendum est quod dupliciter facit inuocationem, scilicet ad Apollinem et ad Domi-*
> *cianum imperatorem.*

The third detail that is not in the Carpentras *accessus* is the discussion as to whether the poem is complete (24–26). This discussion is found in several other *accessus*,[77] such as the *accessus* in Wolfenbüttel, cod. 13.10 Aug. 4°, but the passage is so rewritten that a clear source cannot be assigned. Such is also the case with the last detail not derived from the Carpentras *accessus*, the discussion of the number of books, which notes Priscian as a source for the division of the *Achilleid* into two books, rather than five (35–39).[78]

The only strengths of the new *accessus* are that it is much more succinct than its original, and avoids hyperbole (e.g., *potissima* at line 23). As such, the *accessus* is a bit disappointing. One would hope that a scholar of Filelfo's stature could end the stalemate of Statian scholarship in this age, but we see no evidence of his "dinamismo intelletuale,"[79] and no evidence of Filelfo's own wisdom in the actual interpretation of the text; indeed, the only scholarly additions are of tangential material. But even in these, Filelfo is not at his best. In the discussion of the Year of the Four Emperors (ll. 10–11), for example, he curiously reverses the order of Vitellius and Otho, and, in the discussion of Homer (ll. 51–59), he describes the *Iliad* as "bella contra Troiam facta in honorem Acchillis seu Helene" (54), which, considering Filelfo's reputation as a Greek scholar, is surprisingly off-base.[80] Similarly, in the expanded discussion of the *tres artes* (ll. 66–74) the translation of the opening of the *Odyssey* is not by Filelfo but, rather, is taken from Horace (*Ars* 141–42, without citation).[81]

If this *accessus* is actually by Filelfo,[82] it demonstrates us the major problem in Statian scholarship in his day. Filelfo, it seems, was content to add no critical judgement of his sources, or even of the text. Further, we see no attempt to modernize or contemporize the previous tradition. All that we see, outside of the desire to refine and improve the tone of his model, is a desire to compose a "complete" *accessus*; that is, to compile all the information that was at hand.

---

[77] See de Angelis 1984.168 n. 121

[78] In the manuscripts of the poem, Priscian is mentioned as a source for the proper division of the books only here and in the fourteenth-century manuscript, Venezia, BNM, Zan. Lat. 541.

[79] This is the judgement of R. Bianchi ("Note di Francesco Filelfo al «De natura deorum», al «De oratore» e all' «Eneide» negli appunti di un notaio senese," in *Francesco Filelfo nel quinto centenario della morte, atti del XVII convegno di studi maceratesi*, Medioevo e umanesimo 58 (1986), 325–68 [328]); she contrasts this quality with the stagnant scholarship in Siena ("l'umanesimo senese rifluì in una fase di ristagno e di emarginazione," p. 328). See also V. Fera, "Itinerari filologici di Francesco Filelfo," in *Francesco Filelfo nel quinto centenario della morte, atti del XVII convegno di studi maceratesi*, Medioevo e umanesimo 58 (1986), 89–135, esp. 91–93.

[80] The spelling "Acchilles" is strange for a scholar who fought so bitterly for the proper spelling and transliteration of Greek words. See R. Ruboli, "Spunti filologici dall' epistolario del Filelfo," in *Francesco Filelfo nel quinto centenario della morte, atti del XVII convegno di studi maceratesi*, Medioevo e umanesimo 58 (1986), 137–62 [151–52]. The spelling could stem from a mistranscription of a Gothic or fractura original, where "Ac" could be seen as "Acc."

[81] On Filelfo's adaptations of Homer in his own poetry, see G. Albanese, "Le raccolte poetiche latine di Francesco Filelfo," in *Francesco Filelfo nel quinto centenario della morte, atti del XVII convegno di studi maceratesi*, Medioevo e umanesimo 58 (1986), 389–458 [414]. For examples of his insistence on transmitting the Greek together with his translations, see M. Cortesi, "Aspetti linguistici della cultura graeca di Francesco Filelfo," *ibid.*, 163–206. The usage of Greek in the commentary that follows the *accessus* is equally atypical. For example, the Greek for *Euhius* (*Ach.* 1.616, f. 17vb) is given as Ευλιοσ [sic], which is supposedly derived ευ (*bonum* [!]) and λιοσ [sic] (*filius*). This etymology is not derived from a Greek source (e.g. Sophocles, *OT* 211), but rather from Pseudacron (*Scholia in Horatium Vetustiora*, ed. O. Keller [Leipzig, 1902]), *ad Od.* 2.11.17. The mistranscription of Εὔιος seems to be derived from the same source: all of the manuscripts of Pseudacron's commentary transmit υἱός as *hios, hyos*, or *chios*; that is, without the upsilon. The author of our commentary to the *Achilleid* further compensated for the missing aspiration in the Greek by adding a lambda. (In all fairness, this could be a scribal error, but since the etymology and the absence of the upsilon derive from the same source, I find that solution doubtful.)

[82] The only other discussion of this text (de Angelis 1985.168 n. 121) occupies itself only with Filelfo's division of the poem into two books, and does not note any problems with the scholarship of the text.

Text 22. Pseudo-Filelfo's *accessus* to the *Achilleid*

M = Modena, Biblioteca Estense universitaria, α.F.8.15 (Est. lat. 331) (XV s.), 9ra–b

inscr.   Commentum Statii Achilleidos editum sub doctissimo uiro Francischo Fidelfo, et in primis, de vita ipsius poete.

<S>icud dicit Seruius in commentario Virgilii, in exponendis auctoribus non nulla prius consideranda esse, videlicet vita poete, titulus libri, scribentis intentio, qualitas carminis, numerus librorum, et poete materia.

5   Statii autem ut paucis expediam, vita hec est: ortus est patre Papino, familia uero Sarcula, ex ciuitate quadam Tolosa ciuis extitit, que ciuitas in Gallia est sita Transalpina. Iste autem a principio oratorie arti diligenter incubuit, in tantum quod rethor erat. Deinde se Romam contulit, tempore Neronis. Quo mortuo, propter eius
10   scelera electi fuerunt tres imperatores, scilicet Gabba, Vitelius, et Otthonus. Quibus extinctis Vespatianus successit, qui duos genuit filios, vnum sceleratissimum Domitianum, qui secundam in Christianos persequutionem ausus sit exercere, alterum uero mitissimum Titum, qui et fama sic est apud auctores, quod
15   quotiens quisque ad eum iratus esset acriter situs, in tanta pietate uitam ducebat, deposita ira recedere uolebat. Statius sub horum stetit imperio. Qui, uidens Romanos in uoluminibus summam poetarum delectationem habere, tunc cepit scribere. Et primo edidit opus Thebaidos in quo bella Thebana continentur. Secundum aliquos in
20   illo simia Virgilii fuit, nam quem ad modum Virgilius in sexto de inferis narrat, etiam Statius in aliis similiter libris. Deinde Statium Acchileidos, quem pre manibus habemus, composuit. <S>et istum propter repentinam mortem nullo modo explere potuit, quamquam aliqui dicant esse completum opus, quod esse non potest, ut in
25   propositione probare possumus, quando ait "Sed tota iuuenem deducere Troia," non ut superius dictum est. Et hoc de ipsius Statii uita.

Titulus operis est Statii Surculi Tholosani Papinii primus liber incipit. Dicitur enim titulus quia tutatur operis editorem.
30   Statii nomen proprium, Surculi familie nomen, Tolosani a ciuitate Tolosa, Papinii patris sui nomen, Acchilleidos, qui<a> tractatur de Acchille. Dicitur "Acchilleis" secundum quod Virgilius etiam in libri descriptione "Eneis" usus est. Et est sciendum secundum declinationem Graecam formatum Acchilleys, Acchillei, Acchilleis.

35   Numerus librorum: in duos tantum diuidit, in primum et secundum. Secundus uero finem non habet, ut dixi. Nichilominus aliqui indocti in V libros diuidere audent, quod nullo modo Priscianus posse fieri probat, quod hunc textum nisi in primo et secundo allegat. Intentionem auctoris duplicem fuisse facile
40   cognoscere possumus. Harum altera est ut possit sicut docti uiri apud posteros phamam ac laudes sibi comparare. Altera ut excitaret adolescentes alios laudibus Acchillis ad virtutem.

Qualitas carminis: ut breui colloquio extrinsecam explanationem absoluam, herroicum siue exametrum est carmen.
45   Heroes enim dicuntur qui sunt plus quam homines, minus quam dei,

ut Theseus et Acchilles. In hoc autem genere metri gesta heroum
describuntur et in eo Homerus semper versatus est. Vnde Oratius,

> Res geste regumque ducum<que> et tristia
> Bella, quo scribi possint numero monstrauit Homerus.

50   Exametrum dicitur eo quod habeat sex pedes, ab εξ, sex, et μετροσ, mensura.

Materia huius uoluminis est de Achille tractare, et est
sciendum Homerum duo uolumina edidisse, vnum Odissephs
nominatum, in quo facta scripsit Ulixis, alterum Illiados et ibi tractat
bella contra Troiam facta in honorem Acchillis seu Helene. Opus
55   illud in 48 libros diuisum est, quod Virgilius in XII transtulit,
nam quem ad|modum in Homerico opere Hector et Acchillis   9rb
ad inuicem bella conserunt, ita in Virgilio Eneas et Turnus. *Prelia
de Acchille in nono anno describere incepit, proceditque usque ad
Hectoris mortem.* Statius hec animaduertens dicit se uelle ab
60   infantia Acchillis incipere nec solum manere in interfectione
Hectoris, ut Homerus perfecit.

Hiis itaque diligenter inquisitis, paulatim potero litteram
exponere. Igitur etiam notandum est tres esse poeticas partes,
propositio, per quam proponunt de quibus siue rebus
65   tractaturi, quam omnes sequuntur poete, vt Virgilius, "Arma
uirumque cano," Lucanus,

> Bella per Emathios plus quam ciuilia campos
> Iusque datum sceleri canimus, populumque potentem;

inuocationem quoque duplicem facit Statius, unam ad deum
70   Apollinem, alteram ad imperatorem Romanum; narratio dein
per quam incipit tractare quo modo res sit gesta. Primo
uidetur facere secundum Homerum qui similiter inuocat et
proponit,

> Dic mihi, musa, uirum, capte post tempora Troie,
75   qui mores hominum multorum uidet et vrbes, et cetera.

---

1 Servius, *ad Aen.* 1.*praef.*1

17 qui... describere (18)] cf. Carpentras accessum, 5–7

19 secundum... fuit (20)] cf. *ibid.* 10–11

25–26 *Ach.* 1.7

38 videlicet *Inst. Gramm.* 7.65 (*GLK* 2.342.5–6)

40 possit... comparare (41)] cf. Carpentras accessum, 22–24

41 posteros] cf. Petrum de Caneffis de Parma, *Prohemium in Achilleidem* (Berkeley, CA, University of California, Bancroft Library, MS UCB 145), 76

41 ut... virtutem (42)] cf. accessum in Escorial f.III.11, ll. 70–72

48–49 *Ars* 73–74

65–66 *Aen.* 1.1

67–68 *BC* 1.1–2

69 inuocationem... Romanum (70)] cf. accessum in Düsseldorf, K2: F.49, ll. 18–19

74–75 Horatius, *Ars* 141–42

---

3 lib<ri> *post* qualitas *eras.* M   **6** familie M   **18** describere M   **57** prelia... mortem (59)] *fort. nota ad lin.* 54   **58** usque] videlicet M   **71** g (*pro* igitur?) *post* gesta *eras.* M

Conclusion

The fourteenth and early fifteenth centuries were a period of stagnation in scholarship on Statius. Even though we begin to find authorial texts and even though we find mention of contemporary scholars—suggesting some climate for scholarly debate—we find no originality in the *accessus*, either in their approach or in their form. The source of this problem seems to be the lack of firm details on Statius' biography, such that scholars had nothing more to work with than the scanty details in the *Quaeritur* and other early *accessus*, together with the fabrications of the previous centuries. Once again, scholars were reluctant to improvise. As we will see in the following chapter, when new information does enter the scene, *accessus* begin to show a great deal of scholarly activity, and the *accessus* that reflect this information, even though they are contemporary with the *accessus* we have just seen, have a markedly different flavor, tone, and style.

INTERPRETATION AFTER THE REDISCOVERY OF THE *SILVAE*

The rediscovery of classical texts in the fifteenth century was a powerful catalyst for a rebirth of classical scholarship. Newly recovered works, including those of Tacitus, Ausonius, Cicero, Catullus, Manilius, Silius Italicus, and Statius' *Silvae*—which represented a genre previously all but unknown to scholars—gave scholars the fodder needed to break from medieval scholasticism and return to humanist scholarship. This is, at least, the picture of themselves that scholars of the period paint of themselves. To be fair, previous scholars were, for the most part, well-trained philologists. What they lacked was resources. The coincidence of the newly discovered works and a more advanced way of promulgating these works—the printing press—led to a need to reevaluate all criticism since the ninth century and to the impetus needed to devise new academic methodologies. More importantly, it infused life into a discipline that had been unable to escape the shadows of the great scholars of the past and had thus grown stale and unoriginal.

The reception of the *Silvae* seems to have gone through three phases. In the first, scholars simply adapted the new data from the *Silvae* to the old data, resulting in very mixed treatises. In the second phase, scholars tried to correct the medieval interpretations by adapting the newly discovered materials to established forms of medieval exegesis. In the final stage, scholars began to introduce new information from Statius' *Silvae* and to rewrite Statius' biography almost completely.

Phase 1. The Wien 3114 *accessus*

Texts in the first phase typically display little knowledge of different *accessus* traditions and base their information only on indirect knowledge of the *Silvae*. A good example of this is the brief *accessus* in Wien, ÖNB, cod. 3114 (dated 1481; Incipitarium 268).

There are actually two *accessus* in this manuscript of the *Achilleid*, the first of which is loosely based on the *Quaeritur accessus*; the second is a representative of a fifteenth-century German tradition that shows no knowledge of the *Silvae*.[1] It is the first that we shall treat here.

The *accessus* begins with a restatement of the *Quaeritur accessus*, with a minor correction: Statius is now *Neapolitanus* (1–2). There then follows a typical catalog of virtues, including the familiar *doctus eloquio* and the note that he was *insigni morum vrbanitate conspicuus* (which we saw in the *In principio accessus* to the *Thebaid*). This *accessus* then lists the typical *intentiones* of the *Thebaid* (namely, that Statius sought to prevent the imperial brothers from fighting) and of the *Achilleid* (that he sought to sharpen his poetical abilities), but does not mention the *Silvae*.

The allegory of the name *Sursulus* that follows expands on the "shoot" interpretation that we have seen before, with the exception that here, the name is used to reflect Statius' superiority over his contemporaries (12–13):

> *Quidam autem dicunt Sursulus, quoniam surculus frons est nouellus. Ergo et ipse excreuit inter alios poetas quasi iterum nouellus suo euo, uero successiue excrescebat in succis.*

To the author, the validity of the name *Surculus* does not come into question. However, the text continues and the author sets himself against previous tradition by noting that Statius did not

---

[1] The *accessus* seems to be descended from the same original which Augsburg, 4° Cod. 21 (25v–26v) and Kraków, Biblioteca Jagiellońska, 525 III (111r) rewrite. The *accessus* in Olomouc, Státní vědecká knihovna, M.I.167, is related to the Wien version, and may represent a Bohemian tradition; see sigla O and V in Appendix I).

come from Gaul. The confusion, he goes on to explain, stems from confusion with Caecilius Statius, the comic poet and contemporary of Ennius (and a Greek)[2] who, according to this *accessus*, came from Gaul.[3]

This text shows one of the most prominent trends that we find in Statian scholarship before the development of the printed book. The *Silvae* are specifically mentioned in only a handful of *accessus* to Statius, and outside of the major commentaries and extremely learned *accessus*, most authors are content only to change the notes about Statius' homeland, without realizing that much more was critically at stake. We see again that Statius' biography was seen as comparatively unimportant. Here, for example, even though evidence concerning his personal life was available, this scholar chose not to use it (other than to correct the most glaring error). It is, rather, the style and the rhetorical and moral aspect of the poems that were of greatest interest. Why this was the case is unclear, but I suspect that the scholarship reflected the work at hand. Statius is personally present in only some 30 lines in his epics, but he plays a very emphatic (and certainly exaggerated) role in the *Silvae*, and, as we will see below, it will be the scholars who are familiar with the *Silvae* who are interested in Statius' personality.

---

[2] The source of this may have been Aulus Gellius, 2.23, where passages from the *Plocium* are placed alongside their Greek originals and used as examples of the process of *vortere*.

[3] The source of this is undoubtedly Volcacius Sedigitus (1.5), who claimed that the poet came from Cisalpine Gaul. Jerome (*Chron. a. Abr.* 1839, taken from Suetonius) claims that he was an Insubrian, likely having been born in Milan. Aulus Gellius (4.20.12 and 13) claims that he was a slave. Politian also suggests Caecilius Statius as a possible source of the confusion. See his *Vita Statii* in L. Martinelli Cesarini, 8.9–12. The only instances I have come across in which Caecilius Statius is identified with our Statius are all late: Bruxelles, BR, 21891 (XV s.); Paris, BnF, ital. 557 (XV s.); and chapter 61 of Vincentius Burgundus' *Speculi maioris* (first printed in the late fifteenth century).

Text 23. The Wien 3114 *accessus* to the *Achilleid*

W = Wien, Österreichische Nationalbibliothek, 3114 (dated 1481), 109v

Stacius Neapolitanus tempore Vespesiani imperatoris fuisse dicitur et
ad Domiciani filii sui tempora vsque peruenisse. Homo quid fuit
ortu et ingenio non degener. Doctus eloquio et insigni morum
vrbanitate conspicuus, priusquam Thebaidem scriberet ad
5   instructionem Tyti et Domiciani fratrum ne de imperio dissiderent,
ad examinandum et exercendum ingenium suum, hoc opus
aggreditur, nam sibi Achilleiden, i.e. hystoriam de Achille
assumpsit ut ad animositatem et virtutes eos cohortetur. Est ergo
tytulus Stacii Pampinii Sursuli liber Achilleidum incipit. Stacius
10   proprium nomen, Pampinius cognomen, Sursulus uero agnomen,
quasi sursum canens. Quidam autem dicunt Sursulus quoniam surculus
frons est nouellus. <Er>go et ipse excreuit inter alios poetas quasi
iterum nouellus suo euo, uero successiue excrescebat in factis. Licet
et alter Stacii Grecus et poeta fuerat tempore Ennii poete quem
15   Tolonensem vocant, Gallicum fuisse ayunt, plerumque igitur ab
ignoranti<b>us nomina confunduntur eorum. Hic in omnibus
operibus suis honestis et artificiosis prohemii<s> vsus est ut per hoc
auditores excitet ad materiam preelectam anteponendo eis de quo in
opere suo toto sit dicturus. Cum exordiis auditorum beneuolentia,
20   docilitas et attencio conpara<n>tur, ut habet.

---

1 tempore... peruenisse (2)] cf. *Quaeritur accessus*, ll. 1–2
3 doctus eloquio] cf. *Quaeritur accessum*, l. 7 et *In principio accessum* 19–21: *Fuit autem
    morum honestate preditus... doctus eloquio.*
8 animositate] cf. Linc. 27, 79 (sed de Diomede)

---

2 sua W   **4** thebaidum W   **5** institucionem W   **12** nouellos W

Phase 2. Nicolaus Perottus and Pomponius Laetus

The first *accessus* that realized the scholarly importance of the *Silvae* poems sought to incorporate the poems into old and respected traditions.[4] This is best exemplified by the *accessus* to the commentary on the *Silvae* of Nicolaus Perottus (1430–1480), which he wrote in 1472.[5]

The *accessus* mimics the style and language of the *Quaeritur accessus*, the only additional material being the correction of Statius' nationality in lines 1–2 ("P. Papinius Statius poeta Neapolitanus fuit, ut ipse diuersis in locis testatur") and 11–13:

> *Quidam ignari eum Tholossensem dixerunt fuisse, ducti in errorem similitudine nominis alterius Statii Ursuli oratoris qui Tholossensis fuit et Neronis tempore rhetoricum in Gallia celeberrime docuit.*

The only "new" part of the *accessus* is at the very end, an 11-line discussion of the genre *silvae* (which he derived from the Greek word ὕλη) and a citation from Quintilian on the merits of the genre, which is probably meant to mirror the citation from Juvenal as an ancient authority.

The most noteworthy aspect of this text, aside from its similarities to the *Quaeritur accessus* is the emphasis placed on correcting Statius' bibliography. All manuscripts of the *Silvae* that contain any annotation whatsoever have notes to the passages that identify Statius as being Neapolitan, especially passages in 1.2,[6] 3.5[7] and 5.3,[8] and some other *vitae* and *accessus* have been corrected by later hands,[9] which shows to some degree what a matter of academic debate it was.

The debate was to no little degree fostered by the *editio princeps* of the *Thebaid* and *Achilleid*, which was apparently publshed in Rome in 1470 or 1471. The edition, as I have demonstrated elsewhere, was copied, glosses and all, from the Carpentras manuscript and transmits the *accessus* to the *Achilleid* as well several mythological prefaces to the *Thebaid* that are no longer part of the Carpentras manuscript.[10] It was printed using the same type as Flavius Blondus' *Roma instaurata*, likely edited by Gaspar Blondus and printed perhaps in Rome, before 6 August 1471, when the copy in the Bibliothèque nationale in Paris was purchased.[11]

The edition is fraught with errors. First, the chosen manuscript had several poor readings, had many lines added in the margins and had a very sloppy format,[12] and as a result, many corrections in the manuscript, including corrected words and inserted lines, were not transmitted to the printed version. The manuscript had two advantages: it was written in a clear hand that used

---

[4] On this practice in late–fifteenth century scholarship, cf. Coulson 1997, especially in the treatment of Bonus Accursius.

[5] It is worth noting that *accessus* to the *Thebaid* drop off heavily in number in the end of the fifteenth century. I have found only a few *accessus* to the *Thebaid* that mention the *Silvae*, while there are several *accessus* to the *Achilleid* that do.

[6] E.g. Firenze, BML, plut. 38.13, *ad* 1.2.260: "Papinius Statius Neapolitanus fuit."

[7] E.g. Firenze, Biblioteca del Seminario maggiore Archivescovile, B.V.2 *ad* 3.5.78: "hec excerpsi quoniam omnes Gallum et Tholosanum Statium fuisse dicunt cum ipse patriam Neapolim recognoscat."

[8] E.g. Vaticano, Vat. lat. 3282 *ad* 5.4.104–106: "Neapoli plane fatetur et in epicedio defuncti patris ita ad Neapolim apostrophat."

[9] In one witness of Giovanni Colonna's *De viris illustribus*—Vaticano, Barb. lat. 2351—the word *Tholosa* has been scratched out, and in one witness of Petrus Decembrius' *Lives of the Poets*—Firenze, Ricc. 907—a marginal note corrects the text. Cf. too, Vaticano, Chigi, H.VI.210 where a hand has underscored *Surculus* and *Tholosanus*.

[10] The first gathering and the first two folia of the second gathering in the Carpentras manuscript are now wanting.

[11] See BMC IV.143, and plate XIII*.

[12] The pages seldom have the same number of lines, which made casting off difficult, and the marginal notes fill the page, making scribal corrections difficult to find on the page.

little abbreviation and it had a commentary. Second, two compositors (or type-setters) worked on the project. The first, who did not have good Latin skills, copied the manuscript doggedly, including the spellings *maijster* for *magister* and *michi* for *mihi*. The second type-setter modernized the spelling of the manuscript and made a few emendations. As a result, the edition is rather Janus-like, looking both backwards and forwards at once. The most important aspect of the edition for us is the commentary, which most noteably says that Statius was from Toulouse and that the *Achilleid* was written in response to an argument about predestination.

Some time between spring of 1469, when he was released from prison, and July 26–27, 1471, when Paulus II died,[13] Pomponius Laetus composed a commentary on the *Thebaid*, now Vaticano, Vat. lat. 3279. The manuscript contains two texts that are of immediate interest to us: a *vita Statii* on ff. 1r–2r (Incipitarium 179) and a mythological preface to the *Thebaid* on f. 2v (Incipitarium 95). The second of these is transmitted in only one other witness, the *editio princeps* (on f. 2r), and the relationship between the two witnesses becomes clearer when we see that the commentary is dedicated to the son of a certain Blondus. As there was no other prominent Blondus active in Italy at this point, this must refer to Caspar Blondus, the editor of the *Roma instaurata* and the probable editor of the *editio princeps* of Statius. When we further consider that the details discussed in the *vita* are only those issues found in the Carpentras *accessus*, it becomes clear that Laetus' *vita* was written in direct response to the *accessus* in the *editio princeps*.

In the *vita*, Laetus begins with a description of his methodology:

> *Nuper de Papinii vita sermo fuit quae ignota est ut aliorum fere poetarum. Scripsere ueteres sed neglegentia quadam talia posteri contempsere. Nec mirum, nam illustria Romanorum monumenta pene extincta sunt et nisi Grẹca lingua opem tulisset de tam magna re publica atque imperio maior pars desideraretur. Necesse ergo est hinc inde colligere, ut faciunt agricole in inculto campo, plerumque tamen siquẹ bone herbe sunt sub insalubribus ita latent ut inueniri nequeant* (1–8).

Essentially, Laetus associates himself with the Greek tradition as opposed to the *posteri* who have allowed Rome to perish. His methodology, which is a typical claim for this time, is to constantly dig and examine. Essentially, the key to good research is a good search.[14] Now, Laetus is very careful not to directly insult his dedicatee's father, but he depicts him, ipso facto, as part of the ignorant *posteri* who believe that the true and the obvious are the same. But how valid are Laetus' claims?

What Greek there is in the commentary is etymological only and all the details that Laetus "researched" are taken directly from the *Silvae*, although he does include some details that were taken from other medieval traditions, including the identity of Statius' mother (line 19). He seems to have used few other works and seems not to have investigated all of the data he used. In essence, although Laetus espouses "modernity," only his facts are modern—his methods are not. This becomes more apparent when we examine the brief explanation of the *Achilleid*.

---

[13] He is mentioned in the notes on, 1.2.484. See Zabughin 1909.2.25.

[14] Cf. Bonus Accursius Pisanus, *Vita Ovidii*: "... Qua quidem in re nihil equidem noui ex me ipso afferam, id quod facere nonnulli consueuerunt, ostentationis magis cupidi quam ueritatis. At ego ita de hoc poeta uerba facturus sum ut quicquid dixero, id ex eiusdem operibus a me collectum liquido appareat..." (ed. Venetia, 1486, I.2r). See Coulson-Roy 84.

In the Carpentras *accessus*, the origin of the *Achilleid* was traced to a debate about predestination. In discrediting the *accessus*, Blondus posits a different explanation: the *Achilleid* was written to guide Crispinus in his military training, a statement that he derives from *Silvae* 5.2.8–9:

> *Quid? si militiae iam te, puer inclite, primae*
> *clara rudimenta et castrorum dulce vocaret...*

This is not advanced criticism. Although Laetus is eager to point out errors in the tradition, he only points out errors that are contradicted directly or indirectly by the *Silvae* and then provides the "correct" information. That is, he does not examine the validity of the preexisting information. The *Silvae* are thus the programmatic and allegorical source for all of Laetus' corrections. This methodology effectively ties Laetus to the scholarly interests and methodology of his predecessors, and this is something that medieval scholars could have (and perhaps would have) done, had they had the *Silvae*.

Text 24. Nicolaus Perottus' *accessus* to the *Silvae*

V = Vaticano, Città del, Biblioteca Apostolica Vaticana, Vat. lat. 6835 (anno 1472), 55r

P. Papinius Statius poeta Neapolitanus fuit, ut ipse diuersis in locis
testatur. Claruit tempore Domiciani imperatoris, quanquan
Vespasiani temporis Thebaida incepisset. Nobili ortus est prosapia et
magno honore habitus. Huius satyrus noster ita meminit <Juv., *Sat.* 7.82–86>:

5   Curritur ad uocem iocundam et carmen amice
       Thebaidos, letam quum fecit Statius urbem:
       Promisitque diem. Tanta dulcedine captos
       Afficit ille animos tantaque libidine uulgi
       Auditur, sed cum fregit subsellia uersu
10   Exurit (!), intactam Paridi nisi uendat Agauen.

Quidam ignari eum Tholossensem dixerunt fuisse, ducti in errorem
similitudine nominis alterius Statii Ursuli oratoris qui Tholossensis
fuit et Neronis tempore rhetoricum in Gallia celeberrime docuit.

       Hoc opus in circo Siluarum inscribitur quia, ut ipse poeta
15   inquit, hi libelli subito calore et quadam festinandi uoluptate ei
       fluxerunt. Hoc enim festinum scribendi genus silua dicitur, quod
       sit quasi prima materia, nam ὕλη, unde silua dicitur, apud Grecos
       materiam significat. Quintilianus libro decimo <*IO* 10.3.17>:

       Diuersum est huic eorum uitium, quod primo decurrere
20   per materiam stilo quam uelocissimo uolunt et sequentes
       calorem atque impetum ex tempore scribant, hanc
       siluam uocant. Repetunt deinde et componunt quae
       effuderant, sed uerba emendantur et numeri manet in
       rebus temere congestis, quae fuit leuita<s>.

2–13 claruit... docuit] cf. *Quaeritur* accessum
15–16 cf. *Silv.* 1.*praef.*3–4

---

3 incoepisset (*subpunc.*) V

Text 25. Pomponius Laetus' *Vita Statii*

V = Vaticano, Città del, Biblioteca Apostolica Vaticana, Vat. lat. 3279 (XV s.), 1r–2r

Nuper de Papinii vita sermo fuit quae ignota est ut aliorum fere
poetarum. Scripsere ueteres sed neglegentia quadam talia posteri
contempsere. Nec mirum, nam illustria Romanorum monumenta
pene extincta sunt et nisi Grẹca lingua opem tulisset de tam magna re
5   publica atque imperio maior pars desideraretur. Necesse ergo est
hinc inde colligere, ut faciunt agricole in inculto campo, plerumque
tamen siquẹ bone herbe sunt sub insalubribus ita latent ut inueniri
nequeant. Blondus pater tuus summa diligentia multorum saeculorum
historias in lucem reduxit; ipse uero si non adeo diligens, eo quo potui
10   labore, de qua locuti sumus uitam perquisiui nec patre in silentium
dato in haec uerba digessi.

P. Papinius Statius pater Greca et Romana lingua eruditus ad
nouissimum usque diem professus est summo honore apud
Domitianum habitus. A quo auro donatus et corona digno principe
15   erga praeceptorem munere. Primus genus suum propter inopiam
oblitteratum, celebritate nominis celebre fecit, adeoque claruit, ut   1v
quod Homero, ei contig<er>it. Due enim urbes, Selle Epyrotarum et
Neapolis Campanorum de <eius> natali solo certabant. Ex qua intelligi
facile potest quanto in pretio littere fuerunt. Ex Agelina uxore, quam
20   unicam habuit, et cuius superstes fuit, P. Papinium Statium suscepit,
cuius pueritiam ac iuuentutem litteris fouit, copia varietateque rerum
refersit, et omne eius studium, quoad vixit, juuit operaque castigauit.
Senex vicio inexpergibilis somni periit.

Papinius filius, juuenis admodum, Claudiam Claudii Apollinaris
25   filiam impatiens amoris uxorem duxit, cui tanta modestia atque castitas
et amoris obseruantia fuit ut matrimonialem fidem absentia mariti XX
annis non fraudarit. Vergens ad senium eam Neapolim comunem
patriam reuocauit. Ambigitur quis superstes fuerit. Albe, Domitianus
Cesar, eadem qua patrem qui prẹsens erat, filium corona muniuit, et
30   auro insigniuit. Qua ex re non ingratus, Poeta Thebaida et Achillem
dignissimo Cesaris numini consecrauit.

Thebaida uero ut ipse ait, multa cruciauit lima, ac Junii Maximi
eloquentissimi viri iudicio publicauit. Cum Achillis etatem caneret,
absentem Crispinum, Vectij Bolani filium, clarum militia juuenem   2r
35   mente formauit; vtrumque opus graue uero et in altero copia rerum
magnitudo ingenii et ineuitabile mortalium fatum. In altero indoles
magni ducis exprimitur unde cognoscimus Virgilii quem ipse
magistrum fatetur sepulchrum coluisse, Siluarum libros V edidit, in
quibus et amicos et fortunam poete nosces. Hos ex omni parte
40   corruptos multa uigilia et laudabili industria Niclaus Perotta Pontifex
Sipontinus, in quo ut mea fert opinio tantum acuminis atque doctrine ad
interpretandum est, quantum ueteres habuerunt, emendat aperitque.
Habes non de filio tantum sed et de patre que legi; perquire tu, forte
aliquid amplius adicies, nam elucubratio duorum maior est quam unius.

45   Interea, non minus hoc legentibus si probaueris quam quod de
Lucano superiore anno Fabio Ambusto scripsimus gratum fore spero.

Vale.

17 Selle] *Silv.* 5.3.127: Sele Mss.

31 numini *ex* nomini V

Phase 3. The Ottob. lat. 1261 *accessus*

Laetus' *vita Statii* demonstrated the limits to which medieval styles and methodology could be used to correct previous traditions, in that the scholar was trapped as to what aspects of a text he could discuss or explain. In this third phase, scholars began to do what Laetus claimed to do but didn't do—that is, to dig for information. Unlike Laetus, their interest is not so much in correcting the previous information as in adding new information and expanding their interpretation and rewriting Statius' biography. This would result much more in a break from tradition, in that scholars began to ask new questions and to see aspects of a text that would not fit into the Servian mode of exegesis. It is this path that would eventually result in the removal of the previous academic definitions and norms.

A good example of the beginning of this process is the *accessus* to the *Achilleid* in Vaticano, Ottob. lat. 1261 (dated 1435; Incipitarium 223), which rewrites the Carpentras *accessus* by adding details from the *Silvae*. The *accessus* is methodologically very awkward, in that it juxtaposes old and new information, as the author tries to fit all of the new information into the *accessus* scheme. The tension is apparent from the very beginning (1–2):

> *P. Statius Papinius ortus fuit patre P. Statio Papinio libertini generis homine, matre uero Agelina, ciuis fuit Neapolitanus.*

The author of this *accessus*, who apparently knew several other *accessus* to Statius,[15] used the Carpentras *accessus* as a basis to change only the information that was contrary to that in the *Silvae*, adding some information from Servius.[16] The reason for this is that the author saw only two errors with the previous tradition, Statius' birthplace and when he wrote, both of which he attributed to confusion with Jerome's Statius Ursulus (120–23).[17] The author, then, only corrected the glaringly wrong aspects of the tradition and perpetuated some non-evident errors, including the name of Statius' mother (2) and the fact that he wrote the *Thebaid* before coming to Rome (131–32); further, he retains the fictive *intentio* (i.e. the *questio* in Domitian's court, 133) and *qualitas* of the poem (58 ff.) that are found in the Carpentras *accessus*.

The details that are added show a wider interest in Statius' personal life. From the *Silvae*, the author took the name of Statius' wife (26–28, from *Silv.* 3.*praef.* 22), which falls under the category of *vita*; his Alban success and Capitoline loss (23–25, from *Silv.* 3.5.28–31), which fall under the category of *modus tractandi*; and his friendship with Crispinus (147, from *Silv.* 3.2), under the rubric of *quibus auxiliis*. What is most interesting in these additions is the beginning of a new interpretation of Domitian. Although the emperor retains the image of the philosopher-king (arising from the tale of his court), the author of this *accessus* adds the note that Statius—who seems here to retain his moral character—returned to Naples because of the emperor's increased vices (50–53).[18]

---

[15] He shows direct knowledge of the fourteenth-century Carpentras *accessus*; the late–twelfth century KP *accessus*; and the *accessus* in Venezia, BnM, Lat. XII.61 (XV s. ex.) (Incipitarium, nrr. 31 and 294), and indirect knowledge of the Oxford, Lincoln College 27 *accessus* (XII s. in.); Thomas Walsingham (XV s.), and the *In principio accessus* (XII s. ex.).

[16] The *titulus* (54–57) and *stilus scribendi* (58–63) are taken from the Servian *accessus* (see p. I).

[17] The author of this *accessus*, like Politian, Perottus, and Gevartius in their commentaries, is vituperative and hastens to find as many faults with previous scholars as possible. It is worth noting that the discrepancy between Jerome's date and the date preferred by the *Quaeritur accessus* never really caused much dispute before the discovery of the *Silvae*.

[18] This information ultimately derives from *Silv.* 3.5, combined with information from Juvenal 7.86 (cf. line 52: *necessarium egens*). Statius' problems with Domitian become a sort of a *topos* in later criticism, with one example being the tradition mentioned by Crinitus that Statius was murdered by Domitian (above, p. 66 n. 10).

What we see, then, in this *accessus*, is a curious, intentional mixture of details from the old and new traditions,[19] using a wide breadth of sources, including all three of Statius' poems, as well as Aulus Gellius, Juvenal, Ovid, Terence, and even Dante, [20] mixing Greek, Latin, and Italian. The author did not wish to break fully from the previous tradition (or did not think it necessary), although he does make an issue of the errors that have been committed before, especially, as is often the case with the late humanists, those of Dante. More importantly, this *accessus* anticipates one aspect of criticism that would come to the forefront in the next century: the undermining of medieval boundaries and methodologies, specifically in the dissolution of the medieval idea of *circumstantiae*.[21]

This *accessus* proved very influential in the following centuries. The text is found in two manuscripts, Vaticano, Ottob. lat. 1261 and a sixteenth-century *codex descriptus*, Ottob. lat. 2027,[22] it is transmitted anonymously,[23] and it displays an overwhelmingly broad knowledge of the different *accessus* to Statius. In spite of its thin pattern of transmission, the text was heavily used and rewritten in the following centuries. The *De Achilleide* of Franciscus Maturantius (*editio princeps* Roma, 1475); Domitius Calderinus' commentary to the *Achilleid* (*editio princeps* Roma, A. Pannartz, 1475); Ioannes Britanneus Brixeus' *Interpretatio in Achilleida Statii* (Brixiae: Iacobum Britannicum, 1485); and the *vita Statii* in Gyraldus' *De poetarum historia dialogus*, Book 4 (ca. 1535), are at least heavily indebted to it. Indeed, Maturantius'[24] treatise, which is extant in at least two versions,[25] is so similar that it is probably only a rewriting of this *accessus*.

These printed editions present us with another problem. The *accessus* in Vaticano, Ottob. lat. 1261 has occasional interlinear and marginal notes and corrections.[26] The printed editions preserve the non-corrected version of the text for the most part, but also transmit some of the interpolated material.[27] The following table shows some of the relationships among the manuscript and the printed *vitae*.[28]

---

[19] It is not until the commentaries of Politian and Perotti that scholars begin to realize that the entire medieval view of Statius' biography was false.

[20] Although the quotation (102–107) has errors, I have been unable to use them to trace its manuscript tradition. Note the mock deferentiality to Dante in lines 118–28, especially "sed parcant obsecro nobis eius manes" (121).

[21] Cf. the *accessus* to the *Silvae* of Ponticus Virunius (Modena, Biblioteca Estense universitaria, Est. Lat. 677 [α.S.4.4], fol. 1r): "Ad explanationem accedamus, non autem ut barbari qui dicunt "scientiam quero"... et de auctore interrogati nesciant respondere. Sed ut antique facere soliti, tam Græci quam Latini, incipiamus. Ac in primis si quis alterioris doctrinæ quęrereret de operis, subiecto, cui parti philosophię subiciantur hę Syluę, respondeo toti philosophię in generali. Magno enim errore tenentur qui dicunt opera poetarum philosophię morali subiici ob sententias morales et utiles... ."

[22] This was first noted by Sweeney 1969.44.

[23] I have been unable to find a similar hand in the study of A. de la Mare, *The Handwriting of Italian Humanists* (Oxford, 1973).

[24] Francesco Maturànzio of Perugia, 1443–1518

[25] There is a shorter version that is found, *inter al.*, in the 1651 London edition (ed. Thomas Stephens), and seems to be the results of a later recension.

[26] Vaticano, Ottob. lat. 2027 favors the corrections over the original errors.

[27] Cf. the note *inexpergiscibili somno* (l. 21), which is interpolated and favored by the later editions.

[28] I do not reproduce the entire text of the printed editions. Italicized words are direct quotations; italicized words are taken out of sequence for the purpose of clarity; bracketed words are interpolations by the later hand.

Table 6. Derivatives of the Ottob. lat. 1261 *accessus*

Ottob. lat. 1261	Franciscus Maturantius	Ioannes Britanneus
P. Statius Papinius ortus fuit patre P. Statio Papinio libertini generis homine, matre uero Agelina, ciuis fuit Neapolitanus... . Ipse enim pater utraque doctus lingua, omnia filii studia fouit quoad uixit. Qui post suam a Sellis Epiri oppido migrationem ad extremum usque diem antiquorum scriptorum enarrationem professus est magno patritiorum adolescentium conuentu et maxime apud Domitianum gratiosus, a quo quidem et auro et corona donatus. Abiit ut pote grato et principe et discipulo in preceptorem. Is genus suum egestate et inopia obscuratum primus propria nominis celebritate ita clarum reddidit, ut due patrie, Selle et Epiri oppidum et Neapolis Campanie ciuitas suum ciuem esse contendant.	Publius Papinius Statius, P. Papinii Statii Pater, ex Agelina uxore *utraque lingua* eruditus, *ad* nouissimum *usque diem* professus est; et summo honore *apud Domitianum* habitus. nam *auro & corona* ab eo *donatus* est, digno principe erga *praeceptorem* munere. *genus suum* propter inopiam obliteratum, primus *celebritate nominis* celebre *reddidit*: adeoque claruit, ut quod Homero, ei contigerit. duae enim urbes, *Sellae Epirotarum, & Neapolis Campanorum*, de eius natali solo certarunt.	Natus Statio *libertini generis homine*,
Hic demum senex lethargo interiit. [Lethargus et ueternus is traditur esse morbus qui vulgo sobetia dicitur, cum quis inexpergiscibili[29] somno corripitur]	senex *inexpergiscibili* somni uitio periit	
Amoris impatiens, Claudiam Claudii Apollinaris filiam viduam in vrbe duxit vxorem.	*Claudiam Claudii Apollinaris* filiam *duxit uxorem, amoris impatiens*	*Vxorem Claudiam uiduam duxit in urbe* filiam Claudii Apollinaris.
Neapolim se recepit prope iam senex Thebaide prius edita,		senex in patriam secessit. *edita prius Thebaide*
patris et amicorum iudicio, in primisque Iunii Maximi viri disertissimi	Thebaida & Achilleidem optime de se meriti imperatoris nomini consecrauit: & Thebaida quidem, ut ipse ait, multa cruciauit lima: ac *Junii Maximi uiri* eloquentissimi *iudicio* publicauit. Caesar Domitianus *Albae*, eadem qua patrem prius *corona insigni*uit, *bisque auro don*auit	
et Domitiano dedicata, a quo Albe corona fuerat insignitus, et bis auro donatus, quemadmodum prius fuerat pater liberaliter acceptus.		

---

[29] This word is unattested in the standard lexica. The only occurrences I have found are in this context, with specific reference to Statius' father.

Ottob. lat. 1261	Franciscus Maturantius	Ioannes Britanneus
Scripsit idem v Syluarum libros in quibus assentatur imperatori et amicis blanditur. Imperatoris autem animo ad auaritiam, rapinamque conuerso, rerum etiam necessariarum egenus, in patriam reuersus, moritur annum iam agens (ex interiit) circiter L, relicta (ex superstite) filia et obscuris nepotibus.	*scripsit Syluarum libros quinque, in quibus* fortunam & amicos poeta cognoscit. Achillis aetatem scribere orsus; | morte interceptus est	dum Syluas, quo opere *imperatori & amicis blanditur,* scribit. ubi *etiam rerum necessarium egens* mortem obiit, *superstite filia et nepotibus obscuris*

Text 26. The Ottob. lat. 1261 *accessus* to the *Achilleid*

V = Vaticano, Città del, Biblioteca Apostolica Vaticana, Ottob. lat. 1261 (dated 1435), 7r–8r

P. Statii Papinii Vita

P. Statius Papinius ortus fuit patre P. Statio Papinio libertini generis
homine, matre uero Agelina, ciuis fuit Neapolitanus, ad poeticen ab
ineunte pueritia patris cura et eruditione formatus. Ipse enim pater
utraque doctus lingua, omnia filii studia fouit quoad uixit. Qui post

5   suam a Sellis Epiri oppido migrationem ad extremum usque diem
antiquorum scriptorum enarrationem professus est magno
patriciorum adolescentium conuentu et maxime apud Domitianum
gratiosus, a quo quidem et auro et corona donatus. Abiit ut pote
grato et principe et discipulo in pręceptorem. Is genus suum egestate

10   et inopia obscuratum primus propria nominis celebritate ita clarum
reddidit, ut duę patrię, Sellę Epirotarum et Neapolis Campanię
ciuitas suum ciuem esse contendant, quemadmodum de Homero hoc
distichon legimus apud Gellium <*Epigr. in Gell.* 3.11>:

ἑπτὰ πόλεισ διερίζουσι περὶ ριζαν Ὁμήρου
15   Σμύρνα, Ῥοδοσ, Κολοφων, Σαλαμὶν, Ἰοσ,
Ἄργοσ, Ἀθῆναι

id est, sep<tem> v<rbes> c<ontendunt> d<e> s<tirpe>
i<llius?> H<omeri >, S<myrna>, R<hodus>, C<olophon>,
S<alamin>, I<os>, A<rgos>, A<thenę>. Hic demum senex

20   lęthargo interiit. *Lethargus et ueternus is traditur esse morbus qui*
vulgo sobetia dicitur, cum quis inexpergiscibili somno corripitur.

Ipse uero Papinius filius admodum iuuenis Neapoli prima
posuit rudimenta ludis quinquennalibus. Mox Romę quinquatribus
Albanis ter de poetis coronam meruit. In certamine Capitolio antea

25   uictus ruborem et confusionem ętate et occupationibus excusat.
Amoris impatiens, Claudiam Claudii Apollinaris filiam viduam in
vrbe duxit vxorem, ex qua filiam susceptam adultamque quoniam rei
familiaris tenuitate collocare et maritare non posset, Neapolim se
recepit *prope* iam senex Thebaide prius edita, patris et amicorum

30   iudicio, in primisque Iunii Maximi viri disertissimi, et Domitiano
consecrata, a quo Albę corona fuerat insignitus, et bis auro donatus,
quemadmodum prius fuerat pater liberaliter acceptus. In eadem uero
Thebaide, quam ipse ait se multa cruciasse lima, imitatus est
Maronem principem poetarum, atque ita est imitatus ut a nonnullis

35   Virgilii simius dictus sit. Hinc ipse in calce eiusdem operis Ęneida
laudibus efferens, Thebaidem sic suam alloquitur <*Theb.* 12.811–12>:

O mihi bissenos multum uigilata per annos
Thebai

et paulo infra <*Theb.* 12.816–17>:

40   Viue precor, nec tu d<iuinam> Ę<neidem> t<emta> s<ed>
l<onge> s<equere> et v<estigia> s<emper> a<dora>

Hoc idem etiam in libello ad Marcellum scripto sic ipse ingenue fatetur
<*Silv.* 4.4.53–55>:

tenues ignauo pollice chordas

45 Pulso Maroneique sedens in margine templi
Sumo animum et magni tumulis accanto magistri.

Quantum autem huius extiterit flumen eloquentię Iuuenalis ostendit,
quamuis satyrice, cum ait <*Sat.* 7.82–83>:

Curritur ad uocem iuucundam et carmen amicę
50 Thebaidos, lętam dum fecit Statius vrbem.

Scripsit idem V Syluarum libros in quibus assentiatur imperatori et
amicis blanditur. Imperatoris autem animo ad auaritiam rapinamque
conuerso, rerum etiam necessariarum egenus, in patriam reuersus,
interiit, superstite filia et obscuris nepotibus.

55 Titulus huius operis est Achilleis, deriuatum nomen ab Achille ut ab
Ęnea Ęneis, a Theseo Theseis, vt illud quod diximus <*Theb.* 12.816>:

Nec tu diuinam Ęneida temta

et item illud <Juv., *Sat.* 1.2>:

Vexit toties rauci Theseide Cordi.

60 De carminis qualitate nulla hic dubitatio. Patet enim metrum esse
heroicum. Actus uero est mixtus, vbi et poeta loquitur et alios
inducit loquentes. Est autem carmen heroicum quod et epicum
dicitur diuinorum rerum et heroicorum humanorumque
comprehensio, nam constat ex diuinis humanisque | personis 7v
65 continens uera cum fictis actis et si poeta hic noster omnibus in
scriptis suis grandis est et resonans, in hac ipsa tantum Achilleide ita
surgit ut hic multo sublimius ferri uideatur quam quo potuerit tota
Thebaide peruenire, nam Achillem teste Pausania historiographo
diligentissimo in Actica Sciron insula expugnasse uerum est.
70 Thetim uero matrem Achillis, filium in Sciron translatum Lycomedique
regi pro filia in puellari habitu commendatum inter illius uirgines
occultasse constat esse compositum. Licet Polignotus pictor
elegantissimus hanc fabulam pinxerit et ea pictura eiusdem Pausanię
tempore uideretur. Sed quia fatorum ius est inuiobile, inuentus est
75 ab Vlysse, ad Troiam profectus est, et in ęde Apollinis Smynthei ut
infra dicemus Paride arcum intendente, pede vulneratus interiit. Stilus
uero est grandiloquus, qui constat alto sermone magnisque sententiis.
Scimus enim tria esse genera dicendi, humile, medium,
grandiloquum.

80 Intentio Papinii hęc est, primum ut in poetica se exercens,
adeptam iam famam ex Thebaide ęternam posteris faciat, quam
potissimam poetarum intentionem esse sic Ouidius perhibet <*A.A.* 3.403–404>

Quid petitur sacris nisi tantum fama poetis?
Hoc uotum nostri summa laboris habet.

85 Deinde ut Achillis educationem apud Chironem ab ineunte pueritia
scribere exorsus, omnia dicturus esset quę ille a prima gessit ętate,
propterea quod multa Homerus intacta pręteriit, nisi morte pręuentus
fuisset. Ea enim dumtaxat absoluit quę illi in Scyro insula occultato
contigere. Illuc enim Thetis ipsius Achillis mater eum a Chirone
90 ablatum ad Licomedis regiam transtulit sub habitu puellari pro sorore
sua latentem, eidem regi Licomedi commendauit. Quam quidem rem

tractans, poeta significat Thetidem uoluisse fatis resistere. Hinc
authori nostro causa intentionis ea est ut doceat neminem debere
uoluntati deorum repugnare. Atque ita suum poema ethicę subiicit
95   philosophię. Moraliter enim agit tractatque subtiliter quid honestum
et quid vtile sit.

De numero librorum ea est questio et contentio, vt quidam
dicant hoc opus in V esse diuisum libros, sed propterea quod Achilles
ab Vlysse inuentus narrat tantum qua disciplina sub Chirone centauro
100   fuerit enutritus, ex quo apparet duos tantummodo esse libros, ac ne
secundum quidem perfectum esse.

Dantes etiam Florentinus poeta doctissimus quamuis
uernaculus ita testatur in Purgatorio eum sic loquentem inducens <21.88–93>:

     Tanto fu dolce el mio vocale spirto
105   Che Tolosano ad se me trasse Roma
        Doue mertai le tempie ornar di myrto.

     Statio dì la lagente ancor mi noma
        Cantai de Thebe e poi del grande Achille
        Ma caddi in via colla secunda soma.

110   *Sunt tamen qui unum dumtaxat esse existiment et opus perfectum*
esse, quoniam propter illud <Ach. 1.17–18>,

     Patere hoc sudare parumper
     Pulvere

tum etiam quia cum in fine dicat "scit cętera mater" <2.167>, uidetur
115   *in compendium conferre narrationis prolixitatem vt Terencius propter*
longum actum ait <An. 980–81>:

     Intus desp<ondebitur>
     Intus transigi siquid est quod restat,

et quod etiam uidetur nolle aliud quam latebras Achillis describere
120   *cum cętera Hom<erus> antea scripsisset.* Quatenus autem Dantes
ipse in his uersibus Tolosam Gallię oppidum Statio poetę nostro
patriam assignat, videtur (ut a uero contra mendacium stemus) non
nihil aberrare, sed parcant obsecro nobis eius manes, nam etsi forte
legerat apud Eusebium Neronis temporibus Statium Surculum
125   Tolosanum rhetoricen in Gallia docuisse, non debuit tamen ad hunc
Statium Papinium id transferre. Hic enim non rhetoricen docuit,
sed poeticę gloria floruit, non Nerone sed Domitiano imperatore,
cui in hoc opere et in duobus aliis sępius assentatur. Pręterea,
Parthenopen non Tolosam sibi patriam celebrat in multis Syluarum
130   locis.

Causam uero qua poeta pręcipue appulerit animum ad hoc
opus scribendum hanc fuisse non nulli tradunt, quod Thebaide
completa, in qua per annos XII se inuigilasse fatetur, Romam cum
uenisset, a Domitiano imperatore et coronatus ut diximus et
135   honorificentissime susceptus est. Quumque in imperatoris aula hoc
quęsitum fuisset utrum ea quę pręstinata sunt possint necne
euitari, ad quam soluendam fuerat a Domitiano subinuitatus.
Decreuit Papinius hanc ut questionem solueret hunc librum
conficere, quo doceret quemadmodum Thetis uoluit fatis resistere,

140 sed non potuit, propterea quod prędictum fuerat si quis deorum
Thetidem vxorem duceret, ex eo *et illa* filium nasciturum esse
patre maiorem. Sic enim fuerat Protheus vaticinatus *ut est apud*
Ouidium in undecimo Meta<morphosum> <11.222–23>: |

     Concipe mater eris iuuenis qui fortibus armis   8r
145   Acta patris vincet, maiorque vocabitur illo.

Quo quidem uaticinato, dii perterriti eam ducere recusarunt, sed in
primis illa Juppiter *quamuis eius amore captus* abstinuit prouiditque
ut Peleo Ęaci filio nuptum daretur, vnde Achilles est ortus.

     Meditatus itaque Papinius Achillis ętatem uitamque
150 describere, complexus est animo suo Crispinum Vectii Bolani filium,
quem legimus pręstantissimum re militari adolescentem fuisse. *Alii*
poetam hunc suspicantur animo concepisse non Crispinum sed
iuuenem quendam potius Siracusanum, quippe quem
Philostratus testatur adeo charum fuisse Domiciano ut imperatoris
155 *lingua et mens diceretur. Ego tamen poetam exprimere Crispinum*
maluisse contenderim, propterea quod eum celebrat eo libello qui
inscribitur "Protrepticon ad Crispinum" vbi etiam meminit huius
operis quum ait <*Silv.* 5.2.162–63>*:*

     cun<eos>que per o<mnes> te meus absentem
160   *circumspectabit Achilles.*

Ceterum Domitiano de se optime merito hoc opus dicauit ut primum
Thebaidos, ac post propositionem et inuocationem, petit ab ipso
imperatore sibi ignosci quod non assumpserit potius eius res gestas
suo poemate celebrandas, quia se illis imparem ait. Licet
165 fateatur se cupere id pręstare, verum tamen nondum audere tantam
rem aggredi, sed hac Sylua scribenda prius de Achille se ait uti
quodam ueluti pręludio et quasi pręgustatione dum experitur sit ne
idoneus ad describendas res ab ipso principe gestas.

     Nunc superest ut ad contextus explanationem transeamus
170 in qua veterum more interpretum et quid nos et quid alii sentiant
quantum memoria suppetet referemus; diuus enim Hieronymus in
epistula ad Pammachium et Marcellam pro se contra Rufinum docet
interpretis officium esse multorum sententias replicare dicereque
hunc locum quidam sic edisserunt, alii sic interpretantur, alii sensum
175 suum et intelligentiam his testimoniis et hac nituntur ratione
firmare, vt prudens lector *uel auditor* cum diuersas explanationes
legerit *audieritue* iudicet quid uerius sit et quasi bonus trapezita
adulterinę monetus pecuniam reprobet ueramque teneat.

---

2 matre... Agelina] *In principio accessus*, l. 8
26 amoris impatiens] cf. Servius *ad Aen.* 1.*praef.* 10: impatiens libidinis
33 multa... lima] *Silv.* 4.7.26
33 imitatus... bissenos (37)] Carpentras *accessus*, 9–12
42 quantum... vrbem (46)] Carpentras 12–15
55 Titulus... codri (59)] cf. Servius *ad Aen.* 1.*praef.* 75–76
60 patet... fictis (65)] cf. Servius *ad Aen.* 1.*praef.* 77–79; cf. Venezia, Lat. XII.61, ll. 35–36
68 Pausanias 1.22.6

69 thetim... compositum (72)] cf. Servius *ad Aen.* 1.*praef.*79–81; cf. Venezia, Lat. XII.61, ll. 35–39

73 cf. Pausanias 1.22.6

74 inuentus... interiit (76)] cf. KP accessum, l. 11

76 stilus... grandilocuum (79)] cf. Servius *ad Aen.* 1.*praef.*81–83; cf. Venezia, Lat. XII.61, 39–40

80 intentio... habet (84)] Carpentras 22–26

86 ętate... pręuentus (87)] cf. Oxford, Linc. Coll. 27, ll. 27–28

90 habitu puellari] Carpentras 29

91 Licomedi commendauit] Thomas Walsingham (146r), l. 21

94 ethicę... sit (96)] Carpentras 32–33

107 *Lectiones variae in apparatibis criticis non inveniuntur.*

124–25 Eusebius-Hieronymus, *Chronica, Olymp.* 210 (*PL* 19.542)

132 quod... maiorem (139)] Carpentras 36–44

146 dii... daretur (156)] cf. Carpentras 44–46

150 complexus... animo] cf. *Silv.* 5.3.100

151 cf. *Silv.* 5.2.8–11

154–55 Philostratus, *Vita Apollonii* 7.36: Δομετιανοῦ δὲ νοῦς τε καὶ γλῶττα.

167 cf. *Ach.* 1.18–19

171 Hieronymus, *Apologia contra Rufinum* 1.6.10–13 (*CCL* 79.6)

---

1 fuit] est *scr. man. rec. sup. lin.*   **11** duę] tres *scr. man. rec. sup. lin.*   epirotarum] et epiri oppidum V   *ante* et *add. man. rec. sup. lin.*: tolosa gallię   **20** lęthargus... corripitur (21)] *add. man. rec. marg.*   **29** prope *add. man. rec. sup. lin.*   patris et *add. sup. lin.*   **31** consecrata] dedicata *man. rec.*   **36** sic *add. sup. lin.*   **54** interiit] moritur annum iam agens circiter L *man. rec.*   superstite] relicta *man. rec.*   **66** factis... interiit (74)] *add. marg. man. text.*   **69** thetim *ex* euadem(?)   V   **70** achille   V   **86** prima ~~ętate~~ gessit ętate   **87** ab *post* nisi *eras.*   **101** etiam *add. sup. lin.*   **107** la *ante* gente *eras.* **110** sunt... scripsisset (120)] *add. marg. man. rec.*   **130** poeta *add. sup. lin.*   **132** non nulli *add. sup. lin.*   tradunt *ex* tradit V   **133** qua *add. sup. lin.*   **134** et *post* uenisset *eras.* **138** decreuit... solueret *post* euitari (136) *dist.* V   **141** ex illa *post* ex eo *add. sup. lin. man. rec.* **142** patrem V   ut... meta. (143) *add. sup. lin. man. rec.*   **147** quamuis... captus *add. sup. lin. man. rec.*   nepotique suo *post* filio *add. sup. lin. man. rec.*   **148** cuius exemplo ostendit poeta non homines modo sed deos etiam fatali necessitate subiunctos esse *post* ortus *add. sup. lin. man. rec.*   **149** et *post* ętatem *eras.*   **150** vectii] versi *corr. sup. lin. man. rec.*   **151** alii... achilles (159) *add. marg. man. rec.*   **159** cuneosque per omnes *add. sup. lin.*   **166** scribendi V **169** nunc... transeamus *add. in lac. man. rec.*   **175** ratione̅ V   **176** uel auditor *post* lector *add. sup. lin. man. rec.*   audieritue *post* legerit *add. sup. lin. man. rec.*

Conclusion

By the end of the period of manuscript transmission of ancient texts, the Servian *accessus* scheme had begun to show its weaknesses. Discoveries of new texts resulted in *accessus* that were filled with information that was haphazardly thrown into preexisting categories. In the case of Statius, had the *Silvae* been known in the twelfth century, scholars who understood the *accessus* scheme would have been able to include its information much more succinctly into the standard *accessus* scheme. However, in comparison with twelfth-century *accessus* to Ovid and Virgil, these *accessus* are jumbled and self-contradictory, and this betrays both a lack of understanding of the logic and structure of *accessus* composition and interests in a new approach to the texts. As the three phases of *accessus* demonstrated, the new information was not so much as showing the limits of the *accessus* methodology, but in showing its growing lack of applicability. In all three phases, scholars were content with simply tacking new information onto the old model. In the second phase, Laetus made some effort at correcting obviously incorrect information, but his emphasis on correcting information that was intrinsically false—the *intentio* of the *Achilleid*, for example—led him to be as incorrect as the tradition he was trying to correct. This led to the third phase, in which the *accessus* to Statius became essentially an extended narrative only loosely joined to an *accessus* formula, a formula that still proved to be a hindrance, both because it included false information and because scholars tried to get around the limitations of the *circumstantiae* it proposed.

Most of the concerns that we saw in the manuscript age of Statius' reception were internal and intrinsic. That is, who Statius was and what the *circumstantiae* of his works were. In the age of the printed book, these concerns suddenly disappear.[30] This may be because of the sudden availability of large numbers of books or because of a new academic climate, but scholarly activity on Statius suddenly shifts to a more extrinsic approach, in which scholarly attention is suddenly focused on the role that the *Silvae* play in Statius' *opera* and, more importantly, on Statius' role in literature in general. In the next—and final—chapter, I summarize some aspects of medieval exegesis and provide a brief summary of the reception of Statius down to the nineteenth century.

Before we move on, we should discuss the fate of Statius' namesake, Statius Ursulus. Just as errors from the pre-*Silvae* tradition continued to crop up in Statius' "restored" biography, Statius Ursulus maintains some aspects of his previous identity long after he was separated from our Statius in the manuscripts. In the early period, this is quite common, as manuscripts continue to identify Statius Ursulus as Statius Surculus. Even despite some prominent corrections to this,[31] we find references to Surculus as late as the late seventeenth century (Paris, BnF, Languedoc (Bénédictins), 100).[32]

---

[30] This notwithstanding, scholars continued to use lists of intrinsic criteria in the Aristotelian-Horatian vein. See, for example, Beraldus (1685, Paris): "Cum epicum poema quinque partes complectatur, actionem, fabulam, mores, sententiam, dictionem, haec omnia in Thebide reperiuntur." He continues to argue, "actio debet esse una, illustris, completa, certae magnitudinis" and "reperis in Statiana Thebaide nihil desiderari eorum, quae ad poticae laudis perfectionem requiruntur."

[31] Cf. the reference to Scaliger in Oxford, Bodleian Library, D'Orville 327 (XVII s.).

[32] The error in the XV s. manuscript Bruxelles, Bibliothèque Royale Albert 1er, 21891, in which the *Thebaid* and *Achilleid* are identified as works of Caecilius Statius in his biography, seems not to reflect a tradition.

EPILOGUE: STATIUS IN THE PRINTED AGE

As a poet, Statius created his works with a close eye to the structure, phraseology, and styles of his literary predecessors, whom he at times emulates and at times manipulates. He is, thus, often termed a mannerist, a characteristic that has been seen as negative for the past two centuries. His popularity before then is unchallengeable, as is clear from both the manuscript tradition and the number of printed editions through 1671. We have very little data for his reception between the end of the seventeenth century and the beginning of the nineteenth—as was the case for all classical authors, there was very little new publishing activity during this period.[1] By the end of the sixteenth century, Statius had already fallen into some sort of literary oblivion,[2] and by the beginning of the nineteenth century, he had been relegated to the *poetae minores*.[3] Indeed, so much had interest in him dropped off that one of the greatest academic debates in the seventeenth century—and certainly the greatest Statian debate ever—was waged not between two great minds but between a young upstart trying to make a career, Gronovius,[4] and an nobody about whom we know nothing more than his questionable philological skills and his tendency to flights of fancy, Emericus Cruceus.[5] Still, both opponents rose to the occasion in the debate proved to be one of the best discussions ever on Statius in particular and philology and Latin style and language in general.[6] Alas, the result of the debate was that Statius' Latin was—if not bad—not to be emulated, and similar pronouncements are very common thereafter.[7]

---

[1] Cf. W.S. Anderson, ed., *Ovidii Metamorphoseon Libri* (Leipzig, 1982²), XX–XXI.

[2] Cf. Bernartius (Antwerpen, 1595), A2r: "parum is vulgo notus, scio sed dignissimus nototia.... Adeste vos critici et oppressum per iniuriam, certe pressum, alleuate virilem et grauem poetam."

[3] Cf. the 1782, Altenburg edition (reprinted in 1824, Paris) and the 1869, Oxford edition.

[4] Johannes Fredericus Gronovius the Elder, 1611–1671. His major scholarly publication, *Opera Statii* (Amsterdam, 1653) was widely bemoaned as not living up to the scholarly strengths he showed much earlier in his life during the debate.

[5] Of the eight vulgar names that are transmitted, Éméric Crucé seems the most likely. He seems to have lived from 1590–1648, may have been Parisian, and may have been a priest or a monk. Other than his works on Statius, he published a very peculiar work in 1623—*Le nouveau Cynée*–which argues for an international commercial and political body which some scholars since the First World War have argued was a sort of League of Nations or United Nations. See P. Louis-Lucas, *Un plan de paix générale et de liberté du commerce au XVIIe siècle: le nouveau Cynée d'Eméric Crucé (1623)* (Paris, 1919); C.F. Farrell, Jr. and E.R. Farrell, transs., *The New Cineas* (New York, 1972), introduction; P. Van den Dungen, *The Hidden History of a Peace "Classic": Emeric Crucé's Le nouveau Cynée* (London, 1980); and A.V. Hartmann, *Rêveurs de paix? Friedenspläne bei Crucé, Richelieu und Sully*, Beiträge zur deutschen und europäischen Geschichte 12 (Hamburg, 1995).

[6] In 1637, J.F. Gronovius published his *Diatribe*, reacting to the heavy corrections Cruceus made, particularly to the *Silvae*, in the 1620 reprint of his 1616 edition. Cruceus responded in 1639 with his *Antidiatribe*, in which he argued that the text, in its transmission, must have been badly distorted by ignorant scribes. The following year, Gronovius, who would deem Cruceus' response not worthy of reading, put forth the explanation (among many others) that Statius stretched Latin to the greatest extent that one could without breaking it; his Latin was not "bad" *per se*, but was certainly not to be emulated. This was the last heated scholarly debate on any aspect of Statius' poems. The debate comprised four volumes: J.F. Gronovius, *In P. Papinii Statii Silvarum libros V diatribe ad Th. Graswinckelium...* ('s-Gravenhage: Theodorus Maire, 1637); E. Cruceus, *Antidiatribe* (Paris: Du Pais, 1639); J.F. Gronovius, *Helenchus Diatribes* (Paris: Soly, 1640); and E. Cruceus, *Ad P. Papinii Siluas muscarium siue helelenchus* (Paris: Michael Soly, 1640). The whole debate (with some additional manuscript notes by Gronovius) was edited by F. Hand in 1812 (I. Fr. Gronovius, *In P. Papinii Statii Silvarum libros V diatribe: Nova editio ab ipso auctore correcta, interpolata, aucta. Accessit Emerici Crucei antidiatribe, Gronovii elenchus antidiatribes et Crucei muscarium*, in two voll. [Leipzig: Ger. Fleischer/Berlin: Moyer und Müller])

[7] Cf. Beraldus (in his 1685, Paris edition), 1r: "Nunc Statius a zoilis uindicatus (quis enim magnorum poetarum zoilos non habet?) qui eum ut tumidum et obscurum damnant. Ad tumorem quod spectat, si constatem et perpetuam elocutionis majestatem tumorem liceat appellari, Statius tumidus appellandus: toto enim suorum operum contextu, nusquam a pulcherrimo stilo degenerat. Si vero tumor vocetur, ut vocari debet, vanus verborum sonus strepitusque, inops rerum et sensuum vacans, aequiores judicabunt, Statius hoc vitio non laborasse. Ad obscuritatem quod attinet, Gronovius optime observat Statium domesticos ac familiares loquendi modos habere, qui non cuivis prima lectione se produnt, sed occultati et velut in alto recessu conditi accurate inspicientibus."

But this debate was only a symptom of Statius' demise. The cause was linked to the advent of the Romantic Age.

Although the Romantics were inspired and fueled by the originality and generic freedom of the *Silvae*,[8] Statius fell into disfavor because he emulated other authors and thus lacked poetic integrity;[9] he lacked *engagement* because he maintained a personal distance from his subject in most of his poetry; he lacked applicability because his poetry did not respond to the problems of his times;[10] and he lacked *auctoritas* because his Latin was not that of the Golden Age. This last element has proven the most damning, and seems to have been prevalent since the early sixteenth century. Even J.C. Scaliger, who was apparently the first to divide Latin literature into ages,[11] made a vehement effort to distance Statius from the wilting aspects of the *aetas tertia* in which he placed him.[12] The question arises, then, why he was so popular in the Middle Ages.

This question is very difficult to answer, since the manuscripts afford us very little evidence. Certainly, Statius does provide us with several moral *exempla*: in the *Thebaid*, he offers examples to children to avoid fraternal anger,[13] or an example to the emperor to avoid fraternal wars;[14] and in the *Achilleid*, an example to the Romans to raise their children and avoid weakness and effeminacy,[15] to obey divine will,[16] or to properly behave with one's teacher/mother or son/student.[17] However Statius was by no means the only poet in whom morality could be found.

There was also the fact that Statius imitated Virgil, much as Virgil himself imitated other authors,[18] that Juvenal extolled him so highly, and that Servius used him frequently in his commentary. It is possible that Statius was read for this purpose, although that would not explain

---

[8] During this age and the following century, Statius did find some sympathetic readers, including Thomas Gray and Alexander Pope and Goethe, in whom he reportedly inspired some awe. Most readers, though, like Thomas Macaulay, found little more than disdain for the poet..

[9] Cf., more recently, the debate between F. Delarue ("Sur deux passages de Stace," *Orpheus* 15 [1968], 13–31) and Venini 1969, in which Delarue finds Statius erudite, but Venini impugns him for adhering too closely to his predecessors and lacking originality. In 1834, J. Nisard argued that Statius was "un versificateur erudite et non un poète" (quoted in Constans 1881.147).

[10] Statius is often criticized, even today, for his praise of Domitian. His silence as to Domitian's wickedness (as attested by Tacitus and Pliny the Younger) does not appease the Romantic view that the artist, endowed with some higher knowledge, should seek to correct society's wrongs without fear of life or limb. Cf. Bernartius' discontent with Statius "qui tam seruiliter Domitiano, monstro non homini, aduletur" (cf. E. Cruceus, ed., *Statii Opera* [Paris: Th. Blaise, 1618], 11). Scholars in manuscript *accessus* seem not to have worried about this issue; indeed, Statius is often put in the position of chastizing the emperor (this, of course, without the view of him as the *poeta adulator* that we have from the *Silvae*). Many late humanists, however, seeking to redeem Statius, said that he wrote the *Achilleid* to avoid the emperor's wrath; for example, Grasserus (Strasbourg, 1609) wrote: "Cum Papinius noster Domitiano imperatori non uulgariter esset familiaris, saepius de rebus eius gestis, poema aliquod illustrare destinauit, unde ut uirium suarum, antiquorum poetarum more, periculum faceret, perfectam Achillis historiam contexere aggreditur" (cf. was the case in the London, BL, Royal 15.a.XXIX *accessus*). The best treatment of Statius' praise of Domitian is in A. Hardie 1983), *passim*.

[11] Scaliger 1561.325aD, 295

[12] See 324bB–325aD; his phrase is "deuergens paulatim efflorescit."

[13] *inter alios*, *Universitatis bruxellensis accessus*, l. 17

[14] *inter alios*, the Bern-Burney *accessus*, ll. 9–11

[15] Oxford, Lincoln College 27, ll. 9–11 and 39–41

[16] *inter alios*, the KP *accessus*, ll. 16–17

[17] *inter alios*, Antwerpen, M 85 and Düsseldorf, K2: F.50

[18] Paris, BnF, lat. 3173, f. 92r: "Virgilius iste in diuersis operibus suis diuersos imitatur auctores" (see B. Hauréau's notes to G. Paris, "Additions et corrections," *Histoire littéraire de la France* 29 [1885], 570). Many other authors were seen as imitating Virgil. An *accessus* to Martianus Capella reads, "Maronem emulatur. Sicut enim apud illum dicitur Eneas per infernos comite Sibilla usque ad Anchisem, ita et hic Mercurius per mundi regiones virtute comite ad Jouem" (H.J. Westra, *The Commentary on Martianus Capella's De nuptiis Philologiae et Mercurii attributed to Bernardus Silvestris*, Studies and Texts 80 [Toronto, 1986], 47, ll. 114–17).

the long "Dark Age" of the transmission of Statius manuscripts between the fifth and tenth centuries.

We could also argue that Statius was read allegorically,[19] but that these interpretations have not been transmitted to us. However, this does not seem to be the case. [20] As Sanford discovered in her survey of glosses of Lucan, the glosses that we find for classical authors suggest that they were read mostly for rhetorical reasons. Thus, most of the manuscripts contain marginal rhetorical finding guides indicating *comparationes*—in the case of Statius, a few manuscripts actually enumerate these.[21] As I said above, Statius was a teacher of rhetoric, and the presence of these and the *utilitas* we occasionally find in *accessus*:[22]

> *ut... pulchras et ornatas sententiarum positiones imitemur,*

suggest that the greatest reason why he was read was to learn rhetorical techniques to imitate.[23] Still, there must have been more than this one aspect that made Statius attractive.

Although this is not reflected in the number of extant and attested manuscripts, the *Achilleid* was certainly the most read of Statius' works. Aeneas Silvius (*De pueris educandis*, 27) attests to the importance of this work in the school. Indeed, the *Achilleid* was more often read in a school context (or so the *accessus* suggest) and the *accessus* offer us three fundamental reasons why: first, it was short and manageable (and considerably easier Latin than that of the *Thebaid*); second it was a good complement to the so-called *Liber catonianus*; and third, it offered lessons on raising children.[24]

Readership of the *Thebaid* seems always to have been more scholarly advanced, and interpretation of the poem avoided the small educational allegories we find in the *Achilleid*. The poem, however, seems to have played a popular role only through the twelfth century, as most academic activity on the poem wanes thereafter, while activity on the *Achilleid* increases two- to three-fold. This may be because the interpretation of the *Thebaid* was cemented at an early age or because the poem had only abstract applicability: it had a contemporary *intentio*, to teach the imperial brothers a lesson, but, at the same time, it was not involved enough in its time to tell later readers more about that period in Roman history. The Statius of the *Thebaid*, moreover, is seen in the poem as a *poeta historiographus*, and an oft-cited *intentio* is to rescue the story of the *Thebaid* from oblivion,[25] and we often see the claim that the poem teaches beautiful *sententiae* and important myths.

---

[19] Cf. the assessment, that "pagan poets were being read allegorically or 'moralised'" (Minnis 1984.6).

[20] The only transmitted allegorical commentary is that of Fulgentius (Incipitarium 200).
The only other allegorical interpretation I have found is in Firenze, BML, Ashburnham 1032 (XIV s. ex.), which argues that the return of Mercury at the beginning of the second book is akin to the return of the soul. I have been unable to examine Vibo Valentia, Biblioteca dei Conti Capialbi, 42, q.v., which reportedly contains a "Allegorizazione o dilucidazione sull' Achilleide di Stazio."

[21] See Firenze, BML, Plut. 91 inf. 10, Salamanca 72 and Vaticano, Vat. lat. 1615. These are discussed in M. Buonocore, "Iohannes Bertus e la *Tebaide* di Stazio," *Aevum* 71.2 (1997), 417–22. Medieval tallies count 187 *comparationes*, while a modern tally counts 202. See A. Luque Lozano, "Los similes en la Tebaida de Estacio," *Habis* 17 (1986), 165–84.

[22] Zürich, Zentralbibliothek, Rh. 53

[23] Cf. the note that Statius was an "offendiculum emulari" in London, Royal 15.A.XXIX (XIII s.) (above, p. 35, l. 13). Cf as well the judgment of Scaliger 1561.325aD: "figuris frequentior et officiorum, habitudinum, animorum prudentior distributor et castigatio<n>um author sententiarum." This judgment continues into the late seventeenth century. Cf. Beraldus (Paris, 1685), 1r, who defends Statius for his *ornatio*, *sententiae*, and moral value.

[24] Reeve 1983.396, on the basis of M. Boas ("De librorum Catonianorum historia atque compositione," *Mnemosyne* 42 [1914], 17–46), *inter al.*, notes that the text was added "for its mythological and moral content." The latter of these is suggested by our *accessus* to the poem; the former seems to be the case only for the *Thebaid*.

[25] Cf., *inter alios*, the *In principio accessus* (above, p. 33, ll. 62–63).

One final *accessus*, actually the *vita Statii* of Petrus Candidus Decembrius from his *Historia peregrina*, Book 3,[26] will illustrate the virtues of the poet.

This short *vita* offers us no new details on Statius, his life, or interpretation of the work (the only novelty is that in what appears to be the autograph [Firenze, Ricc. 907]), a second hand notes that Statius was Neapolitan, not Gallic), and is simply a stringing together of praises and previous plot interpretations. Statius is called *disertissimus*[27] and *dignus* (11 and 10), while his work is *subtilem* and *diligentem* (6). He is praised not for originality or creativity, but for emulating. He copied and remade (*effingat*, 2) Virgil, and did not hesitate to imitate the best poets of both languages (11–13), and he wrote works that are *melliflua* and *iocundae sententiae*.

Text 27. Petrus Candidus Decembrius' *Vita Statii* (from *Lives of the Poets* [*Historia peregrina*, Book 3])

F = Firenze, Biblioteca Riccardiana e Moreniana, Ricc. 907 (XV s.), 138r–v[28]

> Statius Papinius poeta meo iudicio disertissimus et qui Uirgilium non
> emuletur modo sed effingat, ex Gallia oriundus, a Domitiano
> imperatore ad scribendum exhortatus. Ut illius ignauiam effugeret,
> primum duodecim Thebanę historię libros ueluti imperatoris
> 5   uirtutibus alludens, edidit recitauitque. Demum de Achillis uita quasi
> Homeri Iliadam | expressurus unicum subtilem tamen et diligentem   138v
> emisit librum, quem eruditi quidam Gręcorum more in plures sed
> breuiores distinxere libros, ut quę non solum Uirgilius singulari
> opere coniunxisset, sed quę separatim Homerus ediderat duplici
> 10 uideretur uolumine comprehendere. Dignus itaque nobis uisus est
> Pieridum sertis atque choreis, qui tantos uates utraque excellentes
> lingua mellifluo carmine iocundisque sententiis non dubitauerit
> imitari.

---

2 gallia] *nota in margine addita*: Errasti, nam Neapolitanus fuit, ipse de se in Siluis ad Rutilium Gallicum scribens ita ait: "At te nascentem gremio mea prima recepit Parthenope, dulcique solo tu gloria nostro reptasti" etc. <*S.* 1.2.260–62>

---

1 iudice F   **4** imperatoriis F

We can, however, say much more about the attitudes of medieval scholars to his texts. First and foremost, interpretation of Statius was always conservative. We see no overtly religious allegory and—with the exception of the Plut. 24, sin. 12 *accessus*—a stubborn refusal to give into fiction. Scholars were always careful to extract information only from Statius' own words, granted that their interpretations led to some extraordinary "facts."

It was this conservative attitude, combined with the unavailability of new information, that led to the sterility of the *accessus* after the thirteenth century; before the proliferation of the *Silvae* in the 1470s, the only advancements were on stylistic grounds, as scholars adapted their

---

[26] Written ca. 1450. Cf. K. Kreschmer, "Die Kosmographie des Petrus Candidus Decembrius," in *Festschrift Ferdinand Freiherrn von Richthofen zum sechzigsten Geburtstag* (Berlin, 1893), 269; V. Zaccaria, "Sulle opere di Pier Candido Decembrio," *Rinascimento* 7 (1956), 13–74; and Coulson-Roy 315. Our text is Incipitarium 273.

[27] Scaliger 1561.325aD: "At profecto heroicorum poetarum, si Phoenicem [i.e. Vergilium] illum nostrum eximas, tum Latinorum tum etiam Graecorum facile princeps; nam et meliores versus facit quam Homerus."

[28] The text is also extant in London, BL, Harley 2587 (XV s.) and Milano, Codice Trivulziano 817 (XV s.).

information to new questions and approaches, but not to new answers.[29] It is only later on the printed page that scholars begin to let their imagination take flights of fancy, inspired by the abundant details available from the *Silvae*.

This conservative core suggests an important aspect of criticism and the composition of *accessus*, specifically that medieval scholars sought first of all to find a scholarly interpretation of the poem. Tropological allegory and moralization, on the other hand—despite Minnis' claim that they were important aspects of medieval scholarship[30]—do not seem to be a part of general medieval reading.

We have seen, in these 28 *accessus*, distinctive patterns of development. In our first *accessus*, the *Quaeritur accessus*, we saw the careful, conservative development of an authorial biography. Knowing their limitations, the scholars who created and used that *accessus* drew their results only from verifiable facts and sources. In the twelfth century, after a short lull in activity, this caution persisted as scholars adapted the formal rigor of the *Quaeritur accessus* to the questions that were being asked in the newly developing genre of the *accessus*, and the *accessus* began to fill-out.

It is in the thirteenth century and the beginning of the fourteenth that the *accessus* to Statius reached their pinnacle, in which the previously existing data on the author was adapted to Statius' new surroundings. Statius existed in that century in two different environments: the classroom, where his *Achilleid* was intended as a tool for imitation, and among more advanced scholars, where his *Thebaid* was seen as a history and he as a teacher of stories, in this case with a moral background. In this role, he was not so much to be imitated as to be obeyed. Statius was the *poeta doctus* and *doctor*.

After the thirteenth century, scholarship on Statius began to stagnate. *Accessus* in this time tend to simply rewrite preexisting *accessus*, based on five models: for the *Achilleid*, scholars relied heavily on the *Universitas bruxellensis* and KP *accessus* from the twelfth-century and on the Carpentras *accessus*; for the *Thebaid*, they relied either on the *Quaeritur accessus* or on the partially derivative *In principio accessus*. If the jejune *accessus* attributed to Filelfo that we saw in the fourteenth century is authentic, then we see the severe limitations even the best scholars had when dealing with *accessus* to Statius. In such a scholarly conservative atmosphere and without new information, new development was impossible.

It was the rediscovery of the *Silvae* that freed the humanist scholars. These poems contained the data that scholars needed to make the requisite advancements in Statian scholarship. At first, scholars did not realize the full importance of these poems, and simply adapted the information to the older traditions. As scholars came to realize the difference between the information in the *Silvae* and that in the older *accessus* traditions, they began to recast their *accessus*. As we saw in the Ottob. lat. 1261 *accessus*, this entailed a recasting of the form of the *accessus* to Statius, and possibly of *accessus* in general, by virtue of the fact that the author eliminated major parts of the traditional *accessus* form, including the catalogue of *circumstantiae*. By doing this, he effectively separated himself completely from the roots of medieval *accessus*, Servius. Practically, he does not need to abrogate Servius' authority; his own authority is based on something more important and newer: a knowledge of Greek. He stresses this aspect of his scholarship, quoting Greek almost at the beginning of his text, on line 14. That is something we have seen nowhere else in the *accessus* to Statius, and it is typical something that we will see in

---

[29] I should note here the reluctance with scholars to one of Statius' poems borrowed from scholarship to the other poem (see Appendix I). This may have been due to conservatism or simply to a lack of communication between the scholarly traditions of the two poems. If the second is the case, that would support the difference between the readers of the two poems as I suggested in my treatment of the word "historiographus" in the *In principio accessus* (above, p. 35).

[30] See Minnis 1984.6.

scholars from the sixteenth century down through our own, as authority is finally derived more from reason than from tradition. However, with this reason will come a new set of problems. With the information in the *Silvae*, scholars were able to do much more with the text, both for better and for worse. Scholars in the following centuries, freed from the conservatism that controlled criticism of Statius—and other authors—for so long, would (finally) turn to imaginative and allegorical interpretation of the texts;[31] at the same time, we find the beginning of a new assessment of Statius' style, his poems, and his life, this time with a philological basis and with a view to investigating Statius' literary role.

Although the reception of Statius' works since the end of the Middle Ages is a topic better reserved for another forum, I should make some brief mention of the issues that occupied scholars in the following centuries.

Scholarship after the sixteenth century continued to struggle with the problem of Statius' identity. While the question regarding *Statius Surculus* seems to have continued into the seventeenth century,[32] scholars came to struggle with the larger problem of reconciling the epic Statius with the Statius of the *Silvae*. This struggle has resulted in three major questions: the relationship between Statius and his predecessors (i.e., Statius' originality);[33] the relationship between the two facets of Statius' poetry (i.e. the epic Statius and the occasional Statius); and Statius' relationship with Domitian.[34]

Scholars' and readers' opinions of Statius have been equally polarized between Statius' two authorial styles—as epic poet and as author of occasional poems. Still, it has been the *Silvae* that have controlled the way scholars have seen Statius, such that the medieval estimation *Statii urbanitas* (Ps.-Boethius, *De disciplina scolarum*, 1.8) has given way to a view of Statius as representing "free vigour," even in the *Thebaid*.[35] For example, in his reported praise of Statius, Goethe describes the poet in terms that are truly applicable only to the *Silvae*:

> *Poeta est magnopere laudandus assiduoque studio nostro dignus; non me offendunt ea, quae luxurie quadam ingenii effudit, sed admiror in ea artem, qua res conspicuas comprehendere et exacte describere optimum quemque poetam decet—lauta est ei ars rerum imagines percipiendi et representandi.*[36]

---

[31] One example of this is the story of Domitian killing Statius that Crinitus cites (above, p. 66 n. 10).

[32] Cf. Thomas Stephens (*An Essay Upon Statius, or, the First Five Books of Publ. Papinius Statius, his Thebais* [London, 1648]): "For those criticall pens which have published their ingenious disputes, between Ursulus and Surculus, (although, I conceive, neither were of kin to our Statius) would have deserv'd better of the Commonwealth of Learning, if they had held a torce to the darke and mysterious places of the poem: which, I dare say, would not be so much neglected, but that it is so little understood." The claim is likely more than a slight exaggeration.

[33] Cf. Venini 1969.

[34] Modern scholars see Statius as a court poet (cf. J. Garthwaite, *Domitian and the Court Poets Martial and Statius*, Dissertation, Cornell, 1978; and A. Hardie 1983), as a blind flatterer (cf. K. Scott, "Statius' Adulation of Domitian," *AJPh* [1933], 247–59), or devote their studies to reconciling Statius' adulation of Domitian in the *Silvae* with the material of his epics (Cf. J.J. Hartman, "De Domitiano imperatore et de poeta Statio," *Mnemosyne* 44 [1916], 338–72; J. Schilp, *Die politischen Ideen der domitianischen Zeit gesehen aus den Werken der zeitgenössischen Dichter Martial, Statius, Silius Italicus*, Dissertation, Uni-Marburg, 1947; M. Benker, *Achill und Domitian: Herrscherkritik in der Achilleis des Statius*, Dissertation, Erlangen-Nürnberg, 1987). It is interesting that medieval scholars did not consider the close association with Domitian a blemish, even after the *Silvae* were rediscovered.

[35] W. Harte, *Poems on Several Occasions* (London, 1727), 101. In conjunction with this vigor, it is worth noting that most of the representations of Statius that we find in printed editions bear a marked resemblance to those in manuscripts: he is depicted as an unshaven youth with unkempt hair (see the index of manuscripts with historiating decorations in Volume II).

[36] Quoted, from a conversation, in F. Hand, *Hercules epitrapezios Novii Vindicis cum carmentariis* (Jena, 1849), 7. Cf. Bonn, UB, S 1024 a,b,c, 2r. Cf. W.F. von Biedermann et al., edd., *Goethes Werke* (Weimar, 1887–1912), III, 13.1511; and W.F. von Biedermann, *Goethes Gespräche* (Leipzig, 1889–96), 8.330–31.

Still, the polarizing nature of Statius' works is a fruitful starting point for future investigation, in that it is there—from the Middle Ages through today—that individuals betray their esthetic feelings about the poems. I close with three examples of scholars who preferred one poem to the exclusion of the others:[37]

Mapheus Vegius Laudensis (1422–23)[38]

> *Paruo opere ingentem Peliden Statius ornat*
> *Fraternas acies cui male praetuleris.*

Marcus Antonius Sabellicus (1484)[39]

> *Velles Papinium Statium tam dextro genio Thebas, fortissimumque Achillem, quam Silvas decantasse. Si non maius nomen, maiorem certe gratiam inde haud dubio reportasset. Nulli unquam poetarum, quod sciam, magis proprium fuit subito oestro incalescere, atque ibi incaluisset, fortius feliciusque debacchari; ut quantumcunque Phoebum hauserit, ac nescio an etiam maiorem, eodem calore confestim reddat. Cuperes, dixi, omnem eius operam in Silvis locatam: nihil est illis amabilius, floridius, magisque poeticum.*

John Jortin[40]

> I think that the *Silvæ*, though they are not bad poems, are far enough from being very good ones. There is an unpleasant Mediocrity that runs through them all. The *Thebais* is a thousand times better written.[41]

But these topics are better reserved for discussion elsewhere.

---

[37] Appendix III contains a collection of epithets to Statius and his works. Many editions (such as that of Gevartius, 1616) include lists of *testimonia* and *judicia*, the most commly cited are those of Juvenal, Julius Capitolinus, Sidonius Apollinaris, Claudianus Mamertus, Boethius, Alanus ab Insulis, Nicolaus Clemangius, Politian, Domitius Calderinus, Janus Parrhasius, Julius Caesar Scaliger, Joseph Scaliger, and Justus Lipsius. See, too, the citations in *Miscellaneae observationes* (Amsterdam, 1732), 1.2.153.

[38] *Ad Achilleidem* (from his *Disticorum liber primus*), transcribed from Firenze, BML, Plut. 34.53 (XV s.), 14v.

[39] Marco Antonio Coccio (Antonio Sabellico), 1436–1506, *Annotationes in Plinium et alios authores*, Venezia, 1484, quoted in Gevartius, ed., *Statii Opera* (Leiden, 1616), 6r, and in *Miscellaneae observationes* (Amsterdam, 1732), 1.2.154.

[40] *Tracts, Philosophical, Critical, and Miscellaneous* (London, 1790), 424–25

[41] Cf. Bentley, "Hujus auctoris sententiam amplecti non possum. Silvae licet non sint mala poema, longe tamen ab ea perfectione abesse videntur, ut inter valde bona locum obtinere possint. Inest omnibus quaedam ingrata, mediocritas. Thebais multum praestat Silvis" (*Miscellaneae observationes* [Amsterdam, 1732], 1.2.154).

APPENDIX I. STEMMATA OF MAJOR ACCESSUS

The following two figures show demonstrable relationships between individual *accessus* and *accessus*-traditions, organized by approximate location and date of composition. Full lines show visible relationships, dotted lines show probable relationships or minor similarities. Descendancy is shown by the vertical angle of the connecting line. Horizontal lines show relationships among contemporary manuscripts without a clear precedence. I have added a number of *accessus* that are not edited in this collection in order to make stemmata more clear at places. In each figure, sigla in parentheses represent *accessus* to the other poem.

Sigla

Thebaid

λ = the parent of the marginal notes in In
B = the Bern-Burney *accessus*
Br = the *accessus* in London, BL, Royal 15.C.X (not edited here; see above, p. 8 n. 30)
C = the *accessus* in Cambridge, UL, Ii.3.13 (not edited here)
Cz = the *accessus* in Kraków, Muzeum Narodowe, Biblioteka Czartoryskich, 1876 II (not edited here; see above, pp. 46, 50 n. 39, and 95 n. 75)
F = the Freiburg *accessus*
Fi = the *accessus* in Firenze, BNC, II.II.55
I = the *In principio accessus*
In = the marginal notes in the London witness of I
O = the Olomouc *accessus*
P = the *accessus* in Paris, lat. 13046 (not edited here; see above, p. 8 n. 30)
Q = the *Quaeritur accessus*
R = the *accessus* in London, Royal 15.A.XXIX
Rl = the *accessus* in Vaticano, Reg. lat. 1375
Z = the *accessus* in Zürich, Rh. 53

Achilleid

A = the *accessus* in Antwerpen M.85 (not edited here; see above, p. 124 n. 17)
Au = the Augsburg (Staats- und Stadtbibliothek, 4° Cod. 21) witness of Kr (not edited here; see above, p. 103 n. 1)
Bb = The Bruxelles witness of the *Universitatis bruxellensis accessus*
Bl = The Leiden witness of the *Universitatis bruxellensis accessus*
C = the Carpentras *accessus*
Ce = the *Casualis euentus accessus* (not edited here; see above, pp. IV and 94)
D = the *accessus* in Düsseldorf K2: F.50 (not edited here; see above, p. 97)
E = the interpolations in Escorial witness of G
Ff = the *accessus* of Francesco Filelfo
Fm = the *accessus* of Franciscus Maturantius (not edited here; see above, p. 114)
G = the Gronov. 66 *accessus*
H = the *Hoc ex ordine compendium* (not edited here; see above, p. 84)
Ib = the *accessus* of Iohannes Britannicus (not edited here; see above, p. 114)
K = the KP *accessus*
Kr = the *accessus* in Kraków, Biblioteka Jagiellońska, 525 III (not edited here; see above, p. 103 n. 1 and p. 83)
L = the Lincoln College *accessus*
N = the N witness of the KP *accessus*
Ol = the Ottob. lat. 1261 *accessus*
P = the Plut. 24 sin. 12 *accessus*

Pr = the Paris witness of Pu
Ps = the Strasbourg witness Pv (not edited here; see above, p. 28)
Pu = the Plut. 38.10 *accessus*
Pv = the *accessus* in Pal. lat. 1695 (not edited here; see above, p. 28)
Rl = the *accessus* in Reg. Lat. 1556
V = the *accessus* in Wien 3114
Ve = the *accessus* in Venezia, lat. XII.61 (not edited here; see above, p. 112 n. 15)
Vl = the *accessus* in Vat. Lat. 1663
W = the Guelf. 13.10 Aug. 4° *accessus*
Wa = the *accessus* of Thomas Walsingham
Wi = the *accessus* in Wien 13685 (only partially edited here; see above, p. 81)
Wz = the *accessus* in Warszawa, Biblioteka Narodowa, BOZ Cim 50 (not edited here)

α = the parent of Pv and Ps
β = the parent of Bl and Bb
γ = the parent of Ve
κ1 = one of the two parents that were interpolated into the KP *accessus* (ω and Ω); cf. N
ρ = the parent of Kr
υ = the parent of Au

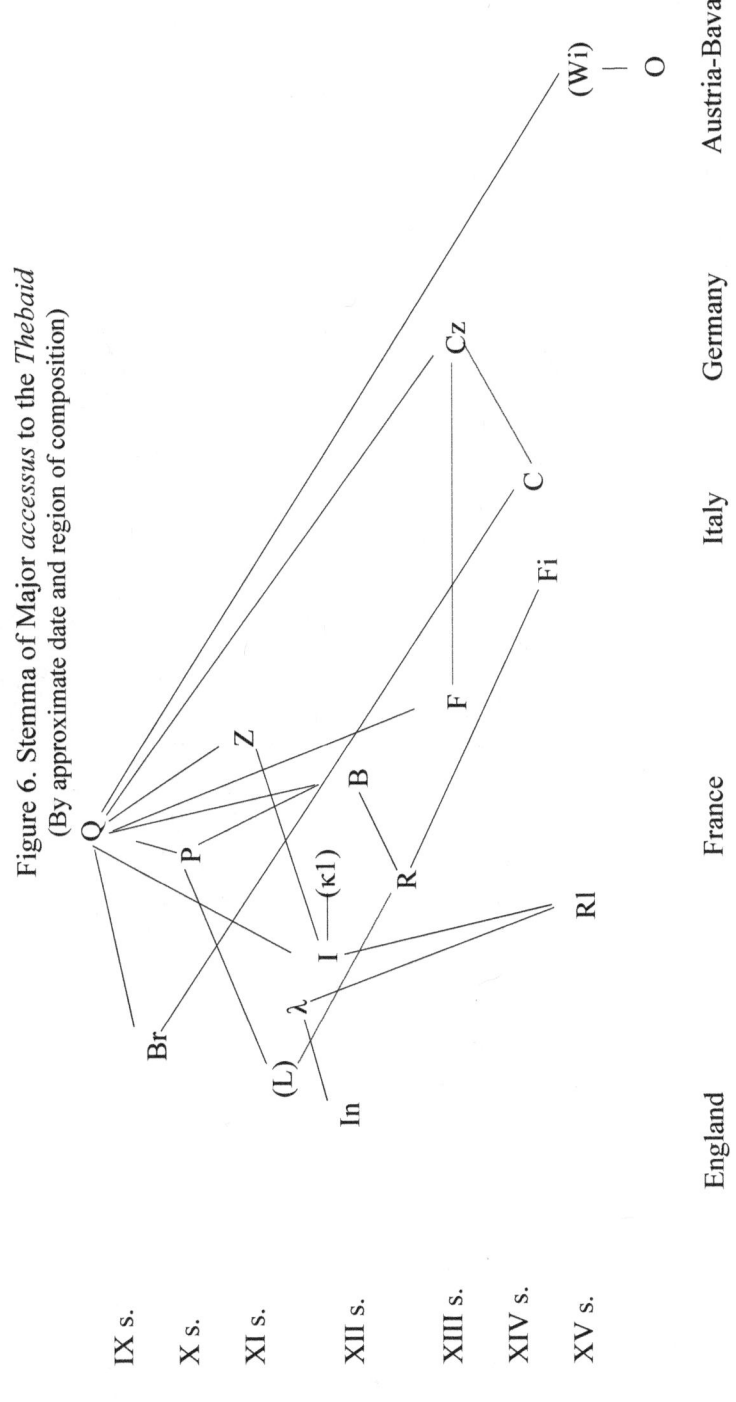

Figure 6. Stemma of Major *accessus* to the *Thebaid*
(By approximate date and region of composition)

Figure 7 Stemma of Major *accessus* to the *Achilleid*

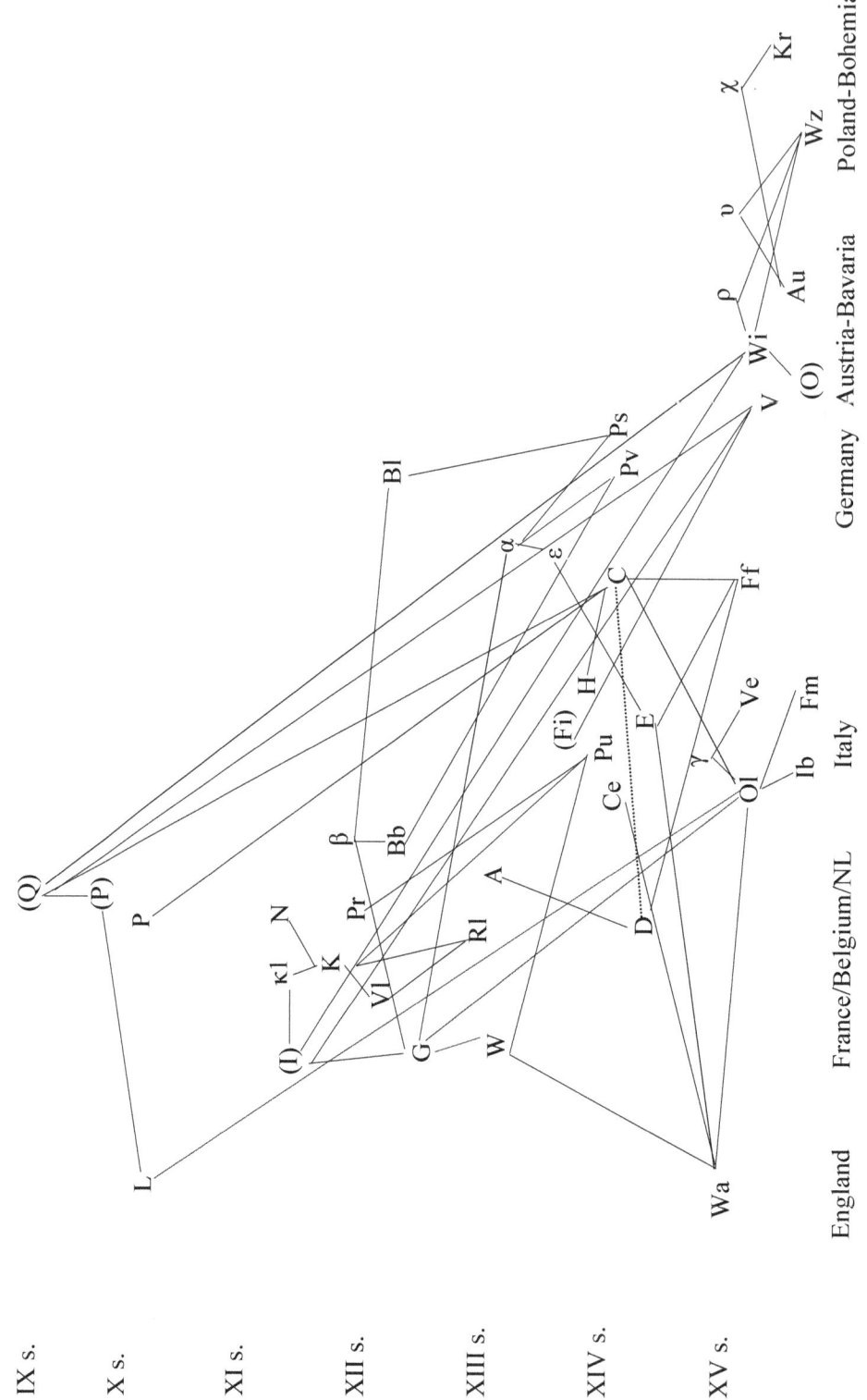

APPENDIX II. CHRONOLOGICAL TABLE

The *accessus* edited above are listed in an approximated chronological order by an abbreviated title.

Century	*Accessus* to the *Thebaid*	*Accessus* to the *Achilleid*
IX	*Quaeritur*	
XII in.	Zürich	Lincoln College
XII	Bern-Burney *accessus*	Plut. 24 sin. 12 KP
XII ex.	*In principio*	*Univ. Bruxellensis*
XIII in.	Freiburg	Reg. lat. 1556 Plut. 38.10 (F)
XIII	Royal 15.A.XXIX	Gronov. 66 Guelf. 13.10 Aug. 4°
XIII ex.		Vat. lat. 1663
XIV in.	Firenze, BNC, II.II.55	Carpentras
XIV		Genova
XIV ex.		Plut. 38.10
XV	Reg. lat. 1375	Walsingham Ps.-Filelfo Candidus
XV ex.	Olomouc	Wien 3114 Perottus Laetus Ottob. lat. 1261

APPENDIX III. ANTHOLOGY OF EPITAPHS AND POEMS ON STATIUS

I.   An epitaph of Statius

Strasbourg, Bibliothèque universitaire et régionale, Ms. 3370 (anno 1811), Ir (secundum Burman)

Impressus

Alat. Burman 2.234; Meyer-Burman 842

inscr.   Statii epitaphium

> Statius hic situs est, iuvenem quem Cypris ademit,
> 2   Praeconem Aeneae carmine quod premeret.

II.   An epitaph of Statius

Paris, Bibliothèque nationale de France, lat. 5929 (xiv–xv s.), 81v

> Assurgunt ididem Stacio venienti poete.
> Virgilius quantum Stacius ipse suo
> 3   Edidit Thebaidos duodecim carmine libros.

III.   A four-line epitaph of Statius

M =   Milano, Biblioteca Ambrosiana, H 21 inf. (anno 1416), 155v

> Inclitus hunc Statius merito poeta uocatus
> Edidit ut magno polleret nomine fame
> Vt propaganda totum foret sua fama super orbem
> 4   Diuinam Eneydan unctis secutus in actis.

---

2 vti(?) *post* fame *del.* M   **3** super *e* sub M   **4** *post* actis *add. not.*: hunc librum scripsit composuitque metra M

IV.   An epigram on Statius

impressus: ed. 1496?, Poitiers, J. Bouyer and G. Bouchet, 28r

inscr.   Epigramma in laudem Statii

> Clarus Burdegala nobis ex vrbe poeta
> Statius emicuit Surculus alta petens.
> Alter Virgilius de virga Surculus exit,
> 4   Qui post loca ipsum iure secunda tenet.

---

3 surculis *ed.*

V.   Adam Werner von Themar, *Epitaphium Statii poetae* (1492)

Karlsruhe, Generallandesarchiv, Ms. 65/723 (xv s. ex.), 114r

> Ille ego sum Statius uestigia certa Maronis
> Cui ire fauens uati maxima Musa dedit
> Thebas Eacidem Siluas quoque uersibus orno
> Hinc mihi qua uiuo candida phama nitet
> 5   Nomine et ore patrem refero, satus ex Agelina

Dic rogo quisquis ades, 'chare poeta ualę.'

VI. An apostrophic poem to Statius by Domitius Calderinus

impressus: ed. 1475, Roma: A. Pannartz, A3v

inscr. Domitius hortatur Statium Papinium ut redeat Neapolim in patria vbi ei
blandiet Franciscus Aragonus Regis. Ferd. F.

Nuper non fueras in vrbe notus
Incultus, lacer, horridus, retonsus
Nunc uultus reparatus in priores
Splendens integer elegans politus
5　　O quot millia fronte basiorum
Gaudendti excipies. Nouem sorores
Tam lętis cupiant sedere Syluis
Hic tecum pariter uelit Papini
Phoebus Castalium nouare carmen
10　　I nunc Euboicos celer Penates
Qua surgens tumulo canora uirgo
Nomen nobile pandit et nepotes
Illic nam tibi cuncta blandientur
Et tellus popularibus sonabit
15　　Certans plausibus hos dabit iuuentus
Fossos quę bibit ungula liquores
Proles regia te fouebit Illa
Cui Parcę tria lustra computarunt
Spondentes Pylię situm senectę
20　　Famę ut grandia pensa subministrent
Quę cęli gemino uehetur axe
Huius quom bene noueris Papini
Mores: Ingenium decusque formę
Tum gratum fuerit perisse quondam
25　　Huic nunc ut liceat tibi renasci.

VII. An epitaph of Statius

V = Vaticano, Città del, Biblioteca Apostolica Vaticana, Vat. lat. 3279 (xv s.), 2r–
2v

Papinio genitus nomen studiumque paternum
　　Mite solum fecit patria Parthenope
Donatus pater est auro pacisque corona
　　Atque eadem tribuit Cęsaris alba mihi.　　　　　　2v
5　　Vxor cara fuit seruati pignus amoris,
　　Claudia Laertis uincere docta nurum.
Oedipodam mea Musa canit, describit Achillem
　　Et que praecipiti facta calore fluunt.

VIII. A hexastich epitaph of Statius

Impressi

A = ed. 1506, Paris: J. Petit
B = ed. 1510, Paris: J. Petit.

inscr. Opera Statiana

Tanquam gemma nitens hoc orbe Papinius extat,
Qui Siluas cecinit Thebanaque bella coturno
Altisono et duri primeuum tempus Achillis
Et nisi crudeli preuentus morte fuisset,
5   Statius a forti cesum cecinisset Achille
Hectora et in Paridis finisset proditione.

---

1 urbe A   **2** cothurno A

IX.   An epitaph of Statius

A =   Vaticano, Città del, Biblioteca Apostolica Vaticana, Vat. lat. 1670 (xv s. ex.), 120r

M =   ms. Moroni apud Meyer-Burman

V =   Vaticano, Città del, Biblioteca Apostolica Vaticana, Vat. lat. 3282 (xv s.), 1r

ω =   codices quos vidd. Burman et Meyer

Impressi uel emendationes:

B =   *ALat.* Burman (Amsterdam, 1773), 2.233

Bm =   *ALat.* Meyer-Burman (Leipzig, 1835), 841

N =   emendationes mss. a F. Menke (in Strasbourg, Bibliothèque universitaire et régionale, Ms. 3370 [anno 1811], 1r) (secundum Burman)

inscr.   In statuam Statii poetę Neapolitani

Qui cecinit Thebas primum, mox orsus Achillem
     Occidit; hac colitur Statius in statua.
Hunc genuit tali gauisa Neapolis ortu,
     Ipsa Tholosa licet blateret esse suum.
5   Hęc etiam genuit Stellam fęcunda poetam,
     Ne sit in hoc uno splendida Parthenope.
Quod si uana suum contendat Gallia uatem,
     Siluarum relegas, candide lector, opus.

---

inscr. A : antonius panhormita in statuam statii V : *om.* Mω   **1** thebas primum A : primo thebas V : primo cecinit thebas Mω   orsus AV (*spec.* Schrader *apud* Bm, *laud.* Jacobs *ibid.*) : rursus Oudendorp *apud* Bm (*laud.* N) : casus ω   **2** occidit] occinit Oudendorp *apud* Bm (*laud.* N)   **3** tali] thalia M   blateret] *legendum blacteret uel blatteret* (*cf. Alat.* Burman 5.143.50) *notat* Bm   **4** tolosa V   **5–8** *ordinem seru.* A : *ordinem* 7–8–5–6 *seruu.* BBmMVω   **5** etiam] eadem V   stellam genuit N peperit V   fecunda AV : paritura ω (*in* pariterque *emend.* B)   **6** sblendida A **7** quod si] quasi V

X.   An *exordium* to a prose argument to the *Thebaid*

K =   Kassel, Murhardsche Bibliothek der Stadt Kassel und Landesbibliothek, 2° Ms. poet. et rom. 8 (xvi in.), 1r

Impressus

C.W. Weber, *De codice Statii cassellano*, Prog. U. Marburg (Marburg, 1853), p. 7

inscr.   Argumentum totius Thebaidos. Exordium argumenti.

Quo Staciana tibi leuius voluenda patescat
    Thoebais. Scriptum conspice lector opus.
Cum modo quae maduit fraterno Ysmęnia tellus
4   Sanguine succinctim chartula scripta refert.

---

inscr. exordium argumenti *post* refert (4) *dist.* K   **2** Scriptum conspice *e* conscriptum (asscriptum, *Weber*) despice K

XI.   An epitaph of the *Thebaid*

Eberhard of Béthune, *Laborinthus* 3.35 (ca. 1212)

B =   Bruxelles, Bibliothèque Royale Albert 1er, 21891 (1981) (xv s.), 193v

Impressus

L =   P. Leyser, *Historia poetarum et poematum medii aevi* (Halle, 1721), p. 826 (cf. M. Manitius, "Beiträge zur Geschichte römischer Dichter im Mittelalter," *Philologus* 52 [1894], 542)

Statius eloquii iucundus melle duorum
2   Arma canit fratrum sub duce quaeque suo.

XII.   An epitaph of the *Achilleid*

Eberhard of Béthune, *Laborinthus* 3.21 (ca. 1212)

B =   Bruxelles, Bibliothèque Royale Albert 1er, 21891 (1981) (xv s.), 193v

Impressi

L =   P. Leyser, *Historia poetarum et poematum medii aevi* (Halle, 1721), 826
M =   M. Manitius, "Beiträge zur Geschichte römischer Dichter im Mittelalter," *Philologus* 52 (1894), 542

Statius Aeacidem stantem cultu muliebri
2   Virtutem prodit calliditate uiri.

---

1 cultu M : stultu L   **2** sui LM

XIII.   A two-couplet epitaph of the *Achilleid* by Focaudus Monierus

Impressi

ed. 1496?, Poitiers: J. Bouyer and G. Bouchet, aiv
ed. 1506, Paris: J. Petit, aiv

inscr.   Focaudi Monieri tetrastichon in Achilleida Statii

Inclyta gesta viri Eacide celebrauit Homerus
    Ast adolescentius Statius acta canit
Thebais hunc etiam culte Silueque decorent
4   Hortulus iste tamen cultius vber habet.

---

1 eacido *edd.*   homexus *edd.*

XIV.   A two-line argument to the *Achilleid*

Impressus

ed. 1506, Paris: J. Petit, aiv

inscr.   Totius Achilleidos Compendium

        A Chirone Thetis ad Sciron ducit Achillem
2   Et (Pirrho genito) Troiam petit arte repertus.

XV.   An epitaph of the *Achilleid*

Parma, Biblioteca Palatina, Ms. Par. N. 3065 (anno 1368), 150r

        Vndecies centum uigenti iunge sed octo
2   Statius Eacide uersus dedit ore diserto.

XVI.   A five-couplet epithet to the *Achilleid*

Impressus

ed. 1515, Wien: per Hieronymium Victorem, Air

        Pelidae non usqueadeo prius alter ad annos
           Venerat et uitæ singula gesta suæ
        Statius in tali quam carmine Parthenopeus
           Infantis quoniam prima elementa canit.
5   Phillyridæ præcepta senis tælique chelisque
           Et clandestinæ furta parentis habet.
        Pulchrum est, nosse uiri Mauortia principis acta,
           Quae faciant fortem constituantque hominem.
        Hoc legisse modo uates, laudabile censet
10   Quisquis et huic studio, certum habet, esse locum.

XVII.   A five-line epitaph of the *Achilleid*

F =   Firenze, Biblioteca Medicea Laurenziana, plut. 91 sup. 34 (xiv s.), 21v

        Dum frena laxaret Muse dum altius ire
        Pollicitus uates moribundus ad astra meauit
        Proh dolor! ecce (heu!) remansit alba papirus
        Auctoris ergo magni casum doleamus acerbum
5   Quattuor in fine subiunxit Ghesea rudes.

---

1 lapxaret F   **5** *nota est*: "*i.e. franciscus filius Ghesis.*"

XVIII.   An epitaph of the *Achilleid*

R =   Roma, Biblioteca statale Angelica, 1721 (xv s.), 102v

        Quam cultus Danis et Formidatus Achilles
           Carus Amynthoride quam fuit usque suo
        Tam mihi grata mei uenerandaque numina Pauli
           Et constant placida cum pietate fides.
5   Et quantum ingenio formaque excesserat annos
           Eacides, tantum Paulus et ipse suos.

Ergo qui ueterem probat et miratur Achillem
Viventem Paulum diligat ille meum.

XIX. An epitaph of the *Silvae*

R = Roma, Biblioteca statale Angelica, 1721 (xv s.), 80v

Ingenio quantum hec celeri composta feruntur
Precipiti tantum scripta fuere manu.
Aspicis errores: veniam concede vetustas
Temporis has mendas non mea dextra tulit
5 Preterea in Sylvis non errare licebit
Cum solent nostrum fallere campus iter.

ADDITIONAL BIBLIOGRAPHY TO VOLUME III

Accessus to Other Authors

Boethius

Silks, E.T., ed., *Saeculi noni auctoris in Boetii Consolationem Philosophiae commentarius*, Papers and Monographs of the American Academy in Rome 9 (Roma, 1935), 5–8.

Cicero

Pellegrin, E., "Quelques «accessus» au «De amicitia» de Cicéron," in *Hommages à André Boutemy* (Bruxelles, 1976), 274–98.

Horace

Botschuyver, H.J., ed., *Scholia in Horatium* λφψ (Amsterdam, 1935), 1–2.

_____, ed., *Scholia in Horatium* πurz (Amsterdam, 1939), 3–5.

Holder, A., ed., *Pomponi Porfyrionis Commentum in Horatium Flaccum* (Innsbrück, 1894), 1–2.

Keller, O., ed., *Pseudacron Scholia in Horatium Vetustiora* (Leipzig, 1902), 1–3.

Juvenal

Löfstedt, B., ed., *Vier Juvenal-Kommentare aus dem 12. Jh.* (Amsterdam, 1995), 3–5 (B), 217–19 (P), and 369 (Bern) .

Wessner, P., ed., *Scholia in Iuvenalem vetustiora* (Leipzig, 1931), 1.

Wilson, B., *Glosae in Iuvenalem* (Paris, 1980).

Lucan

Hofmann, D., "Accessus ad Lucanum," in *Sagnaskemmtum: Studies in Honour of H. Pálsson* (Köln, 1986), 121–51.

Marti, B.M., ed., *Arnulfi Aurelianensis Glosule super Lucanum*, Papers and Monographs of the American Academy in Rome, 18 (Rome, 1958).

Quadlbauer, F., "Lukan im Schema des ordo naturalis/artificialis. Ein Beitrag zur Geschichte der Lukanwertung im lateinischen Mittelalter," *Grazer Beiträge* 6 (1977), 67–105.

Sanford, E.M., "The Manuscripts of Lucan: *Accessus* and *Marginalia*," *Speculum* 9 (1934), 178–95.

Weber, C.F., *Vitae M. Annaei Lucani collectae*, Indices lectionum... in Academia Marburgensi, in 3 parts (Marburg, 1856, 1857, 1858) .

Martianus Capella

King, J.M., *Notker latinus zum Martianus Capella*, Altdeutsche Textbibliothek, 98: Die Werke des Notkers des Deutschen 4A (Tübingen, 1986).

Westra, H.J., *The Commentary on Martianus Capella's* De nuptiis Philologiae et Mercurii *attributed to Bernardus Silvestris*, Studies and Texts 80 (Toronto, 1986), 43–48.

_____ and C. Vester, edd., *The Berlin Commentary on Martianus Capella's De nuptiis Philologiae et Mercurii, Book I* (Leiden, 1994).

Ovid

Coulson, F.T., "New Manuscript Evidence for Sources of the Accessus of Arnoul d'Orléans to the *Metamorphoses* of Ovid," *Manuscripta* 30 (1986), 103–107.

_____, "Hitherto Unedited Medieval and Renaissance Lives of Ovid (I)," *Mediaeval Studies* 49 (1987), 152–207.

_____, "Hitherto Unedited Medieval and Renaissance Lives of Ovid (II)," *Mediaeval Studies* 59 (1997), 111–53.

_____, "Hitherto Unedited Medieval and Renaissance Lives of Ovid (III): The Earliest Accessus," forthcoming.

_____ and B. Roy, *Incipitarium Ovidianum*, Publications of the Journal of Medieval Latin 3 (Turnhout, 2000).

Donnini, M., "L'*accessus Ovidii epistularum* del cod. Asis. Bibl. Civ. 302," *GIF* 31 (1979), 121–29.

Elliott, A.G., "*Accessus ad auctores*: Twelfth-Century Introductions to Ovid," *Allegorica* 5 (1980), 12–17.

Ghisalberti, F., "Giovanni del Virgilio espositore delle *Metamorfosi*," *Giornale dantesco* 34 (1931), 1–110.

_____, "Arnolfo d'Orléans. Un cultore di Ovidio nel secolo XII," *Memorie del Reale Istituto Lombardo di Scienze e Lettere* 24 (1932), 157–234.

_____, "L'*Ovidius Moralizatus* di Pierre Bersuire," *Studj romanzi* 23 (1933), 5–136 .

_____, ed., *Giovanni di Garlandia,* Integumenta Ovidii, *poemetto inedito del secolo XII* (Messina, 1933).

_____, "Mediaeval Biographies of Ovid," *Journal of the Warburg and Courtauld Institutes* 9–10 (1946–47), 10–59.

Jahnke, R., "Eine neue Ovid-vita," *RhM* 47 (1892), 460–62.

Klopsch, P., *Pseudo Ovidius de Vetula*, Mittellateinische Studien und Texte 2 (Leiden, 1967).

Leotta, R., "Un accessus ovidiano," *GIF* 33 (1981), 141–44.

Nogara, B., "Di alcune vite e commenti medioevali di Ovidio," in *Miscellanea Ceriani; Raccolta di scritti originali per onarare la memoria di Mr Antonio Maria Ceriani* (Milano, 1910), 413–31.

Przychocki, G., *Accessus Ovidiani*, Rozprawy Akademii Umiejętności, Wydział Filologiczny ser. 3 vol. 4 (Kraków, 1911) ["Symbolae ad veterum auctorum historiam atque Medii Aevi studia philologa," I, 65–126].

Robathan, D.M., *The Pseudo-Ovidian De Vetula* (Amsterdam, 1968), 41–46.

Rosa, L., "Su alcuni commenti inediti alla opere di Ovidio," *Ann. Fac. di Lettere e Filosofie di Napoli* 5 (1955), 191–231.

Roy, B., *L'Art d'amours: Traduction et commentaire de l'Ars amatoria d'Ovide* (Leiden, 1974).

Ps.-Seneca

Questa, C., "«Accessus» medioevali al «De moribus» dello Pseudo-Seneca," *RCCM* 2 (1960), 183–90.

Terence

Ballaira, G., "Praefatio «Monacensis» ad Terentium quae integra in Cod. Vat. lat. 11455 asservatur," *Bollettino del Comitato per la preparazione delle'dizione nazionale dei classici greci e latini*, n.s. 16 (1968), 13.

Sabbadini, R., "Biografi e commentatori di Terenzio," *SIFC* 5 (1987), 289–327.

Virgil

See W. Suerbaum, "Von der «Vita Vergiliana» über die «Accessus Vergiliani» zum Zauberer Vergilius," *ANRW* 2.31.2 (1981), 1156–262, with bibliography in *ANRW* 2.31.1 (1980), 306–308. The bibliography since then follows.

Stok, F., "Il rinascimento della biografia virgiliana," *Res Publica Litterarum* 14 (1991), 229–40.

_____, "La Vita di Virgilio di Zono de' Magnalis," *RCCM* 33 (1991), 145–81.

Other works

Kihlman, E., *Expositiones sequentiarum: Medieval Sequence Commentaries and Prologues: Editions with Introductions*, Studia Latina Stockholmensia 53 (Stockholm, 2006).

Accessus in General

Allen, J.B., *The Ethical Poetic of the Later Middle Ages: A Decorum of Convenient Distinction* (Toronto, 1982).

Bischoff, B., "Wendepunkte in der Geschichte der lateinischen Exegese im Frühmittelalter," *Sacris erudiri* 6 (1954) 189–279 [201–203] (*Mittelalterliche Studien* 1 [Stuttgart, 1966], 205–73 [217–19]).

Freytag, W, "Otfrieds Briefvorrede 'Ad Liutbertum' und die 'Accessus ad auctores,'" *ZfdA* 111 (1912), 168–93.

Glauche, G., *Schullektüre im Mittelalter: Enstehung und Wandlung des Lektürkanons bis 1200*, Münchener Beiträge zur Mediävistik und Renaissanceforschung 5 (München, 1970).

Hunt, R.W., "Introductions to the «Artes» in the Twelfth Century," in *Studia mediaevalia in honorem... Raymundi Josephi Martin* (Bruges, 1948), 85–112.

Huygens, R.B.C., ed., *Accessus ad auctores — Bernard d'Utrecht — Conrad d'Hirsau, Dialogus super auctores* (Leiden, 1970).

Klopsch, P., "Die mittelalterlichen Lehren a: *Accessus ad auctores*," in *Einführung in die Dichtungslehren des lateinischen Mittelalters* (Darmstadt, 1980), 48–64.

Lutz, C.E., "One Formula of Accessus in Remigius' Works," *Latomus* 19 (1960), 774–80.

Minnis, A.J., "The Influence of Academic Prologues on the Prologues and Literary Attitudes of Late-Medieval English Writers," *MedStud* 43 (1981), 342–83.

_____, *Medieval Theory of Authorship: Scholastic Literary Attitudes in the Later Middle Ages* (London, 1984).

_____ and A.B. Scott, *Medieval Literary Theory and Criticism c. 1100-c. 1375* (Oxford, 1991).

_____, "Late-Medieval Vernacular Literature and Latin Exegetical Traditions," in J. Assmann and B. Gladigov, edd., *Text und Kommentar*, Archäologie der literarischen Kommunikation, IV (München, 1995), 311–31.

Quain, E.A., "The Medieval *Accessus ad Auctores*," *Traditio* 3 (1945), 215–64.

Silvestre, H., "Le schema 'moderne' des accessus," *Latomus* 16 (1957), 684–89.

Spallone, M., "I percorsi medievali del testo: «accessus», commentari, florilegi," in *Lo spazio letterario di Roma antice*, vol. 3: *La ricezione del testo* (Rome, 1990), 387–471.

INDEX TO VOLUME III